Milton's Socratic Rationalism

Politics, Literature, and Film

Series Editor: Lee Trepanier, Saginaw Valley State University

The Politics, Literature, and Film series is an interdisciplinary examination of the inter-section of politics with literature and/or film. The series is receptive to works that use a variety of methodological approaches, focus on any period from antiquity to the present, and situate their analysis in national, comparative, or global contexts. Politics, Literature, & Film seeks to be truly interdisciplinary by including authors from all the social sciences and humanities, such as political science, sociology, psychology, literature, philosophy, history, religious studies, and law. The series is open to both American and non-American literature and film. By putting forth bold and innovative ideas that appeal to a broad range of interests, the series aims to enrich our conversations about literature, film, and their relationship to politics.

Advisory Board

Richard Avaramenko, University of Wisconsin-Madison
Linda Beail, Point Loma Nazarene University
Claudia Franziska Brühwiler, University of St. Gallen
Timothy Burns, Baylor University
Paul A. Cantor, University of Virginia
Joshua Foa Dienstag, University of California at Los Angeles
Lilly Goren, Carroll University
Natalie Taylor, Skidmore College
Ann Ward, University of Regina
Catherine Heldt Zuckert, University of Notre Dame

Recent Titles

Milton's Socratic Rationalism: The Conversations of Adam and Eve in Paradise Lost by
    David Oliver Davies
Walker Percy and the Politics of the Wayfarer by Brian A. Smith
Romanticism and Civilization: Love, Marriage and Family in Rousseau's Julie by
    Mark Kremer
Aldous Huxley: The Political Thought of a Man of Letters by Alessandro Maurini
Sinclair Lewis and American Democracy by Steven Michels
Liberty, Individuality, and Democracy in Jorge Luis Borges by Alejandra M. Salinas

Milton's Socratic Rationalism

The Conversations of Adam and Eve in *Paradise Lost*

David Oliver Davies

LEXINGTON BOOKS
Lanham • Boulder • New York • London

Published by Lexington Books
An imprint of The Rowman & Littlefield Publishing Group, Inc.
4501 Forbes Boulevard, Suite 200, Lanham, Maryland 20706
www.rowman.com

Unit A, Whitacre Mews, 26-34 Stannary Street, London SE11 4AB

British Library Cataloguing in Publication Information Available
The hardback edition of this book was previously catalogued by the Library of Congress as follows:

Library of Congress Cataloging-in-Publication Data

Library of Congress Control Number: 2017945465
ISBN 978-1-4985-3262-4 (cloth)
ISBN 978-1-4985-3264-8 (pbk.)
ISBN 978-1-4985-3263-1 (electronic)

For Becky
and
John and Kristen
and
Rachel

Contents

Acknowledgments

This book investigates a mode of discourse in *Paradise Lost* to which I was introduced many years ago in what Milton had called that "shaded academy offered by Socratic streams." Fortune played some part as well. Happenstance had led me to a classroom lecture on Plato's *Symposium* of Alfred Geier at the University of Rochester. For a number of years thereafter I came to read the dialogues of Plato and Xenophon *et alia* with him and other students of such works. Unlike—I can only hope–Satan on Mt. Niphates, I cannot forget "the debt immense" I yet owe to that teacher and those years.

Later I had the good fortune to be invited to teach in Core Curriculum programs in the undergraduate and doctoral degrees at the University of Dallas. Over the years reading and discussing the works in the curricula of these programs with undergraduate and graduate students and colleagues has provided the fertile ground in which the work at hand was nourished and grew. First of all, I am indebted beyond measure to John Alvis and Tom West for the example in a friendship of many years of their teaching, scholarship and, above all, of their tireless probing inquiry in conversation. Then too I have enjoyed the daily gift of adventitious talk on things Miltonic and otherwise with my colleagues in English, Classics, Politics and Philosophy: Debra Romanick Baldwin, Brett Bourbon, Scott Crider, Katherine Davis, Leo Paul de Alvarez, John Grant, Eileen Gregory, Theresa Kenney, Andrew Moran, Fr. Robert Maguire, Andrew Osborn, R.J. Pestritto, Greg Roper, Steven Stryer and Gerard Wegemer. Dr. Grace West read an early version of "Eve's First Words"; Dr. Bourbon read a late version of "Becoming Dear" and Drs. Alvis and Roper read the completed manuscript. By pointed query, advice and example these colleagues have all refined and advanced my views of my subject. I am particularly grateful as well for opportunity on two occasions in the past to have audited Joshua Parens' graduate seminar on Maimonides'

Guide which opened a new perspective for me on Milton's appropriations of Genesis.

In the summer of 1992 I was a participant in a National Endowment for the Humanities Summer Institute, the *Arizona Milton Institute*, directed by John Shawcross at the University of Arizona, Tucson, Arizona. In AY 2000–2001 I enjoyed the support of the Earhart Foundation Research Fellowship Grant during my sabbatical year, as well as, on two occasions, a summer research grant by the Haggar Fund at the University of Dallas.

Quotations from the text of "Milton: Paradise Lost" by Alastair Fowler (Editor), Copyright (2007) Pearson Education Limited are reproduced with permission of Taylor & Francis Books UK.

Chapter 3, "Eve's First Words" first appeared in *Classical and Modern Literature* 28.2 (1-31) (2008) as "Eve's First Words in Paradise: Ovidian Wit, Platonic Self-knowledge, and Milton's Translations in *Paradise Lost*"4.440-491. I remain grateful for the many helpful suggestions of an anonymous reader and the encouragement of the editor of *CML*, Michael Barnes, in my revision of this chapter. Likewise, I am grateful to the anonymous reviewer and editors at Lexington Books for their aid in revision of the introductory and concluding chapters of this book.

Here I must give recognition to the critical insight and simple generosity of a scholar whose approach to Milton anticipated my own. When I was yet an ABD candidate in Classics at the State University of New York at Buffalo, Paul Dowling of Canisius College, for afternoon's conversation over a few lines of Euripides's Greek as a motto for Milton's tract on the liberty of unlicensed printing, *Areopagitica*, granted me co-authorship in his essay, "'Shrewd books with dangerous Frontespieces'": *Areopagitica*'s Motto." *Milton Quarterly*.Vol. 20, no. 2 (May 1986). Years later, in his completed book, *Polite Wisdom* (Rowman & Littlefield Publishers: 1995) on that Miltonic tract I came upon his call for just such an approach to *Paradise Lost* which I was now beginning to discern in Milton's appropriation of a Socratic Rationalism represented in the dialogues of Plato and Xenophon. I hope I have done justice in this book to his insight.

Finally, I am grateful beyond measure for the never-failing patience and encouragement of my wife, Becky—not to mention her assiduous care in proofreading every draft throughout the years of this project.

The author is grateful for the generous gift from Michael Erlingher of eleven engravings originally added to the French translation, *Le Paradis Perdu*, by Chateaubriand of Milton's Paradise Lost (Paris: Gustave Guérin, Libraire-Éditeur, 1881), one of which, "La Prière," provides the cover illustration of this volume.

Preface

The title of this book, Milton's Socratic Rationalism, identifies a distinct mode of deliberative inquiry that is by design, as I will argue, an objective in the plan of *Paradise Lost*. The poet became acquainted with this mode of discourse—as few[1] at present are—in the Socratic writings of Xenophon and Plato during an extended period of private study after his formal studies at Cambridge had ended.[2] In *An Apology Against a Pamphlet* (*CPW* 1.891, italics in original text) Milton recalled that "riper yeares, and ceaseless round of study and reading led me to the shady spaces of philosophy, but chiefly to the divine volumes of *Plato*, and his equall *Xenophon*."[3]

Socratic rationalism would appear to broadly characterize an approach made familiar in the conversations Plato poetically represented Socrates to have with various individuals in the dialogues. The present use of the term is certainly inclusive of such exempla, but pays particular attention to Xenophon's less well-known if more circumspect and surely more austere report. Differences in these portraits of Socratic conversation invite considered interest. Xenophon concurs with the Platonic portrait of Socrates that represents him "constantly conversing about human things as he considered . . ." (περὶ τῶν ἀνθρωπείων ἀεὶ δ διελέγετο σκοπῶν . . . [*Mem.* 1.1.16]) those 'what is' (τί ἐστι . . . ;) questions that fill the dialogs, yet Xenophon appears to not permit us to observe his Socrates so engaged.[4] Xenophon also tells us that Socrates "did not approach everyone in the same way" (οὐ τὸν αὐτὸν τρόπον ἐπὶ πάντας ᾔει [*Mem.* 4.1.3] yet, unlike Plato, we are not allowed to overhear his talk with those of extraordinary gifts such as an Alcibiades. Instead, the *Memorabilia* chiefly records Xenophon's recollections of Socrates giving other young men sound moral advice. Only in the fourth book we are shown what might be called Socrates' didactic method, but practiced on a young acolyte of Socrates, Euthydemus, who believes that wisdom consists in collecting the sayings of esteemed poets and sophists (*Mem.* 4.2.1ff.).

Commentary on *Paradise Lost* also has been generally disappointing, save that of C.S. Lewis perhaps, with the domestic tableau of the two now embellished with the talk Milton imagined they would have. Yet even Lewis had to concede that, "In considering his (i.e., Adam's) relations with Eve we must remind ourselves of the greatness of these personages" (119).[5] The conversations of Adam and Eve in *Paradise Lost* appear to have shared with Xenophon's portrait of Socrates a neglect born of indifference to the mundane attire of its considerable charms—in the former case, a spectacle of two remarkably intelligent individuals conversing with each other in their complete innocence in wonder of what they each are; who is that other, alike yet different from one's self; what is this place, and whence, and by whom and how.

These objects for inquiry are suggested by the poet's additions to the bare particulars of the Scriptural story in pursuit of his explicit subject in *Paradise Lost*, "Man's Disobedience and the Fruit" (1.1).[6] The poet among other expansions[7] includes five conversations between Adam and Eve—four before and one after the Fall—within an extended scope for the Biblical narrative of several additional days. In Genesis Adam and Eve say not a word to each other before, at, or even after the fatal events of that day they were created and then fell. Adam talked with God, and Eve with the snake, but they did not converse with each other. The only thing Adam says to Eve is this name he gives her after they are judged (Gen. 3:20). With the addition of the conversations of these two to *Paradise Lost*, however, Milton now places an implicit anthropology in Scripture's account of the events in Paradise in counterpoise to the most evident sense of "Let us make man in our own image, according to our likeness" (Gen. 1:26): rational discourse.

This plan of counterpoise as well begins to reveal a Socratic pedigree in its recognition of distinct audiences to whom these alternatives might appeal. Milton's expansions upon the Scriptural narrative must surely cultivate generally accepted opinions of these events if the poem hopes to "justify the ways of God *to men*" (1.26, italics added). But Milton's report of their overheard conversations must also render in a plausible fashion the unique circumstances of their nascent consciousness and intelligence. They both begin, "much wondering where/ And what I was, whence thither brought, and how" (4.451–452, cf. 8.270–271), in full possession of their rational faculties though without that reservoir of experience and consequent opinions that for all their descendants populates, so-to-speak, the infancy, childhood and adolescence of their growth as rational beings. Adam and Eve are innocents, and are without any awareness of accepted notions—not to mention fallen ones— of the matters they in wonder ask of themselves and eventually each other. Their pristine experience, unclouded by authoritative opinion of any sort is available to be examined since it is described by their own undiminished rational faculties. To view such beings with wonder, to listen to their talk as they make sense of themselves and each other without resort to a knowledge of good and evil—that inheritance from the Fall—even the general audience of the poem might assume would seem an attainment of a "fit audience . . . though few" (7.31).

At present it is worth noting that the peculiar circumstances of these conversations of Adam and Eve and the particular discernment required of both in several essential respects also resembles conversations which Xenophon said Socrates had with certain interlocutors "whose souls were naturally well disposed towards virtue." "Socrates took as a sign," Xenophon reports, "of such good natures those who were quick to understand what they put their mind to, and could remember what they had learned, and (among other things, they were those) . . . who desired to learn anything at all by which it was possible to deal with men and human things in a fine manner" (*Memorabilia* 4.1.2). These very qualities will be active in "Eve's First Words" to Adam (chapter 3) and Adam's account of Eve's dream of the Forbidden Tree in "Becoming Dear" (chapter 5).

In Genesis Adam and Eve after a fashion briefly converse with their Creator; they speak and understand speech, both declarative and interrogatory. Milton expands upon[8] this rational nature they share with their Creator. In *Paradise Lost* both Eve and Adam begin by their own account, "much wondering where\ And what I was, whence thither brought, and how" (4.451–452, cf. 8.270–271). The few days of their life together before the Fall will be punctuated by conversation *with each other* marking the discovery and growth of a rational nature *in each other*. They find themselves and their "other self" in a "self /Before me" (see 8.450 & 495–496). These discoveries and still others animate their conversation in Paradise. A passing remark in the introductory chapter of Milton's *Artis Logicae* states the obvious. Citing a comment of Socrates in Plato's *1st Alcibiades*, Milton remarks, *idem vult esse* τό διαλέγεσθαι, *quod ratione uti.* ("he was of the view that 'to converse' was the same as to use reason" [*WJM* 11.20]).

Milton as early as the divorce tracts had argued that "a fit and matchable conversation" was not only "essential to the prime scope of marriage" in the ordinary sense but also provided a glimpse, at least, of "that serene and blissful condition it was in at the beginning" (*CPW* 2.239 & 240). Thus, his poetic expansions in *Paradise Lost* upon the tight-lipped particulars of Genesis not only reveal his sense of, "And God created the human in his image\ in the image of God He created him,\ male and female He created him" (Gen 1:27),[9] but now also revise the terms of inquiry into the explicit subject of the poem.

SOCRATIC RATIONALISM AND THE
PROBLEM OF AUDIENCE

No audience of the poem need be told that "Man's Disobedience and the Fruit" refers to an event of dire consequence—with redemption but a distant prospect. They know the story all too well. But to identify a "serene and blissful condition" that would be lost along with those charms of Adam and Eve reasoning their way—first, to their own marital accord (Books 4 & 5); then to show that accord interrupted by an angel (Books 5 through 8); then fractured thereafter by a quarrel; and thereafter violated in the solitude of their own choices (Book 9); and finally, perhaps restored by the grace or graces bestowed upon them by their Creator (Book 10)—all this would enable one to measure both what they had learned they had, and then apparently lost, and then perhaps, what they regained or retained—and what still might obtain to us to some degree. The means of measurement would be deduced from principles they discover in their own talk. To that talk—as this book endeavors to show—Milton grants a unique status in the poem: it is not conversation narrative persona imagines, but rather, that which he overhears. Thereby these conversations take the pose of a mere report rather than a poet's invention.

The audience that reads *Paradise Lost* is aware of moral certainties, the "generally accepted opinions," τὰ ἔνδοξα[10] as Aristotle called them, about goods lost and evils done and got that surround the poem, the sacred text and the multitudinous interpretations of both. Adam and Eve had no such awareness before the Fall. By the Fall they obtained such an awareness.[11] Thus their talk before and after can make possible an examination of our talk—rife as it is with such certainties. One can examine these opinions. This according to Aristotle is the office of dialectic (*Top.* 100a25–101b4). To do so neither defers to these generally accepted opinions—as if one, though fallen, possesses a knowledge of good and evil as a moral truth—nor simply casts them aside—as if one's own notions, or those borrowed from some poet, can replace "what seems good to everyone, or most people for the most part, or what the wise, either all of them or most of them or those especially renowned and respected think is true."[12] This mode of inquiry this book calls Socratic rationalism. Some account must be given of the name.

Socratic rationalism is imitated in the poetic compositions of some of his students and contemporaries. Plato wrote dialogues; Xenophon intimated[13] Socrates's distinct mode of address to his close associates among his other acquaintances in the fourth book of the *Memorabilia*; and Aristophanes parodied Socrates's public and private instruction in *The Clouds*. Still later Aristotle described a means of inquiry when he explained how rhetoric is a counterpart (ἀντίστροφος [*Rhet* 1354a1]) of dialectic. He also gave notice to the grounds of kinship and difference among his treatises on logical, dialectical and rhetorical syllogisms and the art of poetry. All as disciplines are expressive of our rational nature and all, Aristotle implied, make distinct demands upon and are suited to the peculiar needs of various audiences.

In the absence of a logical demonstration from self-evident principles some are inclined to reason with a degree of caution from and about "generally accepted opinions" (τὰ ἔνδοξα). Yet others are persuaded by what only at first seems a generally accepted opinion, and thus others will see a need to distinguish a rhetorical syllogism from a dialectical one. For others still, it will suffice to be merely persuaded of what requires no further scrutiny. And poetry, indifferent to these considerations, possesses powers to persuade without resort to syllogism. All these modes are rational but they answer to different needs of different audiences.[14] Xenophon, once again, merely observed of Socrates's relationships with his associates that "he did not approach everyone in the same way" (οὐ τὸν αὐτὸν δὲ τρόπον ἐπὶ πάντας ᾔει . . . [*Mem.* 4.1.2]).

Xenophon also recalled (*Mem.* 4.6.15) that Socrates was wont to cite Homer's Odysseus as an example of attending[15] to these differences in an audience: "Homer gave credit to Odysseus for being an unerring orator since that very man was quite adept at *carrying out his speeches by means of the things that seem good to men* (διὰ τῶν δοκούντων τοῖς ἀνθρώποις ἄγειν τοὺς λόγους). Given the great variety of—oftentimes contradictory— "things that seem good to men," Xenophon seems to have learned from Socrates a way speaking about Socrates's way of speaking which muted to some degree the sense of a discriminate address to his audience. "By far of all those I have known," Xenophon adds, "he above all tried to achieve agreement among those who were listening to him." This study will suggest that Milton in *Paradise Lost* is engaged in *this* Socratic project. He speaks to a diverse audience but endeavors to preserve a ground of agreement for all in an articulate respect for generally accepted opinion.

AN EXCURSUS ON THE "DIFFICULTIES" IN THE CRITICISM

That Milton in *Paradise Lost* was also aware of the difficulties of a divided audience and had resorted to a Socratic mode of address emerges from the preliminary matters concerned with audience that first appear in the third printing of the first edition of 1667. Subsequent additions and corrections culminate in the two verse appreciations of A.M. and S.B.M.D. added to the second edition of 1674. All these perhaps otherwise plausible addenda concern audience. The printer pleads that some concession be made to a supposed popular incomprehension; he asks that the poet provide an argument.

The poet grants the request albeit with some pique. He adds further unsolic-
ited comments on the "The Verse," and goes on to describe what he will soon
call his "fit audience . . . though few" (7.31): they will not "vulgar readers,"
but familiar with the verse "of *Homer* in *Greek*, and of *Virgil* in *Latin*," they
will esteem "an example set, the first in English, of ancient liberty recover'd
to Heroic poem from the troublesome and modern bondage of Riming."
A distinct difference between these audiences first presents itself in two distinct ways to understand these remarks on rhyme. Finally the two poems, one
in Latin elegaics and another of rhymed couplets in English, offer—in one,
notes of enthusiastic praise, and in the other, mixed with lingering doubts—
their dubious credentials to be enrolled in the desired audience for the poem.
Chapter 1 examines these matters as ironic commentary on the poem's present and possible reception.

  Paradise Lost is and has always been seen as a "difficult" poem. Jonathan
Richardson (1734) had described the stresses imposed upon a certain kind of
reader:

> A Reader of *Milton* must be Always upon Duty; he is Surrounded with Sense, it
> rises in every Line, every Word is to the Purpose. There are no Lazy Intervals, All
> has been Consider'd, and Demands, and Merits Observation. Even in the Best
> Writers you Sometimes find Words and Sentences which hang on so Loosely
> you may Blow 'em off; Milton's are all Substance and Weight; Fewer would
> not have Serv'd the Turn, and More would have been Superfluous. His Silence
> has the Same Effect, not only that he leaves Work for the Imagination when
> he has Entertain'd it, and Furnish'd it with Noble Materials ; but he Expresses
> himself So Concisely, Employs Words So Sparingly, that whoever will Possess
> His Ideas must Dig for them, and Oftentimes pretty far below the Surface. If
> This is call'd Obscurity let it be remembred 'tis Such a One as is Complaisant
> to the Reader, not Mistrusting his Ability, Care, Diligence, or the Candidness
> of his Temper; . . . if a Good Writer is not Understood 'tis because his Reader
> is Unacquainted with, or Incapable of the Subject, or will not Submit to do the
> Duty of a Reader, which is to Attend Carefully to what he Reads. (cxliv–cxlv)[16]

Nevertheless there was early on a consensus of sorts in behalf of Addison's
"great Moral" of *Paradise Lost*—"that Obedience to the will of God makes
men happy, and that Disobedience makes them miserable" (*Spectator* #369).
The demands on a reader aside, it was not hard to get the basic point. Milton,
we may think, would have been pleased with both appreciations.

  About 75 years ago, however, a critical consensus of sorts in behalf of
Addison's "great Moral" of *Paradise Lost* began to disintegrate. An awareness was growing of so-called "difficulties" of the poem and of the poet.
Charles Williams (1937), however, in speaking of "The New Milton" was
optimistic that certain adjustments in the basic sense of the man himself and

in the critical appreciation of the works he produced were "likely soon to justify Milton's ways to us much more than we have hitherto realized" (19). Herein Williams deftly echoed both Milton's declared subject and the Aristotelian standard by which all great poetry—and fine criticism no less—are to represent the poet's success: "Ah, this is *that* !"[17]

C.S. Lewis (1942) then thought it necessary to remind the audience of the poem just what sort of thing they were reading. As he put it—playfully predicting the strands of appreciation and misapprehension to come—"The first qualification for judging any piece of workmanship from a corkscrew to a cathedral is to know *what* it is" (1). Lewis could see where things were headed. If cathedrals were not for "entertaining tourists" nor corkscrews for opening potted meats, Lewis nevertheless knew that Milton's poem did provide occasion for his figured examples to perform their *actual* functions in the poem. Charles Williams had brought him into the nave of a cathedral (see Dedication, v–vi), but Lewis also saw racks of modern intoxicants waiting to be opened.

A.J.A. Waldock (1947), however, was dismissive of Lewis and, in his own way, of difficulties in Milton's poem: "Only grasp what Milton is driving at, [Lewis] seems to say, and the battle is over; only understand what Milton meant and you will see that there are no real difficulties at all." No, there were problems, Waldock thought, but "[i]t was possible . . . to overrate very much Milton's *awareness* of the peculiar difficulties of his theme" (17). Waldock was attracted to this barely plausible excuse to explain a peculiar fact of narrative progress. With his daring choice of subject Milton "was bound . . . to discover the rigidities and awkwardnesses of his subject." Some would have come as a surprise—

> the subject had traps and pitfalls that Milton, for various reasons easy to understand, could not have been foreseen; it was only to be expected that from time to time he would come to the edge of one of these, and seeing it, would veer sharply away. The traces of such veerings are . . . perceptible in the poem. (25)

Milton had been drawn to a grand theme in Genesis wherein "God does not show to advantage" (18). His choice of the epic form required of him to add embarrassing motives to make acceptable if not attractive characters for whom the spare details of the Biblical narrative had observed a respectful silence. Then there were the intricacies of the Scriptural traditions, and varieties of interpretation. In the end, Waldock thought, that Milton,

> as his work progressed, . . . came on problems that he had not expected to encounter. It is of great interest in reading *Paradise Lost* to note that here, or here, a sudden difficulty has checked Milton slightly—that here, or here, a faint

uneasiness shows itself. And yet we may take it for granted, I suppose, that
Milton never to the end became aware of the real nature of the gravest of the
narrative problems he had been grappling with. (21)

In one sense Waldock was right; the objects of great interest, problems
of Milton's subject and difficulties in the narrative could not be ignored.
Waldock however did not interrogate his own aesthetic judgment that found
defects which might have been arranged as rhetorical directives.

For William Empson (1961), however, difficulties were not defects to be
explained or excused, but the reason why, for him at least, the poem was
good. He had the good sense to examine what these so-called "defects" point
to; their prevalence in the poem could not be accidental. He would also praise
C.S. Lewis for bringing some clarity to the motives of foes no less than admirers of the poem. Aesthetic judgments pro and con were, Empson thought, a
pose to mask "various theologies and world-views" (9). Lewis showed the
way: "Many of those who say they dislike Milton's God only mean they dislike God" (*Preface*, 130). Borrowing then the title for his own book from this
remark, Empson seemed to parade his own confession. As he mischievously
observed, "'Dislike' is a question-begging term here. I think the traditional
God of Christianity very wicked, and I have done so since I was in school,
where nearly all my little playmates thought the same" (10). What opinion
he personally held about God was beside the point; it was the questions that
intrigued him. As he went on to explain,

> to worship a wicked God is morally bad for a man, so that he ought to be free to
> question whether his God is wicked. Such an approach does make Milton himself
> appear in a better light. He is struggling to make his God appear less wicked, as he
> tells us at the start (1.25), and does succeed in making him noticeably less wicked
> than the traditional Christian one; though, after all his efforts, owing to his loyalty
> to the sacred text and the penetration with which he makes its story real to us, his
> modern critics still feel, in a puzzled way, that there is something badly wrong
> about it all. That this searching goes on in *Paradise Lost*, I submit, is the chief
> source of its fascination and poignancy; and to realize that it is going on makes the
> poem feel much better at many points, indeed clears up most of the objections to it.
>   I thus tend to accept the details of the interpretation which various recent
> critics have used to prove the poem bad, and then try to show that they make it
> good (11).

In almost casual terms Empson was raising the question, *quid sit deus?*,
that stands bestride the boundary between the way of faith and a way of
philosophic inquiry.

Anne Ferry (1963) soon pointed a way to discuss these "difficulties"
that turned attention to their role in the poem. These were not unfortunate

oversights or worse "traps and pitfalls," or even pleasing correctives to a doc-
trinaire subject in a poet's performance, but the utterance of a character "as
deliberate an invention as the other characters in the poem and as essential to
its meaning." Ferry had followed Lewis's advice to attend to "*what* a thing
is." Milton's choice of the epic required a narrative voice by convention.[18] In
Paradise Lost she thought its scope was comprehensive:

> everything which is not actually said by this narrator—the speeches of the char-
> acters to themselves or to one another—is reported *and interpreted by him,*[19]
> and therefore only when we have determined who is speaking in the narrative,
> descriptive, and discursive passages, and to whom, can we evaluate the mood
> and meaning of the poem. (20, italics added)

Ferry stressed a complexity in the task. Narrative persona's task was to
account not just for the ways of God but also his own ways and those of his
audience and in fact all men. "We, the readers," Ferry observed, "are immediately included in the events of the narrative with the first line of the poem,
because its subject is 'Man's First Disobedience'" (22). At the same time the
poem and its narrative persona Ferry thought supplied ample testimony "that
as human beings we need divine inspiration because our minds cannot tran-
scend the limits of our creaturely nature, and as heirs of Adam, we are fallen,
bereft, miserable, and mortal" (23). Thus, narrative persona "is . . . not only
one of 'us' because he shares 'our woe'; he is also apart from us, instructing
us in his role as the poet" (24).

Attractive as her proposal might be to account for the difficulty of shifting
perspectives in the poem, Ferry did not explain why this deliberately invented
narrator, nevertheless, should not be identified with John Milton.[20] If he was
distinct, then the author's design for the poem as a whole would begin to
become visible with an account of that persona that explained its close resemblances to John Milton, Englishman—his blindness; a public persona already
familiar from the prose tracts and one immersed in the political, theological,
philosophic controversies of his day—as well as the peculiar difficulties that
persona's own performance instanced or produced in his characters. Why was
this vehicle required?

Ferry had come close to raising the right question—What is the place of
narrative persona in the account of the ways of God to men?—but her labors,
however, were soon to be eclipsed by a study which proposed an entirely
different locus of interest for the poems' notorious "crises of interpretation."
Setting aside the intricacies of plot, character, narrative strategy and the like,
Stanley Fish (1967, 2nd ed. 1997) in *Surprised by Sin* offered to describe a fit
response of the poem's audience to these crises. All the crises had the same
shape and purpose. They were intended to unsettle the audience. It did not

take long for his thesis to gain wide notice and nearly as wide if oft-grudging acceptance.

By his own account in the preface to the second edition Fish's aims originally had been modest. Faced with a long-standing quarrel among critical camps that "accused one another of various heresies and congealed orthodoxies, each side claiming that the other was not really reading the poem but skewing it to fit a preconceived idea," Fish offered to heal the rift:

> By shifting the field where coherence was to be found from the words on the page to the experience they provoked, I was able to reconcile the two camps under the aegis of a single thesis; *Paradise Lost* is a poem about how its readers came to be the way they are; its method, 'not so much a teaching but intangling' is to provoke in its readers wayward, fallen responses which are then corrected by one of several authoritative voices (the narrator, God, Raphael, Michael, the Son). In this way, I argued, the reader is brought to a better understanding of his sinful nature and is encouraged to participate in his own reformation. ("Preface," 2nd ed., x)

In confining interpretative interest to "fallen responses" of an audience of readers, *Surprised by Sin* tacitly assumed the scope of *Paradise Lost* was coincident with that of Genesis, though the former was replete with expansions upon the narrative of the latter. Both taught the way of faith. For a sequence of entanglement, surprise and conditioned impulse to reform that came to view in these additions. Fish had offered the penitential practices and handbooks of Milton's Protestant contemporaries as precedent.[21] That something quite different—which in this book goes by the name of Socratic rationalism—is at work in dialectical counterpoise to Scripture will rest in a sense on the same material evidence though possessed of a more inclusive pedigree in "generally accepted opinion," τὰ ἔνδοξα. Nevertheless, the widespread deference to the approach of *Surprised by Sin* to *Paradise Lost* and to "reader-response criticism"—which Fish celebrated in his preface to the second edition of 1997 requires explanation.

Fish's account of his resolution for the rift in the critical discussion of the poem had deftly avoided the source of disagreement: contending proposals for authorial intent.[22] In broad terms, was Milton of the devil's party or God's? Instead, Fish would confine himself to the "words on the page"[23] and "the experience they provoked." Relieved of the difficult task of discerning what words *this author* used in what particular sense to create what particular effect *he wished* in conveying what matter in the poem *with which he was concerned*, and so on, Fish nonetheless had to say they, the words, did give rise to some experience. But where was that to be found, but in a climate of generally accepted opinion of his own description: an audience of Christian sensibilities, attachments and practices that would become unsettled by the poetic admixture of an epic tradition. Only now did Fish re-introduce authorial intent but now constrained to cultivate the tensions that might arise among *these* "generally accepted opinions" as he delimited and defined them. Herein the intellectual pedigree of "reader response" in historicism becomes visible. Under the Hegelian principle that "every man is a child of his own times" the audience of reader response and the poet, Milton—who out of self-interest surely needs must attend to that audience—,[24] are both creatures of their own time. How then will Fish and the host of his sometimes reluctant admirers explain the postmodern doubt of authorial intent that impels him to abandon any project for his poetic endeavors save cultivating their present wavering beliefs which he as well shares. There is, after all, ample evidence that both the poet and his contemporaries did not have such doubts.[25]

Socratic rationalism and the theory of reader-response criticism begin in a sense with the same material, the difficulties the poem presents in a resort to τὰ ἔνδοξα, generally accepted opinions. No less do the prisoners in Socrates's allegory the Cave begin to engage in conversation about the shadows they behold, those dim shadow reproductions cast by the unseen artifacts of equally unseen makers. In spite of these deficits the prisoners talk about what they behold. Their talk is not of an intent of the makers of the artifacts; their talk is of the realities of their experience. Understandably, nevertheless, they fall into disagreements—it is very dark in this place—about what they are seeing. Fish would argue that Milton, himself one of those prisoners, obtained authority to resolve those disputes because his talk authorized his own and their own pious beliefs.[26] After all he was a prisoner too. What is not allowed in this resolution of conflicting opinions is Milton's interest in cultivating a different audience, a "fit audience," an audience that, when faced with these disagreements—those "difficulties" that some began to encounter in the poem—ask "What is . . .?" questions.[27]

Any author who attends to the audience that he has as well as an audience that he wants—for Milton, his desire to "fit audience find, though few" (7.31)—is rhetorical and political. Milton in his comments in the Verse will speak of the exemplary practice of "learned Ancients in Poetry and all good Oratory" who would not be "vulgar readers" of his poem. As chapter 1 will show, preference for an audience which Milton did endeavor to cultivate is specific to the praise which Xenophon once (*Mem.* 4.6.15) bestowed upon his teacher, Socrates. In short, Milton attended to an audience that was neither oppressed by the postmodern doubts of Fish's contemporaries, nor exclusively concerned to gratify or assuage pious orthodoxies awakened among of his own contemporaries[28]—though Milton obviously could not ignore the latter's sympathies. Rather, he desired to address an audience of excellent natures (see *Mem.* 4.1.2), few to be sure, with which he might raise fundamental questions which only are apprehended in counterpoise.

Surprised by Sin in its advocacy for the way of faith anathematizes another way—a way which this study gives the name of rational inquiry. These two ways challenge the claims of each other in their address to the same question, "How ought one to live?" One way to interpret Milton's *Paradise Lost* assumes that the poem teaches what Genesis teaches—that human kind though created free needs a guide for living other than those powers it has been given to think for itself. This teaching would exclude a 'philosophic' inquiry, especially of the sort that investigates "What is . . .?" questions.

The way of faith asserts its belief in a way, "obedience to the sole Command" which is beyond inquiry by another way, or so it would seem. It believes that knowledge of good and evil is revealed in the Bible as the word of God. But the way of faith cannot—and does not have a need to—prove that the way of inquiry is false, if only because such a proof would refute the very essence of the subject of the proof. Faith names conviction when there is no proof. On the other hand, the way of inquiry cannot invalidate the claim of faith to know good and evil, since it acknowledges no grounds—let alone that which inquiry would accept—of proof save its source in revelation. Nevertheless, inquiry can argue—as these remarks begin to do—the truth of an irreducible dyad of ways presented by means of a unitary but not univocal voice that speaks of and to both.

This unitary but not univocal voice belongs to the narrative persona who gives voice to the "generally accepted opinions" that shape the poem as Anne Ferry had argued that it would. But the narrative expansions of Genesis devised, imagined and managed by this persona[29] naturally will respond to the oft-inchoate stresses of those dominant opinions about the story no less than about the poetic form, and even the poet himself. Milton had a public persona, the outlines of which are sketched in the poem. Everyone knows how the story goes, but wishes it would have been otherwise—if there just had been a "warning voice" the judgment of God would not seem so harsh. So, the narrator supplies one. An epic needs a magnificent hero but Satan's heroism has to be exposed as pose. The totality of these stresses is managed by narrative persona in service to the ends of rhetorical persuasion—his interests are, after all, the same as those of the printer, as chapter 1 will show—and this will give rise to those so-called "difficulties" Waldock thought would have surprised the poet. In a sense it a plausible surmise—about the narrative persona.

These difficulties, however, in fact are arranged by the poet, John Milton, not his persona, to invite a dialectical scrutiny of these generally accepted opinions. The aim would be to discover what truth or falsity resides in these opinions about the poem's subject. In Ovid's tale of Narcissus, for example, that young boy is very definition of vanity, but did Milton mean to suggest that Eve was as well at the pool? Empson said such "difficulties" were what for him made the poem good. I am inclined to think Milton expected there might be a few others who did as well. In short, narrative persona speaks to and for the audience of men; Milton, to the "fit audience . . . though few." *Paradise Lost* speaks to both audiences with one voice, in a way that Augustine thought that even Scripture did.[30]

MAIMONIDES' GUIDE FOR THE PERPLEXED

A different view of the Genesis narrative of the Fall becomes visible in the opening chapters (1.1 & 1.2) of Maimonides' *Doctor Perplexorum* (*The Guide for the Perplexed*)—which Milton knew[31] in the Latin translation of Johannis Buxtorf (Basel, 1629) of a Hebrew translation of the Arabic text— when Maimonides recalls an objection raised by "a certain wise and learned man" (*vir quidam sapiens & eruditus*).[32]

Maimonides has begun the *Guide* with a discussion of the equivocal terms, "image and likeness" (*imago & similitudo*). His immediate object is to correct a false impression about the meaning of these terms which would lead to a grave error in understanding what God is. If men were to think, as many do, that "image and likeness" refer to "the form or shape of some thing" (*Formam alicuius rei*) (1), then, when the Scriptures says, "Let us make man in our image, in our likeness" (Gen. 1:26) they are likely to think that God too is corporeal, having a body, face and hands, that form and figure that men have. Rather, as he explains, the term *imago*, "is applied in reference to a form in nature, in reference to that actuality through which a thing exists, and is what it is." (*usurpatur de Forma Naturali, h*[oc]. *e*[st]. *de re, per quam res extsitit, & est quod est*) In man it is "that in virtue of which the intellectual apprehension shows itself in man " (*cuius virtute in homine existit Apprehensio Intellectiva*) (2). This, Maimonides adds, is "similar to the intellect of the Creator since it too depends upon no instrument or limb of some body"[33] (3).

In the following chapter Maimonides recalls the objection of "a certain wise and learned man" made once made many years before. But prior to addressing that objection Maimonides first discusses another equivocal term in the Hebrew Scriptures: *Elohim*. The term, he says, is appropriate (*competere*) either "to God, or Angels or judges as governing authorities over provinces" (*Deo, Angelis, & judicibus provinciarum gubernatoribus*). The need for this etymological clarification is not immediately obvious.

Returning to the objection, Maimonides recalls, this "wise and learned man," begins from the premise that "by the simple sense of Scripture, the primary intention in the creation of man was that he be similar to the rest of the animals—without knowledge or intellect, not knowing how to distinguish between good and evil." Why then, he wonders, would the "punishment for disobedience have granted to that very being the perfection of *that* which he formerly lacked, namely the intellect?" (*poena inobedientae eius perfectionem ipsi dederit, qua antea carebat, nempe Intellectum*). He is thinking of Satan's temptation of Eve: "for so—i.e., if you eat—you shall be just as *Elohim*[34] knowing good and evil" (Gen. 3:5), and also, of what they now have become, according to God, after the Fall: "Behold they have become like one of us, knowing good and evil" (Gen. 3:22, cf. *P.L.* 9.107–1073).

Maimonides answers the objection by clarifying what is meant by intellect. The objector assumed that the knowledge of good and evil is a perfection of the intellect; Maimonides argues, however, "intellect" refers to that which he was given at creation. The nature of *that* gift was made clear by the bestowal of commandments since they were not given to animals (*brutis*), he argues, "since they lack intellect and reason" (*intellectu ac ratione carentibus*).

Then Maimonides describes this faculty of intellect:

> *Per Intellectum (. . .) potest homo discernere inter verum & falsum, & hic inditus fuit ipsi ad perfectionem & absolutionem eius. Turpe vero, sive deforme, & Pulchrum, dicuntur de rebus manifestis in sensum incurrentibus, non vero de intellectualibus. Nam non dicimus, quod coeli sunt rotundi, pulchrum est: vel Turpe est, quod Terra est extensa, sed praedicatur de illis Verum vel Falsum. Et sic de rei alicuius certitudine vel incertitudine dicitur in Lingua nostra Veritas & Falsitas: de re vero pulchra vel deformi, Bonum vel Malum, & per Intellectum dignoscit homo verum a falso in rebus intellegibilibus. Quando autem homo adhuc extitit in integritate & perfectione sua, mentis imprimis & Intellectus, cuius respectu dictum est de eo, Et minorem fecisti eum paululum ab Angelis: tum nulla plane erat in eo facultas utendi sensibilibus,[35] vel ea apprehendendi.*

Through the intellect (. . .) man can distinguish between true and false, and this was imparted to him alone for his perfection and consummation. The shameful or ugly and the beautiful, however, are said of obvious facts when they impinge upon sensation [i.e. "that are generally accepted as known"], but surely not of matters entertained by the intellect. We do not say that the heavens are round is beautiful, or it is shameful that the earth is wide, but the truth and falsity are asserted of those things. Thus, in our language truth or falsity is said in relation to the certainty or uncertainty of something; of something beautiful or shameful, good or evil; and through the intellect man distinguishes the true from the false in intelligible things. When man, moreover, was in a state of innocence and his own perfection, it was said in his regard that "you have made him a little less that the angels (translating, *Elohim*)"(Ps. 8:6). At that time there was clearly no faculty of making use of "generally accepted opinions," or having any grasp of those things. (*Doctor Perplexorum*, 4–5)

These two chapters of the *Guide* offer a glimpse into events before the Fall of which Genesis had little to say, and Milton has quite a lot. Critical comment on *Paradise Lost* has consistently viewed these events as derived from

that teaching of a "simple sense of Scripture"—as the wise and learned objector in Maimonides would have it—about good and evil. Milton's additions to
the Genesis narrative, therefore, either are combed for hints of a disobedience
to come, or, as in *Surprised by Sin*, the speech and deeds of Adam and Eve are
seen to provoke an audience's own sense of shame: *those two* were innocent
once; we who try to imagine what they were like obviously are not.

This book, however, begins from a simple fact that grounds the initial
conversations of Adam and Eve in *Paradise Lost*. From their very first
moments they endeavor to discern the true from the false in their judgments
about themselves and that place in which they find themselves. Eve awakes,
"much wond'ring where/ And what I was, whence thither brought and how"
(4.451–452). Her first "unexperienc't thought" will be "to look into the clear/
Smooth lake, that *seemd* another sky" (4.457–459, italics added). Adam
wakes, and immediately turns his "wondering eyes" . . . / And gaz'd awhile
the ample Sky" (8.257–258). He looks about himself, seeing the place and
then, the "Creatures that liv'd, and mov'd, and walk'd, or flew"(8.264), and
thereupon discovers his own powers of locomotion: "Myself I then perus'd,
and limb by limb/ Survey'd, and sometimes went, and sometimes ran/ With
supple joints . . ." (8.267–269). But he too in his wonder has questions. "But
who I was, or where, or from what cause/ Knew not" (8.270–271). He asks
his surroundings and the living creatures, "tell/ Tell, if ye saw, how came I
thus, how here?" (8.277).

These questions in their charming naïveté occupy the thoughts and conversation of these two during the brief span of days they dwell in Paradise. On
them they exercise their powers of inquiry in conversation that they come to
learn they have.

Scripture also offers its own authoritative address to these questions which
we as descendants of Adam and Eve no less are wont to ask. And *Paradise
Lost* appears only to second that endeavor. To postlapsarian meditations akin
to Eve's "much wond'ring where/ And what I was, whence thither brought
and how," it replies, "Man's disobedience, and the Fruit/Of that Forbidden Tree, whose mortal taste/ Brought death into the world, and all our
woe"(1.1–3). This book suggests that Milton's additions of conversation to
the Scriptural portrait of Adam and Eve offer a different mode of address to
these questions: Socratic rationalism. Both modes taken together instance a
"great Argument" (1.24).

The discussion to follow will frequently resort to translation and close commentary of sources in the Classical and Judeo-Christian traditions. Milton to a
degree seldom granted in the criticism anticipates a "fit audience . . . though
few" that is acquainted with his sources in their original languages. Word
play, diction, puns, and at times even the studied arrangements of word order
only possible in an inflected language are borrowed, reinvented or allusively

recalled. Moreover, his command of the languages coupled with years of private study argues caution in historicist appeals to "schools of thought" and modes of religious thought and practice current in his own time. Cambridge Platonism and Neoplatonic readings of Augustine are two obvious temptations. An "ancient art of writing" that employs differential address to the problem of audience respects prevalent opinion as the material of dialectical scrutiny not as its interpretation. A test case central to this study is contemptuous dismissal, as already noted above, in the criticism of the past 80 years of Milton's appreciation for Xenophon's testimony on Socrates.

To compensate for the demands of close commentary some remarks on the overarching structure and course of the argument may be of use. Chapter 1 offers, as noted above, an account of the preliminaries to *Paradise Lost* found in THE PRINTER TO THE READER; THE VERSE and the two verse appreciations as an introduction to the problems of audience. In THE VERSE Milton points to the example of "certain learned Ancients in both Poetry and all good Oratory." This appeal is reminiscent of Xenophon's praise in *Memorabilia* 4.6.15 of Socrates's skill in gaining the agreement of his audience. Xenophon then added that Socrates himself was wont to observe that Homer held up the example of Odysseus as a faultless orator because he conducted his discourse by means of those matters that seem good to men.

Subsequent chapters generally follow narrative sequence—though with recourse to an implied chronology of prior events in Paradise. Adam and Eve converse for the first time several days after the day of their creation. What has happened prior to this day they talk informs how they speak and what they say about "that day" they first met. There are three profound moments of discovery in their understanding of themselves and each other during the conversation of these days. In "Eve's First Words" (chapter 3) Eve, aware for several days of Adam's growing doubts about her (see 4.446–447), tells Adam of the revolution in her thinking about herself and him when he seized her hand "that day" (4.449) they first met. A voice, as she gazed unwittingly at a "fair creature" appearing in the limpid waters of a pool, had told her in terms she could barely if at all understand what she was looking at. That voice then assured her that he would lead her rather to someone who would be hers "inseparably." But when she followed that voice and found a creature "less fair,/Less winning soft" she had turned back to the pool, only to be deterred by Adam's earnest grasp of her hand. Several days later her first words reveal to him how much she has learned from that event.

In chapter 4: "Interlude," Adam, as yet hardly able to understand what Eve has said about herself let alone him, but sensing now since she is talking she might be that one he requested of the Divine Presence (8.416–426), is eager to renew those marital relations he first enjoyed the day they met. Eve, however, is eager to talk. Their endeavor to do so as they walk, hand in hand to the bower, adumbrates the potential topics for their talk they will never enjoy.

In "Becoming Dear" (chapter 5), on the following morning Adam will experience his own revolution in his thinking when Eve's report of her dream of the Forbidden Tree reveals to Adam his recent dream induced confusions about Paradise and her. A voice in her dream had summoned her to the forbidden tree and she feared she could not but have eaten of its fruit. Adam now reassures her. His success in assuaging her distress at first seems due to a preternatural grasp of a psychology of dreams. But Adam on the day he was created also experienced two dreams of his own in an encounter with a "Presence Divine" (see esp. 8.292ff & 8.452ff). In talking with Eve he puts these two dreams together with the other one in his thinking. This deed—συλλογίζεσθαι, "to put together in reasoning"—in Aristotle is a method of inquiry that distinguishes the true from the false by means of a dialectical syllogism (see *Topica* 100a1–3). Adam had been pleased when Eve began to talk to him the day before, but now he finally sees before him what his Creator had promised: "Thy likeness, thy fit help, thy other self,/ Thy wish, exactly to thy heart's desire" (8.450–451).

Chapter 6: "No more of Talk" (9.1) examines the moment at which these two could really have begun to talk, but are prevented by a visit from an angel. Just at the moment that each is now aware of their "other self," Raphael arrives, and after a brief salutation to Eve, ignores her and talks with Adam. Eve eventually loses interest in their talk when Adam once again—as in "the Interlude," ventures into cosmology, and thus Eve goes to tend her flowers. Neither Adam nor Raphael notes her departure. She will return late to their talk, and overhear a parting admonition of the angel. The morning following, Adam and Eve quarrel, separate and fall. As William Empson had surmised—on different evidence though not hostile to thesis of this book—"Adam and Eve would not have fallen unless God had sent Raphael to talk to them, supposedly to strengthen their resistance to temptation" (147). These matters raise the question of the poet's design for the poem.

NOTES

1. Leo Strauss, *Xenophon's Socratic Discourse* 83, in the introduction to his interpretation of the *Oeconomicus* speaks to, "a powerful prejudice which emerged in the course of the nineteenth century and is today firmly established. According to that prejudice Xenophon is so simple minded and narrow-minded or philistine that he cannot have grasped the core or depth of Socrates' thought." For examples of this prejudice in the recent past in Milton studies, see Lewis, 7; Samuel, 29–30, concluding, "Xenophon is often merely a emphatic line drawn under Plato."; and Hughes, 694n32 where, "and his equal . . ." means "contemporary." Milton's near contemporaries, however, clearly thought otherwise. See, for example, Bacon's praise Xenophon as both a philosopher and historian in the *Advancement of Learning*, 163–164 & 180;

and Sidney's sense of Xenophon's reputation in both regards, in *The Defense of Poesy*, 218 & 222, and in the Letters, #8 "To My well-beloved Friend Mr. Edward Denny" & #10 "To Robert Sidney," his brother, in *The Major Works*, ed. K. Duncan-Jones.

2. See Appendix A, "A Brief Chronology of the Life of John Milton."

3. In the immediate context the remark, to be sure, was intended to certify Milton's interest in chastity in matters of love by implying his close study of *Symposium* and *Phaedrus* of Plato as a reply to a charge of moral turpitude during those years after Cambridge by his opponent in the pamphlet to which the *Apology* responds. But there is further evidence from this period which indicates Milton's careful study of both authors during this period, which will be examined in detail in "an excursus" of chapter 6.

4. He does report such a conversation his sometime associate, Alcibiades, had with his guardian, Pericles (*Mem.* 1.2.40ff.).

5. Lewis seems here already to have begun to draw sketches for those "ceremonial" personages of his *Perelandra*.

6. Citations to the poetry of Milton are to the second editions (1997) of Fowler, *Milton: Paradise Lost* and *Milton: The Complete Shorter Poems*. ed. Carey (2nd ed. rev [2007]); to the prose works in English unless otherwise noted, to the *Complete Works of John Milton*, hereafter *CPW;* to the prose in Latin, unless otherwise noted, to *The Works of John Milton,* hereafter, *WJM.* All translations from the Latin and Greek of Milton and of texts of the Classical and Patristic traditions, unless otherwise noted, are the author's own.

7. These elements—Books 1 & 2, the colloquies in Hell; Book 3, the discourse of the Father and the Son in prospect of Satan's advance upon the created world and Eden; Book 5.5.385 ff through Book 8, The discourses of Raphael with Adam, and, finally, Book 11.100 through Book 12; the commission and embassy of Michael—are, poetically speaking, the proprieties of Milton's narrative persona, as distinct from the conversations of Adam and Eve which are "overheard" (see especially The Argument of Book, [Fowler, 214] and 4.400ff.).

8. On occasion Milton may appear to abjure such expansions as a mode of Scriptural interpretation. In *The Ready and Easy Way,* for example, he asserts—and as Hughes noted (895n110)—in accord with the Westminster Confession of 1647 ("The infallible rule of interpretation of Scripture is Scripture itself; . . .") "that the whole protestant church allows no supream judge or rule in matters of religion but the scripture—*and these to be interpreted by scripture themselves,* which necessarily infers liberty of conscience—" and then adds, "[that] I have heretofore prov'd at large in another treatise" (*CPW* 7.456, italics added). The weight of an institutional sanction aside, the principle is clearly a premise for Milton's defense of the liberty of conscience, though at what hazard becomes clear in that other treatise to which he refers. In *A Treatise of Civil Power In Ecclesiastical Causes* as his initial principle in defining "the matters of religion" he avers,

> First, it cannot be denied, being the main foundation of our protestant religion, that we of these ages, having no other divine rule or authority, that is, from without us warrantable to one another as a common ground but the holy scripture,

and no other within us but the illumination of the Holy Spirit, so interpreting that scripture as warrantable only to our selves, and to such whose consciences we can so perswade, can have no other ground in matters of religion but only from the scriptures. And these being not possible to be understood without divine illumination, *which no man can know at all times to be in himself,* much less to be at any time for certain in any other, it follows clearly that no man or body of men in these times can be infallible judges or determiners in matters of religion to any other men's consciences but their own. (*CPW* 7.242–243)

Here a defense of a liberty of conscience leans not upon an institutional consensus but on the mystery of the illumination of the Spirit. Thus, as for the expansions upon the scriptural authority in *Paradise Lost,* one must consider what credence can be granted to the invocations of the Spirit (1.1–26; 3.1–55; 7.1–39; and possibly 9.5–24)—a question that A.M.'s "On Paradise Lost" (see esp. 5–22) surely raised in the front matters of the poem. It should be noted, moreover, that the states of soul described in the italicized passages above each anticipate the fundamental premise, the first, of *Paradise Regain'd* (see 1.8–17 & 206–214), and the second, of *Samson Agonistes* (see 23–67 *in re* Judges 16:20)—a matter relevant to their combined publication in 1671.

9. Citations to the Pentatuch are from the translation of Robert Alter, *The Five Books of Moses,* 19 & see, 18, his note to Gen. 1:26 on the term "*adam*" as the generic term for "the human."

10. See, for example *Nic. Eth.* 1145b5

11. See 9.1071–1072 7 10.84–85 in concert with Gen. 3:22–23, confirming the fact what the serpent, 3:5 had told Eve.

12. See Aristotle, *Topica* 100b21–23 in description of "generally accepted opinions," τὰ ἔνδοξα, the object of inquiry in Aristotle's account of the art of dialectic.

13. As noted above Xenophon does not represent conversations of Socrates with those close associates of an excellent nature (see *Mem.* 4.1.2), but he does provide a glimpse of such a nature and conversation in his report of his own apprehension of his talk with Euthydemus (*Mem.* 4.1–6).

14. On the political significance of the conjunction of these disciplines in Aristotle, see P. Rahe on Averroes (in his chapter, "The Liberation of Captive Minds" in *Against Throne and Altar* (139–174), and in particular (157–162). The same distinctions in audience and degrees of discernment in the kindred arts are also noted in Thucydides, *Historia,* 1.20–21.

15. Socrates seems to have had in mind the political uses of such a skill—as for example in Odysseus's restoration of the order in the assembly of the *Iliad* (2.188–335). He first individually addresses the kings in a far different spirit from the commons and then speaks to all in one speech which gains the assent of all. The political utility, after all, of this mode of address would subsequently become a familiar feature in the theory of the classical republic. See Rahe, *Against Throne and Altar,* esp. "Part II: Revolutionary Aristotelianism" (101–174).

16. Jonathan Richardson *Explanatory Notes and Remarks on Milton's Paradise Lost* (1734), cxliv–cxlv. http://books.google.com/books/about/Explanatory_Notes_and_Remarks_on_Milton.html?id=aYOe2Zfis04C (April 26, 2014, 11:10 a.m. CDT)

17. See *De Arte Poetica* 1448b15–17: διὰ γὰρ τοῦτο χαίρουσι τὰς εἰκόνας ὁρῶντες, ὅτι συμβαίνει θεωροῦντες μανθάνειν καὶ συλλογίζεσθαι τί ἕκαστον, οἷον ὅτι οὗτος ἐκεῖνος· ("For this reason, then, those who look at likenesses are delighted, namely that happens as they gaze in wonder, they happen to learn and put together in reasoning what each thing is, as for example, that *this* one is *that one.*)

18. Ferry cites (21) the conventional demands conventionally fulfilled in the poetic forms of *Nativity Ode*, and *Lycidas* and adds Sonnet XII, though far more striking and unconventional voices might noted also in Sonnet XI as well as in Sonnet XII, and, also would resolve the semi-comical perplexities of Sonnet VIII. Parodic representations of the poet's public persona is a common characteristic of the speakers of these three sonnets and, perhaps, might be entertained also in Sonnet IX if, "Therefore be sure/Thou, . . ." (11–12) is an ambiguous imperative of both stern spiritual reminder and awkward public praise.

19. There are two notable exceptions to this claim which will prove central to the argument of this study, the two overheard conversations of Adam and Eve (4.411–504 & 4.610–688). Their conversation the following morning to some degree also preserves this interpretational reserve (5.17–128). Cf. 9.199–384.

20. Robert McMahon made this very point in his *The Two Poets of* Paradise Lost [1998]: "Although she calls the Bard a narrator, she treats him as a consistent authorial consciousness. In her view, he has already made up his mind about everything in the poem, and he does not change his mind as he narrates it. In this regard Ferry's narrator proves much like Milton the author" (6). McMahon would hang his distinction between poet and narrative voice on a thesis of orality in composition: the poet is making it up as he goes along, and, more to the point, he only finds his way out of 'difficulties' in the concluding books (XI & XII). Thus Milton was someone different because he wanted his poem to include telling a story about this Bard's development as a poet. McMahon had probably been thinking of the note of caution Lewis had originally sounded in his *Preface*: "Even the poet, when he appears in the first person within his own poem, is not to be taken as the private individual John Milton. If he were that, he would be an irrelevance. He also becomes an image—the image of the Blind Bard—and we are told nothing that does not help that archetypical pattern" (59).

21. See especially his discussion of "The Good Temptation" in the initial chapter of *Surprised by Sin* (38–56) at the conclusion of which the notion of a "fit audience . . . though few" is treated as distinction without a difference in the notion of a reader's response.

22. "If we transfer the emphasis from Milton's interests and intentions which are available to us only at a distance, to our responses which are available directly, the disparity between intention and execution becomes a disparity between reader expectation and reading experience; and the resulting 'pressures' can be seen as part of an intelligible pattern" (3).

23. The metonymic substitution of "words on the page" as a name for the author's composition already announces the critical "sleight of hand" that will be employed.

24. How far Milton was from cultivating such an audience becomes clear in his discussion of rhyme in (see "some doubtful matter in the Verse") in chapter 1.

25. Fish, of course, would read "[to] assert Eternal Providence \ And justify the ways of God to men" (1.25–26), if not as an intent, surely as an anticipated outcome of his cultivation of his readership, but if the "fit audience . . . though few" is not identical with that readership, as Fish assumes it is (see Dowling, xxx), then how will he explain this divided address? Consider, moreover, the printer's request for an Argument and the two verse appreciations of S.B. M.D. & A.M., for the discussion of which, see, once again, chapter 1.

26. Fish himself aspired to and gained the same authority to adjudicate the dispute among the warring camps on *Paradise Lost*.

27. Thomas Pangle in his "Introduction" *to Leo Strauss, Studies in Platonic Political Philosophy*, 3, offers a concise account of those 'Socratic' questions in Plato and Xenophon: "our most promising inlet into the classes that constitute reality is through the opinions held among men, and above all through the most serious, trusted, authoritative opinions of the various societies. These opinions, considering the experiences and the evidence they point to, almost always make a great deal of sense; but they contain important ambiguities, obscurities, and contradictions—most important of all, they contradict one another. The path toward the truth about the natural species of things begins from the warring opinions and their confrontation, and proceeds in the direction of needed resolutions to which the confrontations point."

28. See especially Paul Dowling's revealing account of a diversity of opinion among these contemporaries, in his chapter, "Introduction, 'Historicizing Milton'" of *Polite Wisdom* (xvii–xxxi). This study to some degree differs from Dowling's account in an emphasis on the compositional strategy adumbrated in the Socratic writings of Xenophon.

29. .The comments added by the "poet" in response to his printer's original request for an "Argument," discussed in chapter 1 are a parody of this process.

30. See *Confessiones* 6.5.7–8

31. See *The Doctrine and Discipline of Divorce CPW* 2.257.

32. It is not at first clear whether this description names an advanced student of the Scriptures or of philosophy. The premise of his objection, however, would seem at first blush to suggest the former: "It seems from the simple sense of the Scripture that primary intention in the creation of man was that he would be similar to the rest of the animals, without intellect or thought, not knowing how to distinguish between good and evil." (*Videtur ex simlici sensu Scripturae, Intentionem primam in Hominis creatione fuisse, ut esset similis reliquis animantibus, sine Intellctu & cogitatione, nesciens discernere inter bonum & malum* [4]). But the question remains, with what intent does "the wise and learned man" question the meaning of "made in our own image," which in turn queries the capacities of intellect granted at the Creation.

33. This claim, clearly in concert with Maimonides's intent to refute the notion of the corporeality of God in order to affirm His true unity, seems an intentional overstatement. The fundamental issue in man's possession of an intellectual apprehension is its relation to the evidence of perception. Be that as it may in Maimonides, in Milton's dramatization of these matters in *Paradise Lost* in the conversations of Adam and Eve—not in the Raphael discourse—the perceptual faculties of touch and sight will seen to be indispensible.

34. It is worth noting that just prior to his addressing the objection of the *vir sapiens & eruditus* , Maimonides notes that *Elohim* is an equivocal term, referring "to God, to the angels, and to judges as governors of provinces" (*Deo, angelis, & judicibus provinciarum gubernatoribus* [*Doctor*, 3]). The third referent, of course, would remove the objection in that the knowledge would no longer be a perfection of God or the Angels, though it would still be useful as an instrument of rule among humankind. "Generally accepted opinions," that is, "the knowledge of good and evil," therefore are best understood in their political necessity as "those things that seem good to men" (τὰ εὖ δοκοῦντα).

35. In a note to the English translation of Maimonides's Arabic text of the *Guide*, Shlomo Pines (24n7) observes that the Arabic term *al-mashhurat* translates the Greek term τὰ ἔνδοξα, that is, "the words generally accepted as known." Buxtorf's Latin apparently uses *sensibilis, -e* (rare and post Aug., according to Lewis & Short) in light of the derivative sense of *sensus, -us* m, as "the common feelings of humanity, the moral sense."

Chapter 1

Preliminaries

"All Good Oratory" and
"This Great Argument"

The preliminaries to *Paradise Lost*—THE ARGUMENT, THE PRINTER TO THE READER, THE VERSE, and eventually, the two poems in appreciation, *In Paradisum Amissum In Summi Poetae Johannes Miltoni* and "On Paradise Lost"—intimate a strategy of address to distinct audiences of the poem in the poem itself. Added in stages after the original publication of the poem in 1667, the front matter of 1668 and the verse encomia of 1674 all speak to this poet's relations with his audience. It might be assumed that a poet simply wishes for the widest possible readership. This poet surely did when he promised in his proem to "justify the ways of God to men" (1.26). This would be in the interest of a printer as well, as it was for S. Simmons when he asked the poet for something he thought was missing, and set in motion the various additions discussed below. But this poet also had designs to "fit audience find, though few" (7.31) and had made provision for its nurture. When the printer in 1668 asked the poet to provide an argument, we can suppose the poet was surprised and disappointed. What, after all, was his "great Argument" (1.24) but an invitation for that few to seek out the great issues that the proem promised lay ahead?

The printer clearly spoke for the broad readership that frequented the book-stalls, but Milton added a further accommodation, THE VERSE, for his preferred audience under the guise of an additional favor to the printer's audience. The extravagant claims of that addition, however, far from providing reason for "why the Poem Rimes not" (THE PRINTER TO THE READER), now require a reason why the poet had availed himself of such an excuse. That reason will be found in the poet's recourse to certain "learned Ancients in both Poetry and all good Oratory" (THE VERSE), and a mode of inquiry that, for a few at least, results in greater discernment in reasoned discourse. The subsequent addition of two verse encomia in 1674 to the front matter of *Paradise*

1

Lost impersonates in distinct modes of praise the equally distinct concerns of the audiences of the poem.

David Masson[1] provided a chronology for all these additions. In brief, due to lagging sales of the first three bindings of the first edition, the printer had requested an ARGUMENT which Milton supplied. At that time he also added a comment of his own on THE VERSE. Taken together these addenda in fourteen additional pages were to constitute the front matter for the fourth binding of the first edition (1668). For these the printer ventured to preface a brief explanation: "THE PRINTER TO THE READER: *Courteous Reader*, There was no Argument at first intended to the Book, but for the satisfaction of the many that have desired it, is procured. (signed) *S. Simmons*." Some copies of the fourth binding, however, show an amended explanation, which thereafter became standard with the fifth binding: "*Courteous Reader*, There was no Argument at first intended to the Book, but for the satisfaction of many that have desired it, I have procured it, *and withal a reason of that which stumbled many others, why the Poem Rimes not*" (second italics added). Masson surmised that Milton, only distressed with the infelicitous grammar of the printer's original explanation, had asked for and then made a correction while the fourth printing was in process. If so, with the amended syntax Milton now also drew attention to a particular concern of his own in THE VERSE, of which the printer had made no mention. He inserted this concern under the printer's warrant. Both the poet and his printer were worried after the sluggish reception of the first three printings, but Milton apparently wanted the printer to seem to have asked on behalf of the general readership of the poem for what he, Milton, now had added.

This revised address to a *Courteous Reader* now suggested that the poet was required to make several concessions to his audience. Some, including the printer, evidently did not notice that an argument of some sort had in fact been mentioned—a "great Argument" (1.24)—and, as epic proems do, adumbrated by the first 26 lines. Others, we are to assume, took exception to a poem that did not rhyme. If the first sentence of THE VERSE desired an audience familiar with the Greek and Latin epics, this lack of rhyme would hardly have been of concern to what might, for the moment, be called the poet's preferred audience. Rather, the poet appears to also court the approval of another audience shaped by a climate of opinion that considers Rime a "necessary Adjunct and true Ornament of Poem or good verse." The remainder of his remarks in THE VERSE were without doubt intended, so-to-speak, to "stumble" both of these audiences.

Six years later, in 1674—and I shall assume with the poet's approval—two poems commending his accomplishment by two friends, S.B. M.D. and A.M., were added to the preliminaries. Milton, I shall also assume, had some say in the tenor of these encomia: S.B. M.D.'s tribute in Latin would appear to proceed from a familiarity with "*Homer* in *Greek*, and *Virgil* in *Latin.*" A.M. ends his apologetic praise with an ironic nod to the poet's scorn for "tinkling rhyme" ("On Paradise Lost," 46). Oblique commentary on both explicit and implicit standards adduced in THE VERSE is too obvious to ignore. *In Paradisum Amissum In Summi Poetae Johannes Miltoni* of *S.B.*, M.D. seems a testimonial from a member of the poet's preferred audience. "On Paradise Lost" of A.M. on the other hand, seems to dull the edge of diatribe in THE VERSE. One of those "famous modern Poets, carried away by Custom" who, though at first had doubts about this poet's project, has come to see some good in it, and even dares in pointed address—"Pardon me, Mighty Poet, . . ." (23)—to fashion his apologetic tribute in Rime.

All these addenda present the poet's relations with the diverse needs of quite different audiences, and in particular, his concern to "fit audience find, though few" (7.32).[2] How he awakens the considered judgment of a few within his more popular address in a public voice—as will now be argued— is an art of writing[3] taught by "learned Ancients both in Poetry and all good Oratory" (THE VERSE).

AN ARGUMENT IN THE POEM

The poet surely thought he had already provided an argument for his poem; the first clause of THE ARGUMENT that was supplied at the printer's behest says as much: "This first book proposes, *first in brief*, the whole subject" (ARG. 1, italics added). One sense of "an argument" is the "whole subject." The printer—or those that he spoke for—apparently unfamiliar with the poetic conventions of the epic form that provided that "subject" at the beginning of work, was looking for a different sort of argument—some sense of the plot of this poem. Perhaps this is why the printer did not notice the two sonorous periods that spoke to "the highth of this great Argument" (1.24). The scope of matters of which the proem promised to treat—his call to *that* "heavenly Muse, that . . . didst inspire/ That Shepherd, who first taught the chosen Seed/ In the Beginning . . ." and his own hopes for success—all would seem to support his view that it was a great matter that he took in hand. The poet was evidently confident his audience would, therefore, grant the propriety of "this great Argument" as a name for his Scriptural subject.

The very first sentence of that argument the poet eventually did supply— "Man's disobedience, and the loss thereupon of Paradise wherein he was placed" (ARG. 1)—thus gently chided the printer with condensed repetition of his argument in the first four lines of his poem. But thereafter, in sections that were eventually distributed to the individual books, he gave a sense of a sequence of events that sketched the sorts of things one might expect to find in heroic poetry. Little if any notice, however, was given in these "arguments" to the conversations of Adam and Eve—save noting their talk is overheard by Satan: he "thence gathers that the Tree of Knowledge was forbidden to them under penalty of death, and theron intends to found his Temptation, by seducing them to transgress" (BOOK IV: THE ARGUMENT). The immediate subjects of their talk, the deeds that accompany their words, and their subsequent relations with each other—that is, the focus of this present study—are nowhere to be found in these remarks fashioned for the printer's audience. For them, to "justify the ways of God" recapitulates in the sonarities of the epic the reticence of Genesis about the words and deeds of Adam and Eve in Paradise.

The poet, nevertheless, does provide what the printer wants, an "argument" in the sense of an account of what he is doing for an audience that the printer thought needed it, while maintaining his sense of the argument: a summary of the whole subject at the beginning: a proem. However, the identity of a "great Argument" remains vague. Perhaps the printer was right after all. The poet did not really say what he meant by that. In THE VERSE, however, the poet now brings to view an entirely different sense of an "argument" and thus, of his intent for his poem.

AN ARGUMENT IN THE VERSE

THE PRINTER TO THE READER

> *Courteous Reader*, there was no Argument at first intended to the book, but for the satisfaction of many that have desired it, I have procured it, and withal a reason of that which stumbled many others, why the Poem Rimes not.
>
> —S. Simmons

THE VERSE

> The Measure is English heroic verse without rhyme, as that of Homer in Greek, and Virgil in Latin; rhyme being no necessary adjunct or true ornament of poem or good verse, in longer works especially, but the invention of a barbarous age, to set off wretched matter and lame metre; graced indeed since by the use of some famous modern poets, carried away by custom, but much to their own vexation, hindrance, and constraint to express many things otherwise, and for the most part worse then else they would have expressed them. Not without cause therefore some both Italian and Spanish poets of prime note have rejected rhyme both in longer and shorter works, as have also long

since our best English tragedies, as a thing of it self, to all judicious
ears, trivial, and of no true musical delight; which consists only in apt
numbers, fit quantity of syllables, and the sense variously drawn out
from one verse into another, not in the jingling sound of like endings,
a fault avoided by the learned ancients both in poetry and all good
oratory. This neglect then of rhyme so little is to be taken for a defect,
though it may seem so perhaps to vulgar readers, that it rather is to
be esteemed an example set, the first in English, of ancient liberty
recovered to heroic poem from the troublesome and modern bondage
of rhyming.

(Fowler, ed., 54–55)

THE VERSE, as Milton's adjustment to the printer's address to the readers assures, provides "a reason of that which stumbled many others." Thus,
this addendum promises an argument in the sense of Cicero's *Topica*: "one
may define . . . an argument to be a reason which provides trust in a doubtful
matter" (*licet definire esse . . . argumentum autem rationem quae rei dubiae
faciat fidem* [§8]): Why is there no rhyme? "rhyme," he says is "the invention
of a barbarous age" and the practice "of some modern poets, carried away
by custom." His objection to this particular poetic custom, however, seems
overwrought; he is disdainful of a "trivial" poetic effect of "jingling sounds
of like endings," and hyperbolic in praise of his own poetic endeavor "to be
esteemed an example set, the first in English, of ancient liberty recovered
to heroic poem . . .," while finding fault with poets that rhyme "to set off
wretched matter and lame metre." To the printer's "Courteous reader" that
looks for a reason he offers contempt: they are "vulgar readers" that find a
defect where there is none. His approval of other poets "of prime note having rejected rhyme in both longer and shorter Works" would even appear to
mock *The Poems of Mr. John Milton* (1646). If THE VERSE provides a reason
"why the poem rhymes not," it has been procured at the expense of making
the poet's own way of speaking in THE VERSE a doubtful matter.

SOME DOUBTFUL MATTERS IN THE VERSE

It is reasonable to assume that Milton had Dryden's *Of Dramatic Poesy, AN
ESSAY*[4] in hand when he composed THE VERSE. Both *Paradise Lost* and the
Essay had been licensed in August 1667. Masson (6.632–633) was inclined
to think the two authors had exchanged presentation copies shortly thereafter. Apart from such speculation, every assertion of THE VERSE echoes a
topic of discussion in the *Essay* save that the original, cast as a congenial
and teasing exchange of views among four friends boating on the Thames,

is now impatiently reprised in THE VERSE with terse polemic. Milton might have taken the side of Crites in defending the absence of rhyme by citing the example of Latin and Greek, but Crites had promised, to "urge such reasons against Rhyme as I find in the Writings of those who have argued the other way" (¶99). And so when rhyme's advocates argued that it "circumscribes a quick and luxuriant fancy which would extend itself too far on every subject, did not the labour which is requir'd to well turn'd and polish'd Rhyme set bounds to," Crites *replied,* "Latine verse was as great a confinement to the imagination of those Poets, as Rhime to ours: and yet you find Ovid saying too much on every subject" (¶100). On the fundamental point of THE VERSE, "troublesome and modern bondage of Riming," Crites allowed that Ben Jonson was confined "even in the liberty of blank verse" (¶102). Neander too conceded that there was no greater liberty in blank than in rhymed verse: required both "an election of apt words and a right disposing of them" (¶104). Milton had claimed in THE VERSE that bad poets used rhyme to beautify "wretched matter and lame Meter," but Neander would parry that bad poets are bad whether they rhyme or not. If THE VERSE held that "famous moderns" were obliged "much to thir own vexation, hindrance, and constraint to express many things otherwise, and for the most part worse then else they would have exprest them," Neander could claim in Dryden's behalf that "the necessity of a rhime never forces any but bad or lazy writers to say what they would not otherwise" (¶104). In short, rhyme entailed no greater loss of liberty for a good modern poet in any modern tongue than Greek and Latin did for Homer and Virgil. Thus Masson dryly observed of the contemporary debate about rhyme: THE VERSE "was nothing else than Milton's contribution to the controversy in his own interest" (6.634). One can hardly call THE VERSE a "contribution." Rather, Milton borrows the notion of a "liberty" from the talk about "Riming" in the *Essay* because it perfectly suited his genuine concern with "a reason of that which stumbled many others."

That concern—Milton's evident disdain for "the use of some famous modern Poets carried away by Custom"—appears in his dissent from a consensus that all the speakers of the *Essay* share: deference is owed to the Custom residing in the tastes of their audience. Speaking of the absence of rhyme in "serious plays" Crites noted,

To prove this, I might satisfie my self to tell you, how much in vain it is for you to strive against the stream of people's inclination; the greatest part of which are prepossess'd so much with the excellent playes of *Shakespeare, Fletcher,* and *Ben. Johnson,* (which have been written out of Rhyme) that except you could bring them such as were written better in it, and those too by persons of equal reputation with them, it will be impossible for you to gain your cause with them, who will still be judges. This it is to which in fine all your reasons must submit. (¶99)

Neander later argues the opposite on the same ground:

> But I need not go so far to prove that Rhyme, as it succeeds to all other offices of
> Greek and Latin, so especially to this of Playes, since the custom of all Nations
> at this day confirms it: All the *French, Italian* and *Spanish* Tragedies are gener-
> ally writ in it, and sure the Universal consent of the most civiliz'd parts of the
> world, ought in this, as it doth in other customs, include the rest. (¶105)

"Dryden was," Masson notes speaking candidly of his early career, "a
man of very easy conscience. His notion of literature was not that rare one
which would insist on administering to the public what they need whether
they like it or not; . . . It was simply the grocer's notion of finding out the
articles immediately in demand with the best customers and competing for
the supply of these" (6.369–370). And thus the *Essay* served Dryden's own
recent successes. "What was the doctrine of Dryden's E*ssay of Dramatic
Poesy*? That blank verse was unsuitable for all high or serious poetry, even
for the tragic and poetical drama for which, and for which only, it had been
brought into use by the Elizabethans" (6.633). Masson and others since have
assumed that, when THE VERSE commended those who "have rejected Rime
in both longer and shorter Works, *as have also long since our best* English
Tragedies" (italics added), this remark and THE VERSE as a whole was an "all
but contemptuous reference" (6.635) to Dryden's successes. Dryden at this
time may well have yet been a mendicant to the new, yet even so, custom-
bound appreciation of his audience. For Milton he was merely a convenient
representative of—for those who knew his plays and the *Essay*—a poet's
obligatory but oft mercantile relation with his public.

Milton in THE VERSE, however, begins not with a contemporary squabble
among poets but with ancient exemplars. He concludes with his own hopes
for a success not in his representing a sacred subject but in the recovery of an
ancient liberty which is strangely instanced in an absence of rhyme. Both are
themes in the *Essay*. The missing element in the discussion of these preliminaries has been a nod to Milton's wit.

Rhyme is a lucid metaphor and, strictly speaking, precise synecdoche for
the work of custom in the desires of an audience. Rhyme is the musical effect
of the "sounding right" of what comes later solely on the basis of its conso-
nance with something that came before. It is the animate principle of every
binding custom. One does not have to think about it.[5] Thus Milton pretended
his poem would not "sound right" to an audience accustomed to the rhyming
tragedies of Dryden. Neander in the *Essay* had cited the sanction of custom
for rhyme in epic poetry to parry Crites's complaints against its use in tragedy.[6] His arguments against rhyme in tragedy would undermine the custom
in epic. Milton registers none of these arguments that favored his pretended

interests in THE VERSE. In fact, he ignores them because his dissent is not from rhyme per se, but rather from that consensus in the *Essay* that custom is the guide to good poetry. He was going to do something very different. His poem would be "the first in *English.*" It would require a fit audience that discerned "apt Numbers, fit quantity in syllables and the sense variously drawn out from one Verse into another." Such a discerning audience would also have to notice what was not apt, what did not fit, with their customary notion of a heroic poem. That same audience or at least a portion of it would also notice what is not apt and what does not fit in this comment on THE VERSE.

THE VERSE awakens discernment by its extravagant complaints against rhyme. There is much that does not sound right. Some might wonder about the poet's discourtesy in reply to the printer's request on behalf of a *Courteous Reader*. Clearly "vulgar Readers" does not "sound" like the right way to address one's audience. Yet those who the printer thought required an argument would be unlikely to pay much if any attention to THE VERSE. They just wanted to know what they could expect to find in the poem. Others, deaf to Milton's metaphoric wit, would find this discussion familiar; this is what poets are wont to do: argue about technical minutiae. Those who did know the arguments of the *Essay* would not think Milton had added anything to the controversy—as Masson had all but implied. But a few, especially those who were familiar with "Homer in Greek and Virgil in Latin" would have found a doubtful matter in the Verse.

The poet's account of himself is strange at the start. He prefers the precedent of Homer and Virgil in "English heroic verse." He might have said he honors an "ancient custom." There are many other customs in heroic verse his poem does honor: it has a proem; it summons a muse; it begins in the middle of things. Instead he launches into a tirade against rhyme, as "no necessary adjunct or true ornament of poem or good verse." For one who wrote sonnets this is a remarkable claim. He will allow that some modern poets have used it, but they no less than evidently were "carried away by custom." It is "the invention of a barbarous age" and the cause of "vexation, hindrance and constraint." By the time he concludes THE VERSE, this "modern bondage of rhyming" is in counterpoise to an "ancient liberty." For a few in his audience who did read "Homer in Greek, and Virgil in Latin," an "ancient liberty recover'd to heroic verse" is now the doubtful matter by virtue of known rules of their own erstwhile laborious versifying. It was not, after all, "liberty" that Milton described to Samuel Hartlib in his tract, *Of Education*:

> Forcing the empty wits of Children to compose Theams, Verses and Orations, which are the acts of ripest judgment and the final work of a head fill'd by long reading and observing, with elegant maxims, and copious invention. These are not matters to be wrung from poor striplings, like blood out of the Nose, or

the plucking of untimely fruit: besides the ill habit which they get of wretched barbarizing against the Latin and Greek idiom, with their untutor'd Anglicisms, odious to be read, yet not to be avoided without a well continu'd and judicious conversing among pure Authors digested. (*CPW* 2.372–373)

A few in the audience of this poem, therefore, might search for signs of some argument in THE VERSE to restore trust in an author who so strangely represents their own experience of study. Their familiarity with some "learned Ancients in Poetry and all good Oratory" might remind them that this phrase was no generalized praise but a precise identification.

AN ARGUMENT FOR THE VERSE

In the concluding chapter of Book 4 (4.6) of the *Memorabilia* Xenophon reports the views of two of his acquaintances—one personal, the other literary—who both might deserve to be called "learned Ancients in Poetry and all good Oratory." "Socrates," he notes, "was wont to say that Homer gave Odysseus the credit of *being an unerring* [i.e., lit. 'not prone to stumbling'] *orator* (τὸ ἀσφαλῆ ῥήτορα εἶναι), because he himself had the skill to conduct his speeches *through those matters that seem good to men*" (διὰ τῶν δοκούντων τοῖς ἀνθρώποις [4.6.15, italics added]). Xenophon had just made a similar observation about Socrates himself: "Whenever he himself went carefully through some matter in speech, he made his way *through things above all agreed [to be so]* (διὰ τῶν μάλιστα ὁμολογουμένων), since he believed that *this was the safe course in speech to avoid stumbling*" (ταύτην τὴν ἀσφάλειαν εἶναι λόγου [4.6.15, italics added]). At the beginning of this same chapter Xenophon had promised to explain how Socrates tried to make his close associates *more discerning in conversation* [i.e., *in the art of discussion by means of questions and answers*] (διαλεκτικωτέρους). "Socrates," he said, "believed that those who know *what each of the beings are* (τί ἕκαστον εἴη τῶν ὄντων) would also be able to carefully explain them to others, but," he added, "it was not surprising that those who do not know at all, *not only 'trip up themselves' but 'stumble'*[7] *others as well*" (αὐτούς τε σφάλλεσθαι καὶ ἄλλους σφάλλειν) (4.6.1 [italics added]). Xenophon thereupon offers to make clear Socrates's method of inquiry: how Socrates with his close associates went about investigating *what each of the beings is* (τί ἕκαστον εἴη τῶν ὄντων [4.6.1, italics added])—something, he claims (see also. 1.1.16), Socrates never ceased doing. However, he observes, since it would be a huge task to relate in detail the way in which he defined all of the beings, Xenophon recounts a conversation Socrates with Euthydemus which he thinks will make clear (δηλώσειν) his method of inquiry into a number of such beings.

Several points deserve notice. Milton's use in his revision of THE PRINTER TO THE READER of "stumble" as a transitive verb—according to the *OED*, only three occurrences prior to the fourth printing of first edition of *Paradise Lost*—a usage in Greek, σφάλλειν, which is unexceptional—begins to suggest that Milton is here engaged in literal translation from the text of Xenophon. In that text the repeated use (4.6.1 *bis*; 4.6.15 *bis*) of alpha privatives in the adjective (ἀσφαλής, -ές) of this verbal notion, as already noted above, is emphatic in describing Socrates's method and his primary concern in conversation. That *method of investigation* (τὸν τρόπον τῆς ἐπισκέψεως [4.6.1]), moreover, is conducted in its entirety by interrogating the conventional and custom-bound answers—i.e., notions that, so-to-speak, "rhyme" with "things that above all seem good to men"—of one Euthydemus. This Euthydemus, furthermore, was an inveterate *collector of the multitudinous sayings of the most well-renowned poets and sophists* (γράμματα πολλὰ συνειλεγμένων ποιητῶν τε καὶ σοφιστῶν τῶν εὐδοκιμωτάτων [4.2.1, italics added]). It is, therefore, either astonishing or utterly predictable, or rather it is perhaps both that Xenophon concludes his display of Socrates's method with the claim "[t]hat Socrates indeed simply declared *his very own opinion* to his close associates *seems to me* to be clear from the things that have been said" (Ὅτι μὲν οὖν ἁπλῶς τὴν ἑαυτοῦ γνώμην ἀπεφαίνετο Σωκράτης πρὸς τοὺς ὁμιλοῦντας αὐτῷ, δοκεῖ μοι δῆλον ἐκ τῶν εἰρημένων εἶναι. [4.7.1, italics added]).

One can take this statement in two ways. It would be easy to assume that Xenophon merely thought that Socrates's own opinion was the same as those notions expressed by Euthydemus under his questioning. (4.7.1) since he never objects to any remark Euthydemus makes. Xenophon's endeavor to show how Socrates made his close associates *more discerning in conversation* (διαλεκτικωτέρους [4.6.1]) however would then be rendered a nullity. To recognize a generally accepted opinion in the statements of an individual requires no discernment. It rhymes.

The other possibility is that Xenophon as he listened somehow discerned Socrates's own distinct opinion as he made his way *through those matters that seem good to men* (διὰ τῶν δοκούντων τοῖς ἀνθρώποις [4.6.15]) which Euthydemus affirmed[8] in his conversation with Socrates about piety and a few other human things. This way of inquiry that Xenophon claims (4.6.1) Socrates devised to produce such discernment will be examined more closely below. At present, however, there is no reason to reject either possibility since both are represented in Xenophon's account of Socrates's method, the first by Euthydemus's own affirmations and the second, by Xenophon's report of the same in his condensed epitome (4.6.1–11) of the conversations he overheard. This divided—one might say, discriminate—apprehension, moreover, represents the fundamental fact about Socrates's manner with his close associates: "*He did not*," Xenophon says at the outset of his account in Book 4, "approach everyone *in the same manner."* (οὐ τὸν αὐτὸν δὲ τρόπον ἐπὶ πάντας ᾔει [4.1.3, italics added]). This divided address is visible in the addition of two verse appreciations of the poem. These two verse encomia of *S.B.*, M.D. and A.M. offer two very different "takes" on *Paradise Lost*. By way of impersonating potential audiences of the poem, they instance distinct views of the poet's accomplishment.

TWO LEARNED FRIENDS

In the second edition of 1674 two verse appreciations—one in Latin elegiacs and another in English in rhymed couplets—were now added to the front matters of *Paradise Lost* along with a division of THE ARGUMENT the printer had requested for the edition of 1667 now arranged as individual headnotes to each of a reconfigured poem of twelve books. The verse encomia of Milton's poem, superficially at least, provide two instances of the poem's reception and coincidentally invite closer scrutiny of the poet's own sense of that preferred audience that he described in THE VERSE.[9] *In Paradisum Amissum In Summi Poetae Johannes Miltoni* of *S.B.*, M.D. with its final couplet proclaims not just a familiarity with the poet's implied standard of judgment—*"Homer* in *Greek* and *Virgil* in *Latin"*—but also dares to assert this standard has now been surpassed: *Haec quicumque leget tantum cecinisse putabit/ Maeonidem ranas, Virgilium culices* (Whoever reads these things shall think/Maeonides only sang of frogs, Virgil, of gnats, nothing more [41–42])[10]. In the closing lines of "On Paradise Lost" A.M. seems to bashfully confess that he too is one of those "famous modern Poets, carried away by Custom, but much to their vexation, hindrance and constraint to express many things otherwise" (THE VERSE). But in his concluding couplets, the rhyme ("offend"/"commend") constrains him to do "otherwise" than just "praise" the poet. Thus, he playfully suggests he now has to "commend" the "Verse" and the "Theme Sublime" as well. This is to say that he has been constrained by rhyme in his verses in praise of Milton to be more comprehensive. Here one suspects Andrew Marvell indulges in the confidant's wink with the author of THE VERSE:

I too, transported by the mode offend,
And while I meant to praise thee must commend
Thy verse created like thy theme sublime,
In number, weight, and measure, needs not rhyme. (51–55)

The authors of both these encomia were aware to some degree, it seems safe to say, of problems of audience this poet and his printer faced, and perhaps, if their contributions were invited, of the company their own verse tributes were to keep, placed before the other front matters of Milton's poem.

Though the authors of both were identified solely by initials, their identity has not been in dispute. The Latin elegaics[11] of *S.B.*, M.D. are attributed to one Samuel Barrow, a physician, whose circumstances are described in Masson.[12] Formerly attached to the army of Monk in Scotland, in the period of the Restoration he had been made physician in ordinary to the King, had a large practice in London, and Masson assumes, was "on terms of kindly familiarity with Milton in his later years" (6.715). Possibly these lines were already in Milton's possession as "a private testimony of Barrow's regard" or they were offered for the new edition. Either appears a reasonable hypothesis for literary history lacking other evidence. Of the nature of a possible friendship between Barrow and Milton there is only Milton's circumstantial remark in the *Areopagitica* that, "[w]hen a man writes to the world, he summons up all his reason and deliberation to assist him; he searches, he meditates, is industrious, and likely consults and confers with his judicious friends" (*CPW*, 2.532).

The circumstances of Marvell's contribution are clearer since notice is taken in "On Paradise Lost" (ll. 45–51) to Dryden's projected opera in rhyme—*The Fall of Angels and Man in Innocence: An Heroick Opera*—which was licensed for publication just two and half months prior to the licensing of second edition of *Paradise Lost*.[13] Masson therefore entertained the possibility that an impetus to a second edition could have been the publication of the text of Dryden's opera—though it never did reach a stage. Masson assumed (see 6.710–711) that Milton must have been privately amused at Dryden's request to "put his *Paradise Lost* into a drama in rhyme." Milton's remarks in THE VERSE had, of course, been current since 1667 and Masson dates Dryden's visit to Milton sometime in the winter of 1673–4. Of that meeting Aubrey reported, "Mr Milton received him civilly, and told him he would give him leave *to tag* his verses" (Hughes, 1023, italics added). That Milton's metaphoric assent to Dryden's request reappears in A.M.'s closing lines led Masson to think that Marvell had been given Milton's first hand an account of Dryden's request:

While the *town-Bayes* writes all the while and spells,
And like a pack-horse tires without his bells
Their fancies like our bushy points appear,
The poets tag them, we for fashion wear. "On Paradise Lost," 47–50

In any case, Milton may well have thought he had a chance to revive his ironic comments in THE VERSE with these two productions. In the 1674 edition both are placed before THE PRINTER TO THE READER and THE VERSE.

The two poems of appreciation pose as advertisements to a potential audience for the poem, but in fact are, "in Poetry and all good Oratory," impersonations of an anticipated approval of two different audiences. *S.B.*, M.D., as the poet seemed to wish in THE VERSE, draws upon his familiarity with *"Homer in Greek* and *Virgil in Latin"* to praise Milton's poem according to a conventional expectation of epic—cosmological scope: *Qui legis Amissum Paradisum, grandia magni /Carmina Miltoni, quid nisi cuncta legis?* ("You who read *Paradise Lost,* lofty verses / Of great Milton, what do you read but everything?" [1–2]). But to judge by the poet's own account of "first in brief, the whole Subject" (THE ARGUMENT, BOOK I) of *his* poem in the proem (1.1–26), this praise will leave nearly "everything" of Milton's subject out. Not a single prominent notion, topic, event nor personage of the proem, save an oblique reference to Christ—"till one greater Man/Restore us, . . ." (1.4–5)—that is referenced by *In Christo erga homines conciliatus amor* ("the love towards men obtained in Christ" [14]). Rather, this impersonated audience in S.B. focuses on the so-called "War in Heaven" and its aftermath in Hell. "Beginnings" and "ends of things" also briefly receive their due, but in diction borrowed from Lucretius: *Res cunctas, et cunctarum primordia rerum/ Et fata, et fines continet iste liber.* ("All things, and the first beginnings of things,/ And things foretold as well, and ends." [3–4]). Adam and Eve, in their innocence, Man's disobedience, and events in Eden after the Fall are nowhere found among those wonders the encomiast catalogues as praiseworthy. Rather, the human pair disappears into a generality for creaturedom: *Quaeque colunt terras, pontumque et Tartara caeca/ Quae colunt summi lucida regna poli.* ("And all that inhabits lands, and sea, and benighted Tartarus/that which peoples the shining realms of highest heaven" [9–10]). So much for that which was made in the image of its Creator.

The rhetorical stance S.B. employs for his praise, however, permits scrutiny of such an approach. Written in Latin its appraisal of the poem would have been beyond the ken of the common stall-reader[14], the general readership over which the printer is concerned. Only those that know they are addressed by the very first words of the front matter, *Qui legis Paradisum Amissam* (1), will be fit to take notice of his praise. Their prior knowledge of the language of this address will have been acquired by study of those very works, perhaps *"Homer in Greek,"* but surely *"Virgil in Latin,"* which also provides the standard of judgment for this poem's claim on them as readers. Following upon that partial catalogue of contents (lines 1–16) which those revered Classical epics do not in fact describe but only remotely imply, S.B. then, at the heart of his poem (lines 17–26), resorts to a trope of interrogative exclamation—(*O quantos in bella duces, quae protulit arma!/* . . . ("O how great the leaders in war, what arms on the march/. . . etc.")—confident that his Latinist readers have prior knowledge of these matters. The trope imitates the role of custom in judgment as rhyme since the exclamation and delight proceed first from recognizing a familiar type and then inviting the reader of these lines to expect that type as a standard that may have just been surpassed by poem they hold in their hands. What they hold in their hands will "rhyme" with what they think they know. It is the same, but only better.

After six elegaic couplets repeating this promise of delight and surprise at the same only better, S.B. brings the Latinist audience into a present of the perilous moment of the War in Heaven: *Sat dubius cui se parti concedat Olympus/ Et metuit pugnae non superesse sua/At simul in coelis Messiae insignia fulgent/* . . . ("Doubt there is to which side Olympus will yield herself/And she fears she will not survive her own assault./ But at that moment the standards of the Messiah blaze forth/ . . ." [27–29]). Most of this readership caught up in the action, will be carried along to anticipate another thrilling spectacle of war like those in Homer and Virgil. But all of this is at a great distance from "Of Man's Disobedience, and the Fruit" (1.1). as even Adam seems to notice when he hears of them: "Great Things and full of wonder in our ears,/Far differing from this World" (7.70–71).

S.B., M.D. needless to say impersonates an audience for *Paradise Lost*, a learned audience, but not that "fit audience . . . though few" (7.31) though the poet in THE VERSE appears to ask for one that knows "of *Homer* in *Greek* and *Virgil* in *Latin*." In fact, it is his knowing of those types that conditions his custom-bound enthusiasms. A.M., however, is a learned audience of a quite different sort.

DISCERNING A REASON IN RHYMING VERSES

Rather than feel confident he recognizes what sort of thing he holds in hand, A.M.'s acquaintance with "Fable and old Song" (8) has raised his doubts:

When I beheld the poet blind yet bold.
In slender book his vast design unfold,
Messiah crown'd, God's reconcil'd decree,
Rebelling angels, the forbidden tree,
Heaven, hell, earth, chaos, All, the argument
Held me a while misdoubting his Intent
That he would ruin[15] (for I saw him strong)
The sacred truths to fable and old song; (1–8)

He needs look no further than S.B.'s own breathless suspense at the impending fate of an "Olympus" to fear the demise of "sacred Truths" as a fable. His own tendentious use of a Scriptural story, "So Sampson grop'd the Temple's post in spite/ The world o'erwhelming to revenge his sight" (9–10) as analogue for his own fears shows the problem. But A.M. has the good sense not to think he knows what he is looking at. He is, perhaps, deaf to the rhyme of custom. And thus, as he reads he comes to reconsider, "growing less severe,/ I lik'd the project, the success did fear" (11–12). His appreciation of *Paradise Lost* was, as he indicates, a work in progress. He is not opposed to looking at things in a different way, but he is ill at ease that things he holds to be true no longer are held so. He wonders about the "Poet blind, yet bold": "Through that wide field how he his way should find/ O'er which lame faith leads understanding blind" (13–14). He is cognizant of human limitations, and no longer doubting (6) this poet's intent, now he fears, "Lest he perplex'd the things he would explain/ And what was easy he should render vain" (15–16). He is wary of difficulties, but he does sense that the poet's task is to explain those truths.

Nevertheless, in spite of, or rather, because of these doubts he will come to change his mind completely:

Pardon me, Mighty Poet, nor despise
My causeless, yet not impious, surmise.
But I am now convinc'd, and none will dare
Within thy Labours to pretend a share.
Thou has not miss'd one thought that could be fit,
And all that was improper dost omit: (23–28)

A.M. does not describe what convinced him to see *Paradise Lost* in a different way, but his praise is without qualification. The work, he tells the poet, the way it was written, has made him, as Xenophon would have said, διαλεκτικώτερος ("more discerning of intent"). A.M. in other words in this tribute impersonates the circumstances propitious to a birth of a "fit audience . . . though few" for *Paradise Lost*. That birth derives from a dawning sense of doubtful matters in the poem that provoke more careful scrutiny. One may note that in this encomium A.M. does not provide any specific insights of his own to support his now seemingly boundless (see 36–42) praise. He has an opinion about what this poet is doing, but, in accord with the example of Xenophon's Socrates and Xenophon himself, he does not speak openly of that opinion.

A METHOD OF INQUIRY IN XENOPHON'S *MEMORABILIA* 4.6

But how he tried to make his close associates more *discerning in conversation* (διαλεκτικωτέρους), this too I shall try to explain. Socrates, you see, was in the habit of thinking that *those who know what each of the beings is* (τοὺς μὲν εἰδότας τί ἕκαστον εἴη τῶν ὄντων), would be able to explain them to others. But he also said that it was not at all surprising that those who did not know *made both themselves stumble and stumbled others* (αὑτούς τε σφάλλεσθαι καὶ ἄλλους σφάλλειν). For these reasons, he never ceased examining *in the company of his close associates* (ἐν[16] τοῖς συνοῦσι) *what each of the beings were* (τί ἕκαστον εἴη τῶν ὄντων). Now of course it would be a huge task to go through everything in the way he defined them, but I will give an account of as many things as I think shall make evident *his method of inquiry* (τὸν τρόπον τῆς ἐπισκέψεως). (*Memorabilia* 4.6.1)

Xenophon's account of Socrates's method of inquiry[17] displays Socrates doing what Xenophon says he never ceased doing in the company of his close associates, examining *what each of the beings is* (τί ἕκαστον εἴη τῶν ὄντων). He says he will try *to give an account* (λέγειν) of how Socrates made his close associates *more discerning in conversation* (διαλεκτικωτέρους). This account begins with Socrates asking Euthydemus what sort of thing he believes piety to be. Euthydemus is not one of those associates with an excellent nature (see 4.1.2) but rather, an inveterate collector of the sayings of the most esteemed poets and sophists (4.2.1). Thus to all appearances he would seem to be one who could explain this or another particular extant thing as one who believes he knows what it is. Socrates's inquiries of Euthydemus—if they are not assumed to be a pose—would be indicative at least of Socrates's own interest to examine his own sense of the matter in the light of generally accepted opinion. Thus the Socratic method of inquiry that Xenophon attempts to make clear conceivably might have several outcomes, and, distinguishing among these various outcomes might itself be evidence of greater discernment in conversation.

Socrates might come to have a better understanding, possibly gain some knowledge of his ignorance—that he perhaps had merely of himself assumed—about what piety is, since inquiry seeks to understand something not yet understood. Or, he could come to some understanding, perhaps even know something about piety by asking Euthydemus, since Euthydemus does offer his remarks as one who, rightly or wrongly, thinks he knows. Or, Euthydemus may come to some understanding of his own ignorance about something he believed he knew, but now sees that he does not. Or finally, though Euthydemus may not recognize his own ignorance, another auditor, for example, Xenophon, in that company of Socrates's close associates may. Some of these outcomes—and there may be still more—might prevent one from stumbling oneself or making others stumble; others might allow one to anticipate certain risks and dangers of stumbling.

As the course of the conversation will show these risks also multiply when their inquiry into the sort of thing piety is, to Socrates at least, invites them to consider what they might say about other extant things. Their discussion of *piety* or *reverence* (εὐσεβεία)—asking what Euthydemus believes about the proper relations toward the gods leads Socrates to ask if there are analogous proprieties among human beings themselves. What they say about the need for a knowledge of those relations leads Socrates to think they might need to say something about *wisdom* (σοφία). Their talk about wisdom and its relation to knowledge and a human limit to knowledge Socrates suggests might involve talking about *the good* (τἀγαθόν) in the same way. And talking about the good in that limited way leads Socrates to wonder whether they might have to talk any differently about *the noble* (τὸ καλόν). Speaking of the noble as the useful leads Socrates to wonder if Euthydemus thinks that the noble so considered will include the usefulness of *courage* (ανδρεία) as one of these extant noble things. And the usefulness of courage leads inevitably to a discussion of *both the terrible and the dangerous* (τὰ δεινά τε καὶ ἐπικίνδυνα).

One further aspect of Xenophon's epitome of a Socratic method of inquiry is of note if only to distinguish Xenophon's account of a Socratic method from a more familiar aspect of a Socratic elenchus in Plato. At the conclusion of Xenophon's extended account of Socrates's gradual "courtship" of Euthydemus (4.2) and the latter's eventual indefatigable attachment to Socrates (4.3–4.6) as one of his close associates, Xenophon stresses that *"by far beyond all I have known, when he was speaking, he (Socrates) tried to bring about a shared sense of a reasonable accord among his auditors"* (πολὺ μάλιστα ὧν ἐγὼ οἶδα, ὅτε λέγοι, τοὺς ἀκούοντας ὁμολογοῦντας παρεῖχε [4.6.15]). This epitome of Socrates's method displays this "accomplishment" in—at first sight at least—a most implausible way: Socrates constantly asks questions of Euthydemus and, thereafter, he never disagrees with, let alone attempts to refute, as it seems, anything Euthydemus says. He does raise further questions which draw further responses, and so forth. This concatenation of questions and responses Xenophon gives the name of a *reasonable accord* (ὁμολογεῖν). The meaning of this "accomplishment" for all involved will be found in close scrutiny of the implications Socrates and some of his close associates discern in these responses from generally accepted opinions, that is, those *things that seem good to men* (τῶν δοκούντων τοῖς ἀνθρώποις), for their own inquiry in conversation.

A caveat of interpretation is required before proceeding to Xenophon's account of Socrates's *method of inquiry* (τὸν τρόπον τῆς ἐπισκέψεως) as exemplary of those "learned Ancients in Poetry and all good Oratory," and thus, to the differential address to distinct audiences employed by Milton in *Paradise Lost*. The priority this book grants to Xenophon's account of Socratic rationalism does not identify similarities of dramatic situation or character, but rather of countervalent stresses at work in the poem. In the conversations of Adam and Eve in *Paradise Lost* there is no Socratic surrogate. Adam and Eve will pose "what is . . .?" questions to themselves and each

other. Narrative persona in outlook is, so-to-speak, Euthydemean. He interprets events rather than participates in them. He cannot be identified with the
poet of *Paradise Lost*, but he bears a plausible likeness to that poet's public
persona—a "learned" man in the customary sense, that is, an inveterate collector of the sayings of poets and sophists—which one audience of the poem
will take as explanation since it is in accord with generally accepted opinion.
It rhymes with what they think they know already about these events. But
another audience, troubled by the difficulties it finds at first—as was A.M.
with *Paradise Lost*—begins to examine matters more closely and grows in
discernment. Euthydemus at the end of his conversations with Socrates in
Book 4 of the *Memorabilia* is little if at all changed by his talks with Socrates.
But Xenophon present as silent auditor to their conversations said he, "was of
the opinion that Socrates simply revealed his own opinion to those who spend
time in conversation with him" (Ὅτι μὲν οὖν ἁπλῶς τὴν ἑαυτοῦ γνώμην
ἀπεφαίνετο Σωκράτης πρὸς ὁμιλοῦντας αὐτῷ, δοκεῖ μοι δῆλον . . . [Mem.
4.7.1]). An attentive reading of *Paradise Lost* might begin to do the same for
Milton.

Socrates's inquiry into piety (εὐσέβεια), begins with asking Euthydemus
about his belief (νομίζεις;) about the sort of thing it is. Someone who believes
he has some sense of what a thing is would be able to say something of *what
sort of thing* (ποῖόν τι) he believes it to be. Euthydemus clearly does believe
he knows something about it. He is quite confident—he swears an oath—he
can say what sort of thing it is. It is the finest thing. Socrates infers (οὖν),
therefore, that he, Euthydemus, will be able to say what sort of person is the
pious (or, reverent) man. Euthydemus says he is one who honors the gods.
His oath might imply that he himself is one who does.

Socrates now wonders if it is possible to honor the gods *in whatever way
one wishes* (ὃν ἄν τις βούληται τρόπον[18]). Euthydemus has honored the
god with his oath. His sense of the finest thing, to honor the gods, was first
instanced with an oath. Socrates apparently wishes to know if *his own present
deed* of inquiry into piety is in the view of Euthydemus also a way to honor
the gods. Without this attention to the belief of Euthydemus any reasonable
accord would be unlikely. Euthydemus, however, appears not to be aware of
the scope of this question. "No," he replies, "rather there are laws *in accord
with which one must honor the gods*" (καθ᾽ οὓς δεῖ τοὺς θεοὺς τιμᾶν [4.6.2]).
He speaks merely of his sense of such laws. Xenophon's audience of the
Memorabilia, however, would be aware that for a decisive number of his fel-
low citizens in Athens Socrates' present practice—in which he was always
engaged in (see 1.1.16)—was believed to be in violation of such laws (1.1.1).
Thus it is reasonable to assume that Socrates's tacit scrutiny of his own activity in the light of generally accepted opinion will determine the direction this
conversation in epitome takes.

The conversation therefore turns to consider what follows from a knowledge of those laws: Socrates asks if the *one who knows these laws* (ὁ τοὺς νόμους τούτους εἰδὼς [4.6.3]) knows *how one must honor the gods* (ὡς δεῖ τοὺς θεοὺς τιμᾶν). Euthydemus agrees that these laws define a way to fulfill the obligation. At this point Socrates questions the relation of the knowledge of these laws to the obligation to act accordingly. He asks Euthydemus, "Then does the one who knows how one ought to honor the gods not think he ought do this differently than the way he knows?" [4.6.3]. This appears to be a sensibility of the morally serious man. Euthydemus does not disagree. This question, of course, also leaves open the possibility that some other unspecified way might also carry the same obligation to act. To this point their talk has established the necessary prior condition of that obligation: one needs to know how one ought to honor the gods—which, for Socrates might yet be an object of inquiry, if these laws are not a self-evident source of such knowledge.

The immediate consequence of the question and Euthydemus's confident agreement, now allows Socrates *to not do otherwise than what he knows* (οὐκ ἄλλως . . . ποιεῖν ἢ ὡς οἶδεν [4.6.3])—and since he does not know what piety is, and, thus whether piety prescribes what he ought to do, he can continue to honor the gods by his own inquiries. Now to further strengthen the claim of that way he asks Euthydemus if *anyone honors the gods in any other way than as he thinks he ought* (ἄλλως δέ τις θεοὺς τιμᾷ ἢ ὡς οἴεται δεῖν [4.6.3]). Euthydemus does not think they do. Thus, Socrates's questions—his mode of inquiry—tacitly reveals two views of piety as one of the human things: it is either a permissible authority in private judgment that arises in the absence of certain knowledge of how one ought to honor the gods; or the belief that the knowledge of how one ought to honor the gods resides in the knowledge of *laws* (οἱ νόμοι).

It is to the latter that Socrates now draws to the attention of Euthydemus. Previously he spoke of the knowledge of *laws* (οἱ νόμοι), but now he speaks of knowing the *customary or lawful things* (τὰ νόμιμα [*incipit* 4.6.4]) about honoring the gods. This change from laws (οἱ νόμοι) to *lawful things* or *customary things* (τὰ νόμιμα) follows from a private judgment about what one ought to do in the absence of that knowledge. If the laws had the authority of a god's pronouncement, there would be no room for private judgment. The gods simply declare—or as in the Judeo-Christian notion of "sacred Truths" might say, reveal—how they require that they be honored. In that case, however, piety would not belong to *human things* (τὰ ἀνθρωπεία) which Xenophon had originally declared (see 1.1.15–16) was Socrates's exclusive interest. But absent such a pronouncement, the stipulations of laws according to Euthydemus are in Socrates's view merely lawful or customary (τὰ νόμιμα): what people are wont to do is based upon their *belief.*

Several points are to be noted in this concluding exchange about piety
(4.6.4). Euthydemus is unaware of any difference between laws and the lawful or customary. He who knows the customary things will honor the gods
in the customary way; he who honors in the customary way, honors as one
ought; and he who honors as one ought is pious. Euthydemus agrees to all
three of these proposals of Socrates (4.6.4). But Socrates now concludes with
a question whose tone might give some pause: "Could he then who knows the
customary things about the gods be correctly defined by us as pious?"(ὁ ἄρα
τὰ περὶ τοὺς θεοὺς νόμιμα εἰδὼς ὀρθῶς ἂν ἡμῖν εὐσεβὴς ὡρισμένος εἴη;
[4.6.4]). Euthydemus replies, "To me, at least, it seems so." It is doubtful that
either Socrates or Xenophon would agree. This difference of opinion might
be seen to arise from an awareness of an unclear sense of what ought be owed
the gods in thinking about a difference between laws (οἱ νόμοι) and customary things (τὰ νόμιμα).

It is not necessary for present purposes to follow out step by step the
remainder of Socrates' inquiries into *other extant things* (τῶν ὄντων) Xenophon includes in his account. But it is noteworthy that in Xenophon's account
of Socrates' method of inquiry, analogous "Socratic" alternatives consonant
with Socrates present inquiry can be observed in these remaining discussion
topics—but most notably, in the discussion of wisdom (σοφία [4.6.7]) and
courage (ἀνδρεία [4.6.10–11]). This same triad of virtues shortly will be seen
to be of central concern to both Milton's proem (1.1–26) of *Paradise Lost* and
A.M.s "On Paradise Lost."

In the *Memorabilia* when Socrates comes to discuss wisdom, he cautiously wonders (4.6.7) "Tell me, do the wise seem to you to be wise about
the things that they know, *or are some perhaps*[19] *wise about that which they
do not know?* (ἢ εἰσί τινες ἃ μὴ ἐπίστανται σοφοί;)" Since Euthydemus is
incredulous at the second alternative, Socrates points out to him that wisdom will therefore be identified with knowledge. He agrees. But in their
concluding remarks on wisdom Socrates seems to restore that second notion
of wisdom—one might call it, a "Socratic wisdom"—as a possibility when
Euthydemus with no difficulty concedes that it is impossible for a man to
know everything. Therefore, Socrates asks, and Euthydemus, as always, willingly agrees that "thus, what each person knows, he is also wise about this"
(ὃ ἄρα ἐπίσταται ἕκαστος, τοῦτο καὶ σοφός ἐστιν [4.6.7]). The prior discussion of piety alone would suggest that Socrates possesses some wisdom about
that which he knows he does not know. Here Euthydemus unaware of such
a knowledge would also be unaware of whether such knowledge would be a
good in the sense of beneficial (see 4.6.8).

At the conclusion of Xenophon's epitome (4.6.10–11), Socrates and
Euthydemus also agree that courage is a fine thing (καλόν) because they
have agreed that the useful is something fine (καλόν) in regard to what is

useful. Here their discussion is occupied with describing the proper relation of the courageous man to *things both terrible and dangerous* (τὰ δεινά τε καὶ ἐπικίνδυνα). At first glance it might appear as if the discussion of courage will be conducted in the abstract: the identification of specific things that are both terrible and dangerous seems not to be at issue. But Euthydemus vigorously asserts that courage is useful with regard to things of *the very greatest import* (πρὸς τὰ μέγιστα μὲν οὖν) and, moreover, he cannot but just as strongly deny that it would be useful to be ignorant of things both terrible and dangerous.

Socrates now asks if those who are not afraid of such things *on account of not knowing what something is* (διὰ τὸ μὴ εἰδέναι τί ἐστιν) are courageous. The phrase, τί ἐστιν, is the form of the questions Xenophon tells us (1.1.16 & 4.6.1) Socrates was always investigating extant human things in the company of his close associates. Euthydemus denies that this ignorance deserves that name of courage and thereby seems once again to give an implicit priority to those investigations of Socrates—investigations which to Socrates, granting the unclear status of piety as one of the human things, have a claim to be pious and, therefore, inquiry into which might be considered wise.

Be that as it may, it would be impossible, it seems, to identify anything as both terrible and dangerous without first knowing what it is. That seems to be Socrates's point of asking as well about those who are afraid of things that are not terrible. With another oath Euthydemus affirms that these individuals are even less courageous than the former. Taken together Euthydemus's two replies appear to establish a need of inquiry into what things are both terrible and the dangerous. One might well think that such an inquiry with Euthydemus might itself be dangerous.

But now Socrates [4.6.11] apparently sets aside these arguments from need to simply ask about those who are, so-to-speak, *in a good state of mind in regard to the terrible and dangerous* (τοὺς μὲν ἀγαθοὺς πρὸς τὰ δεινὰ καὶ ἐπικίνδυνα ὄντας). Evidently there are some who already have—or think they do—an adequate knowledge of the terrible and dangerous in the conventional sense. Euthydemus here without difficulty assents to their description by a moral distinction: the good in this regard are courageous, the bad (κακοὺς) are cowards. He is familiar with both notions. In that confidence Socrates asks him if he believes that any others than the good are able *to manage in a fine manner those things* (αὐτοῖς καλῶς χρῆσθαι)—i.e., the terrible and the dangerous. "None but these," he says. Socrates now adds the obverse: "And the bad are the sort to manage these things badly?" Again Euthydemus agrees, "Who else?," he asks.

Here Socrates poses a decidedly strange question—"Well then, do each (of them) manage [it] *as they think they ought* (ὡς οἴονται δεῖν)?"—to which Euthydemus casually replies, "How else could they?" Euthydemus surely is aware that no one would or could *intentionally manage his own affairs* in such matters *badly* (κακῶς χρῆσθαι). That would lack all common sense, and Euthydemus surely has no lack of that. But Euthydemus clearly misses the thrust of a question which Xenophon did not miss. The good and the bad are both equally ignorant of a truly terrible and dangerous thing: their inability *to know whether they manage* their affairs well or badly since they both think they do it as they ought. Their sense—the moral sense of what one ought to do—that they do so assures them they are doing a fine thing in a fine manner. There would be a danger to expose this difficulty inherent to the moral sense for a man like Euthydemus who depends exclusively on its guidance. But there is little risk that he will discern the problem.

Socrates' subsequent questions now make a not so obvious point very clear. Socrates asks Euthydemus if some that are incapable of managing their affairs in a fine manner know how they ought manage them. With little enthusiasm he replies, "They probably don't." This possibility cannot have relevance to Euthydemus since he is capable in a moral sense though he does not know how. With two more queries he sharpens the grounds of distinction. Those that do know how they ought manage them, are able to manage them; and *if they are not completely mistaken* (οἱ μὴ διημαρτηκότες) Euthydemus admits, they will not manage them badly. This case does apply to Euthydemus; he does know to manage them in a conventionally moral sense. Euthydemus, then, is not completely mistaken about managing his own affairs in a fine manner: As they had agreed, the useful is a fine thing for whom it is useful. Such one would say are the conventional notions of the noble for Euthydemus; they are useful. At the same time, the point of these somewhat tedious questions and equally obvious answers may be easily missed, as it is by Euthydemus. He does not see a thing both terrible and dangerous for him that is inherent to his moral sense, his notion of wisdom.

This discussion of courage is, in a sense, the coping stone of Xenophon's account of Socrates's method of inquiry. Having made clear a necessity of inquiry in regard to the terrible and the dangerous, Xenophon's account drifts in the end unnoticed back into the familiar moral categories of good and bad, noble, and base.[20] The extent to which a Socratic method of inquiry will inevitably fade into the sensibility of a Euthydemus—confident that his own knowledge resides in his collection of the sayings of others and his perpetual attachment to the talk of Socrates with his associates (4.2.40)—is both an ever-present obstacle to inquiry and equally at risk and yet a protection for *the matters above all of general agreement* (τὰ μάλιστα ὁμολογούμενα [see esp. 4.7.1]).

Not a single statement or question in the conversation of Socrates and Euthydemus presents even a whiff of controversy. All the same, Xenophon was equally emphatic that, "conducting conversation always by means of such matters was the practice for which Xenophon said Socrates was wont to say that Homer held up Odysseus as *the orator not prone to stumbling"* (τὸν ἀσφαλῆ ῥήτορα [4.6.15]).

This can perhaps be glimpsed once again in the ambivalence of the final statement of Xenophon's epitomized report of their conversation "Then those who know how in a fine manner to make use of the terrible and the dangerous are courageous, but *those who are completely mistaken about this* (οἱ δὲ διαμαρτάνοντες) are cowards?" Euthydemus will likely have assumed that he is courageous on the grounds of his and Socrates constant agreement about these matters. It seemed, however, to Xenophon that—and considering the risk—he ought to find a way to make clear Socrates's own opinion about these matters that even Euthydemus thought were of greatest import. This would be a way to talk about Xenophon's Socratic rationalism.

THE VIRTUES OF A SOCRATIC
RATIONALISM IN *PARADISE LOST*

The preliminaries to *Paradise* Lost suggest identifying those "learned Ancients in Poetry and all good Oratory" with Xenophon's account of a Socratic method of inquiry epitomized in a discourse on the sort of thing piety is, and thereafter, by investigating the being of other human things, including wisdom and courage. In summary of that account Xenophon notes that the discourse proceeds at all times *by means of those matters most agreed upon* (διὰ τῶν μάλιστα ὁμολογουμένων [4.6.15]), that is, *by means of things that seem good to men* (δία τῶν δοκούντων τοῖς ἀνθρώποις [4.6.15]). Aristotle (*Topica* 100b21–22) would later call them, *generally accepted opinions, things that seem good to everyone, or most people, or the wise, or those of especial repute and renown* (ἔνδοξα δὲ τὰ δοκοῦτα πᾶσιν ἢ τοῖς πλείστοις ἢ τοῖς σοφοῖς ἢ τοῖς μάλιστα γνωρίμοις καὶ ἐνδόξοις)—and, later still, Maimonides (as noted in "A Preface") would explain in response to the objection of a certain "wise and learned man" that these matters are the content of the so-called "knowledge" of "good and evil" (*Dux Perplexorum,*4–5). In Xenophon these matters are sourced in the remarks of Euthydemus, that relentless collector of the sayings of the most esteemed poets and sophists and indefatigable Socratic companion, in conversation with Socrates. In *Paradise Lost* they will be authored in the adopted narrative persona of the poem.

This narrative persona first appears as the blunt-spoken author of THE VERSE and THE ARGUMENT. In THE VERSE his animus against rhyme is, in the voice of the poet John Milton, a poetic pretense. THE ARGUMENT's summary of this persona, as the printer asked, answers to the tastes of a broad audience: it "rhymes" with a common expectation that a poem needs a familiar subject, an easily recognizable plot, and a plausible cast of characters. This persona announces his task in the proem; he is daring, confident of his talent, with no qualms to speak of things both human and divine. He speaks boldly, as it seems, in the invocations of Books 1, 3 and 7; in Book 9 he laments in first person of the change of "Those notes to tragic"(9.6) as the Fall of Man impends; In Book 4 in fear he had called out, "O for that warning voice" (4.1) as he imagined Satan's approach to the earthly paradise and so, soon after, he provided an angelic visitor with such a voice for the human pair before the Fall. Much later he provides another visitor to palliate their expulsion. He has understandable sympathies for this pair.

He appears learned, schooled in the forms of and the expectations for epic poetry; he is a close reader of Sacred Scripture; he is well read in many other authors and has collected the sayings of the most esteemed wise men and poets; and above all, he, like his audience, is a fallen creature. Thus, his narrative is difficult to follow, not in plot, but in the details of characterization and description that on every page echo with notes drawn from the poetry and thought, both philosophical and theological, of his own contemporaries and reaching back to Classical and Biblical antiquity. Since his own experience is the standard of judgment, he rhymes what he imagines he "sees" with what he believes he knows of good and evil—but that knowledge does not produce coherence in the narrative. He is not the author of *Paradise Lost.*

John Milton resembles him, or rather, he resembles Milton quite closely in many, but not all respects. Milton too is a learned and fallen creature, but Milton is the "mighty poet" whose efforts A.M. eventually recognized in the poem. This poet labors to arrange all these difficulties in expectation of a "fit audience . . . though few" (7.31) that is capable of a "true musical delight": that is, a "sense variously drawn out from one Verse into another, not in the jingling sound of like endings" (THE VERSE). Like A.M. this "mighty poet" arranges various elements of generally accepted opinion recited by narrative persona to draw attention to the well-known difficulties that populate the poem. For example, is narrative persona's description of the first sight of the human pair in Paradise (4.288–318) what Satan sees or what narrative persona thinks Satan is seeing? What are both actually looking at? Why associate Eve with Ovid's Narcissus with a nearly identical repetition of Ovid's own narrator's address (4.467–470) to the boy at the pool? And what of Eve's dream of the Tree and Adam's explanation of it?

A clear difference between the narrative persona of the poem and Milton—who created that persona[21] as character, though only an observer of those other characters he added to the Dramatis Personae of Genesis for *Paradise Lost*—first becomes visible in the distinct appreciations of the two verse encomia added to the front matters. *In Paradisum Amissam* names Milton as author of all the things that S.B., M.D. expected to find in an epic and that he now believes has even surpassed the standard of Homer and Virgil. S.B.'s praise for what might now be called the Euthydemean details of the poem is mistaken not in spite of, but due to his acquaintance with *"Homer* in *Greek* and *Virgil* in *Latin."* His is a critical judgment that seeks the rhyme of what he sees with what he thinks he knows.[22]

A.M., on the other hand, admits, "When I beheld the Poet blind yet bold,/ In slender book his vast design unfold" (1–2), that he was troubled. Here one may note that A.M. at first saw *that* poet that was, so-to-speak, *"in* [the] slender book" (italics added); that spoke in the invocations and carries the narrative and at times interprets the events and characters in it. The "mighty poet" (23) that A.M. upon further reflection came to praise *is not in the Book*, but the author of it. Stated simply, A.M. eventually saw what a "mighty poet" was doing, a poet like himself familiar with a "poetry and all good oratory" as taught by certain "learned ancients." What A.M found then transformed his sense of *Paradise Lost*, and how it is to be read. In this sense A.M.'s "On Paradise Lost" though presenting itself as praise of the poet, actually fulfills the promise of its title. It is a précis for the method in the poem.

A.M. at the outset had doubts. He had mistaken the true author's, the "mighty poet's, intent: "the argument/ held me a while misdoubting his intent,/ That he would ruin (for I saw him strong)/The sacred truths to fable and old song" [5–8]. He admits to the poet he now addresses that he initially was afraid of something fearful and dangerous. His doubts questioned both this poet's personified appeal (1.1–16) to a "heav'nly Muse" for support and the subsequent claim of credentials (1.17–26) for such assistance. It was just an artful pose to "ruin sacred truths to poetry and old song." *That* poet asked to be imbued with a triad of virtues—albeit as conventionally understood. The "mighty poet," A.M. comes to see will understand these virtues in a different way.

As if honoring a poetic convention[23] in the call to a "heav'nly Muse" in the proem of *Paradise Lost*, narrative persona as poet had originally requested the triad—piety, wisdom and courage—and then implied that he was a fit vessel for their bestowal. *Seriatim* he referenced first the piety of Moses both at his call (Ex. 3) and at the receipt of the Decalogue (Ex. 19 & 20)—"that on the secret top/Of Oreb or of Sinai, didst inspire/*That shepherd*"(1.6–8); then the wisdom obtained in those encounters by that author of Genesis—*"who first taught* the chosen seed/ In the beginning" (1. 8–9); and with that inspiration, finally the courage to risk like deeds—"I thence/ Invoke thy aid *to my advent'rous song"* (1.12–13). He then repeated the sequence in self-appraisal and self-scrutiny: "And chiefly thou, O Spirit, that dost prefer/ Before all temples, *the upright heart and pure,"*(1.16–17); *"What is dark* in me/ *Illumine"* (1.22–23); and *"That to the highth* of this great argument/ I may assert . . . etc" (1.24–25) (italics added).

A.M. in "On Paradise Lost" at first recalls his fears about this poet's "vast design"(2) in these same terms. But he deftly registers, as it appeared to him at the time, the flaw in that design by pointing to a necessary interdependence of these virtues more visible by their absence, as it then seemed to him, in the poet: daring without wisdom ("the Poet, *blind, yet bold,*/In slender book his vast design unfold" [1]); bold powers with impious intent ("his Intent/that *he would ruin* (for *I saw him strong*)/ *The sacred Truths* to fable and old song" [6–8]) and thereby, a crippled reverence unable to guide an obtuse intelligence ("how he his way should find/ O'er which *lame faith* leads *understanding blind*/ Lest he perplex'd the things he would explain" [13–15]).

But the poem would eventually begin to work its way upon him: "Yet as I read, soon growing less severe/ I liked his project, the success did fear" [11–12] Other doubts follow but in the end, his reading of the poem led him to see it and the poet in a different light:

Pardon me, Mighty Poet, nor despise
My causeless, yet not impious, surmise.
But I am now convinc'd, and none will dare
Within thy Labours to pretend a share.
Thou hast not miss'd one thought that could be fit,
And all that was improper dost omit:
So that no room is here for Writers left
But to detect their Ignorance or Theft. (23–30).

In consequence of his growth in discernment in reading the poem, A.M. now speaks somehow differently about these virtues. He asks this Poet's forgiveness: "Pardon me, mighty poet, nor despise/ My causeless, *yet not impious*, surmise" (23–24, italics added). His initial surmise, "That he (i.e., the Poet) would ruin . . . /The sacred truths to fable and old song" (7–8), was pious in the conventional sense. What then in this apology is the need to explain the obvious?—unless A.M. now sees that initial surmise now must be defended under a different notion of piety: his doubts about what he was doing have allowed him see the poem anew. He has become more discerning.

The immediate context for A.M.'s apology had spoken of a different concern: "that some less skilful Hand/. . ./. . ./Might hence presume the whole Creations' day/ To change in Scenes and show it in a Play" (18, 21–22)—a reference, it seems, to Dryden's ill-conceived attempt to "tag" Milton's verses. If that was once a concern, it is no longer:

But I am now convinc'd, and none will dare
Within thy labours to pretend a share
Thou hast not miss'd one thought that could be fit,
And all that was improper dost omit: (25–28)

Together with his concluding wink at his own rhyming verse, A.M. indicates that he understands that the concerns at the surface of these front matters of *Paradise Lost*—concerns about Dryden's designs on a play and the vexatious custom of rhyme (45–55)—are beside the point.

That majesty which through thy work doth reign
Draws the devout, deterring the profane.
And things divine thou treat's of in such state
As them preserves, and thee, inviolate. (31–34)

A.M.'s new understanding—without ever naming him—of Milton's way of preserving the sacred things of Scripture is expressed in conventional terms. The poet is pious; he "draws the devout." In "deterring the profane." He makes discriminate address to a fit audience for the poem. His wisdom, moreover, is visible in his care for how he treats divine things, "in such a state/ As them preserves, and [himself], inviolate." Here A.M. obviously refers, in the first place, to way the poet represents in words these things in his poetry. If cast in familiar, human or ordinary terms these things would be unlikely to preserve their character as divine. Perhaps this is why A.M. resorts to a poetic flight about such poetic flights:

Thou sing'st with so much gravity and ease;
And above human flight doest soar aloft
With plume so strong, so equal, and so soft.
The bird nam'd from that Paradise you sing
So never flags, but always keeps on wing.
Where could'st thou words of such a compass find?
Whence furnish such a vast expanse of mind? (36–42)

It seems A.M. answers the questions of the last lines in pointing to the poet's own preservation of questions about divine things, that so-to-speak, keeps them in flight. And finally, his courage is implied by the notice A.M. gives to the risk the poet incurs when he expands on the poet's concerns: "As them preserves, *and thee*, inviolate."

Those acquainted with Xenophon's Socrates's discussion of these same virtues with Euthydemus may notice that here too seemingly univocal descriptions in definition may also permit a different sense. In that discussion, examining the sorts of things a man like Euthydemus believes about piety might also be taken as a way to honor the gods; an understanding of one's own ignorance might be granted the name of wisdom; and courage might be needed to discern a flaw in moral judgments.

The pages to follow examine Milton's attempt to revive these "ancient liberties" that he observed in his studies of certain "learned ancients in poetry and all good oratory" which this study calls Milton's Socratic Rationalism.

NOTES

1. Masson, 6.621–634

2. Almost any discussion that seeks interpretative principles from internal evidence of the poem will either openly or implicitly identify a candidate for Milton's "fit audience . . . though few." Lewis, and others as well, thought "Milton intended his poem for an audience familiar with the particular conventions of language and attitude associated with earlier epics" (Ferry, 2). Empson saw his task in *Milton's God* to "recapture the way it was meant to strike a fit reader" (36)—distinguished from a "simpler reader," since Milton wrote on theological matters of "two levels" (38)—who, among other qualities, could appreciate his (i.e., Milton's) sustained analysis of Satan's character" (66). Corns, vii, casually suggested Milton "was probably thinking primarily of moral fitness, of a godly readership capable of responding to the theological perspective his poem contains," and Fish had identified that perspective in *Surprized by Sin, (passim)* with a penitential discipline of Milton's contemporaries. But Dowling, xxvi–xxx, points to a distinction in audience, one *"Popular,* accommodated to the prejudices of the vulgar and to received CUSTOMS and RELIGIONS, the other *philosophical"* found in John Toland's [1670–1722] "Clidophorus" (65–66) and, rejecting reader response criticism's grant of discernment to all readers, argues that "truly responsive reading is rare"(xxx).

3. When my own thoughts on the operations of such an art in *Paradise Lost* were in process, I became acquainted with Paul Dowling's description (*Polite Wisdom* 1994) of this art at work in his commentary on the *Areopagitica.* Dowling argues that after the disastrous reception of the Divorce Tracts, Milton took a new course in his prose. With painstaking attention to anomalies, disjuncts and contradiction in a rhetoric of address to Parliament on the liberty of unlicensed printing, Dowling shows how and why Milton must cautiously advance a politically prudent defense of a liberty to philosophize. At the close of this study Dowling, 106–107, evinces a need to investigate the operation of this art in *Paradise Lost*. The present book hopes to contribute to such an endeavor.

More recently, Paul Rahe, 104–174, has provided circumstantial evidence and congruent citation of the prose tracts that Milton was likely to have been familiar with neo-Latin Averroist writings on the Continent. The evidence Rahe finds of Milton's awareness of the problem of audience, as one element among others of a so-called "political-theological" problem; his practice of an ancient art of writing learned from these writers acquainted with the Medieval transmission of the Arabic commentaries of Al-farabi on Plato and Aristotle, both directly and by way of Maimonides; and the accommodations Milton saw necessary under the new circumstances of Christian polity grounded in revealed Scripture to defend an ancient liberty of philosophizing—all offer welcome but ancillary support to the present argument which rests its case on Milton's familiarity with and extended study of certain "learned Ancients."

4. John Dryden, citations by numbered paragraph.

5. This is the essence of Milton's better known yet disastrously unsuccessful complaint against custom found in the address, "to the Parliament of England, with the Assembly," as the preface to *The Doctrine and Discipline of Divorce*. See CPW 2.222–224.

6. See esp. 1732–1737 & also, 1790–1840.

7. The use of "stumble" here as a transitive verb, as in Milton's emendation to the PRINTER TO THE READER, "and withal a reason that which *stumbled* many others," is intentional. Milton's preference for this rarity is likely a sign that he was translating σφάλλειν, wherein a transitive sense in Greek is unexceptional.

8. Christopher Bruell in his introductory essay, "Xenophon and His Socrates," to the Amy Bonnette translation, Xenophon: *Memorabilia* (Cornell: 1994), calls Euthydemus, "the nonobjector par excellence" (xxi).

9. Critical discussion of the encomia is disappointing to say the least. The sole discussion, if it could be called that, of the Latin elegaics is Micheal Lieb's "S.B.'s '*In Paradisum Amissam*': Sublime Commentary" (71–78). Hardly more than a paraphase larded with enthusiastic references to obvious correlations in text of *Paradise Lost*, the commentary on the Latin rests on the authority of two compared English translations, of N.G. McCrea and J. Milton French, which did not reveal to the author the misconstrued grammar his sources evidently shared [*currus animes*, (30) as if a modified masculine plural noun taken as a singular, "living chariot," instead of, a second person singular present hortatory subjunctive (*animes*) with an plural object (*currus*) substituted for an impersonal passive (see *A&G* §439a), "*Awaken life in those chariots and arms worthy of God!*"] which was then further construed as a minor theme in the poem. No mention, moreover, was made of any metrical considerations that would render praise of an epic poem in elegaic couplets at least peculiar. "On Paradise Lost" of A.M has not shared the fate of such neglect. For discussion of the poem on its own terms, Nigil Smith's (*The Poems of Andrew Marvell*, ed. Nigel Smith [2003]) commentary represents the labors of contemporary comment on Marvell, not Milton. In brief, comment on A.M.'s remarks on Milton has become a display case for modern and postmodern critical trends. Wittreich's "Perplexing the Explanation: Marvell's "On Mr. Milton's *Paradise Lost*" 280–305, for example, reads the poem in light of contemporary events, including attacks on Milton. Kenneth Gross, 77–96, broadly posits Marvell's anxieties as one poet reading and writing on another as the motive principle in the uncertainties and doubts he first reveals. These doubts and their unexplained dismissal, "Pardon Me, Mighty Poet" (23) are relentlessly theorized.

10. The conclusion of course refers to the pseudo-Homer *Batrachomyomachia* "The Battle of the Frogs and Mice," of various attributions but which Martial (*Epigrammata* 14.183: *Perlege Maeonio cantatas carmine ranas/ Et frontem nugis solvere disce meis*.) assigned to Homer, and the pseudo-Virgil *Culex* of the *Appendix Virgiliana*, a collection of 33 poems of various sorts gathered under the name of the Roman poet.

11. See Appendix A for the Latin text and a translation.

12. The most detailed biography of Barrow is A.L. Wyman's "Samuel Barrow, M.D. Physician to Charles II and admirer of John Milton," in *Medical History* v.18 (1974). 335–348. Wyman relies chiefly on Masson for the friendship with Milton (see 344–345) but cites John Toland, Milton's first biographer, *The life of John Milton* (1698) for the identification of *S.B.*, M.D. as the author of *In Paradisum Amissum In Summi Poetae Johannes Miltoni*.

13. For a more detailed account of the relations of Milton and Marvell and recent critical comment on Marvell's contribution to the "front matters," see Smith, 180–184.

14. To judge, at least, by the parodic treatment of them in the two "Tetrachordon Sonnets (XI & XII)

15. Smith, 183n7, citing OED v. I.1. glosses *ruin*, "to reduce [to]."

16. Reading ἐν in manuscript D, rather the σὺν in the text of Marchant, following the preference of Strauss, *Xenophon's Socrates*, 116–117. See also translation of A. Bonnette, 139n.j.

17. The author's translation of Xenophon's epitome of the Socratic method of inquiry, *Memorabilia* 4.6.1–11) is in Appendix A.

18. The phrase employs the same expression, τρόπον, Xenophon used to refer to the manner or mode of Socrates investigations: τὸν τρόπον τῆς ἐπισκέψεως [4.6.1].

19. The second, Socratic, alternative for wisdom is cast as a doubtful assertion (For μή with the indicative, see Smyth, *Greek Grammar*, §1772.).

20. In *Paradise Lost* this sensibility goes by the name of "the knowledge of good and evil."

21. Milton's critique in his *1st Defense of the English People* of Salmasius's quotation of some lines from Euripides *Suppliants* as if they were a warrant for Euripides's own opinion bears notice, *mutatis mutandis,* in this matter: "know then, I say, that we must not regard the poet's own words as his own, but consider who it is that speaks in the play, and what that person says; for different persons are introduced, sometimes good, sometimes bad, sometimes wise men, sometimes fools and they speak not always the poet's own opinion, but what is fitting to each character" (ch. V [Alvis,216]). This is the most economical explanation of the so-called "difficulties" of the poem. They are sourced in the persona of a learned poet, who is, as most are, an inveterate collector of generally accepted opinions of wise men and poets. To expect a coherent vision from such a source per se would be unwise. But a "Mighty Poet" might employ available disjunctions among various opinions at times to raise important questions.

22. Joseph Summers (*The Muse's Method*, 1960) in the finest critical account of this proem in poetic terms noticed this same problem among his contemporaries: "In reading these lines, as in reading the entire poem, we can use all the erudition we possess and all that we acquire from scholarship; but we must beware that it does not blind us. The dangers of scholarship and of genre criticism are that they may lead us *to believe that we know what we shall find before we find it; the result is often that we find exactly what we expected*" (12, italics added).

23. In fact this triad of virtues is exceptional in the conventions of an epic proem. Homer in both epics summons a muse without specifying, apart from a subject, either

the nature of the gift or himself as fit receptacle; Virgil only asks a reminder of the "reasons" (*causas* 1.8); Ariosto follows Virgil's blunting of invocation per se by first person (*Arma virumque cano* 1.1.). This triad, however, is implied in a political context in Homer's invocation for the catalogue of ships (see 2.484–493) wherein the poet doubts his own ability to bring any order to the confusion of those multitudinous tribes which Odysseus, Xenophon's Socrates's "unerring orator," has in some measure just achieved.

Chapter 2

Prologue

"To value right the good before them" (4.202–203)

As Satan comes to roost, "[l]ike a cormorant" in the Tree of Life, narrative persona declares an epistemological problem rendered with moral indignation at anticipated wrongs to come:

> So little knows
> Any, but God alone, to value right
> The good before him, but perverts best things
> To worst abuse, or to their meanest use. (4.201–204)

Expecting the worst—"O for that warning voice, . . . \ . . . that now\While time was, our first parents had been warned" (4.1 & 4.5–6)—from the very beginning of Book 4 as Satan approaches the created world and the earthly paradise, narrative persona establishes an interpretative caveat for the entire spectacle of the human pair in Paradise. Quite soon this fallen creature will instance the problem in his own judgments of them both. He of course is thinking of the use that Satan intends to make of these two, but knowing the story of Genesis as he does, his own design to tell that story misinterprets his own sight. It will be difficult, then, for any audience that knows that tale to value right the good before them. They will undoubtedly look for signs of what rhymes with what they think they know. Narrative persona soon provides an instance:

> the fiend
> Saw undelighted all delight, all kind
> Of living creatures new to sight and strange:

Two of far nobler shape erect and tall,
Godlike erect, with native honour clad
In naked majesty seemed lords of all,
And worthy seemed, for in thir looks divine
The image of their glorious maker shone,
Truth, wisdom, sanctitude severe and pure,
Severe but in true filial freedom placed;
Whence true authority in men; . . . (4.285–295)

At first, it would seem that these remarks relate what Satan sees. None of *these* living creatures were familiar to Heaven; all would be to him "new to sight and strange." Yet in these two he appears to recognize virtues he once might have claimed for his own. Might he be then, *mirabile dictu* for a moment an innocent observer of these two? To narrative persona in *his* mind's eye, however, these two particular creatures and some of the other kinds would not be "new to sight and strange." Yet though familiar in form, can he imagine them to be a kind he has ever seen before?[1] In short, it is difficult to tell from narrative persona's representations who is seeing what, how. Nevertheless, for both these fallen creatures—and no less, the presumed audience of the poem—*what is being seen* will be "rhymed" with what they think they know of it already.

Narrative persona in spite of himself describes what he could imagine Satan would see, not what he, Satan, is seeing. "Valu[ing] right" would otherwise be a distinction without a difference. Narrative persona, and Satan no less, cannot segregate their judgments from a fault of remembering those generally accepted notions about things in the past that these two resemble.[2] They are fallen. At first, narrative persona plausibly assigns a divinity to the looks of these "Creatures new to sight and strange," an image of which the fallen angel would yet recall.[3] Narrative persona, however, would only need to recall the words of the Genesis account he intends to elucidate: "Let us make a human[4] in our image" (Gen 1:27)—if, that is, unwittingly, he, for the moment takes that line in a corporealist sense. But gradually other notes resonant with his prior experience of his own human kind find their correlative objects in what he sees:

                though both
Not equal, as thir sex not equal seemed;
For contemplation hee and valor formed,
For softness shee and sweet attractive grace,
Hee for God only, shee for God in him:
His fair large front and eye sublime declared
Absolute rule; and hyacinthine locks
Round from his parted forelock manly hung

Clustering, but not beneath his shoulders broad:
Shee as a veil down to the slender waist
Her unadorned golden tresses wore
Dishevelled, but in wanton ringlets waved
As the vine curls her tendrils, which implied
Subjection, but required with gentle sway,
And by her yielded, by him best received,
Yielded with coy submission, modest pride,
And sweet reluctant amorous delay.
Nor those mysterious parts were then concealed,
Then was not guilty shame: dishonest shame
Of nature's works, honor dishonorable,
Sin-bred, how have ye troubled all mankind
With shows instead, mere shows of seeming pure,
And banished from mans life his happiest life,
Simplicity and spotless innocence. (4.295–318)

The elemental sign of this prior experience is the way narrative progress in description mimics the way one human being is wont to look at another. Taking in a general sense of bodily comportment and expression of face, one's glance begins at the head, looks to find sight in the eyes, relates the glance to the face, the expression with the hair and thereafter the glance moves down the torso. Milton has his narrative persona represent not only what he imagines Satan would be seeing, but also that persona's human way of seeing. He too is looking at something and representing what he sees. And this looking will come to a crisis when, so-to-speak, the eyes of his mind reach "those mysterious parts." His embarrassed deflection of his own shame at his own imagined gaze at those "parts"—one may say he blushes to imagine it—displays his sense of his own lack of innocence as an heir to the knowledge of good and evil. For him at least there is nothing "mysterious" about them. He knows what he is looking at, even if only in his imagination.

With this brief drama of a guilty conscience in narrative persona, Milton draws attention to the less visible—because "generally accepted"—opinions about this pair's mode of life, character and relations which are imposed on the "sensory particulars." On what grounds—on what evidence, after all—is this narrator able to describe with such confidence the relations of these two with their God and with each other? Why does he take one to be a contemplative, and the other, a dream object of amorous affection? They have yet to say a single word and they are utterly motionless throughout the elaborated catalog of their observers' gaze. Satan, after *his* first sight, will decide he needs more information. He moves closer, "To mark what of their state he more might learn\ By word or action marked" (4.400–401). By these means, even he understands one must discern character and motive.[5]

It will be by these very same criteria that some of Milton's audience will obtain an innocent sight of this pair in their conversation soon to follow (4.411–491). They will talk about their past few days together. How they look from the vantage of the Tree of Life, if purified of narrative persona's imposed reading of character and motive, is not a frozen distillation of their being—as if the drama of their life in Paradise begins from this moment, but the specific result of their recent past life together since they were created.

Milton validates a naïveté to investigate such events and ask such questions by having his narrative persona represent a familiar progress in his very own seeing. This persona is looking at something in the way human beings look at something, drawing upon past acquaintance, their 'knowledge' of good and bad, to represent to themselves and others what they are seeing. But they and he himself do not value right the good because only God does. In Book 3 of *Paradise Lost* God's seeing was described as a "prospect high,\ Wherein past, present, future he beholds, . . ." (3. 77–78). To approximate *that* sight of this pair, therefore, would be to see—as God sees—this motionless present moment as a plausible or reasonable consequence in their freedom of choice of their words and deeds of their past few days together since the day of their creation and as incipient particulars relevant to their future relations. What they said and thought and felt and did those first few days animates the aspect they present to Satan perched in the Tree of Life and, so-to-speak, to the imagination of the narrative persona when he describes what he and Satan see.

Milton by every means available to him would have us believe this evidence in speech and deed (4.411–491) does not spring from the fallen imagination of his narrative persona. The talk of these two about their recent past is granted a unique status in all of *Paradise Lost*. In both the narrative and THE ARGUMENT it is said to be *overheard* (See 4.400–409)[6]—by Satan surely, and—in accord with the fictive parallels[7] noted in the careers of both in prior books—also by narrative persona. Moreover, this overheard speech is introduced by an elaborate play on the locus classicus for anticipatory pleasures in Catullus ("*Ad Fabullum*,") 13.13–14.

Catullus in inviting his friend to dinner had promised Fabullus in recompense for his otherwise penurious board of fare, a whiff of the perfume worn by his sweetheart, *quod tu cum olfacies, deos rogabis,\ totum ut te faciant, Fabulle, nasum* ("which when you smell it you'll beg the gods\ To make you, my Fabullus, all nose." In *Paradise Lost*, Satan creeps closer to the pair "as a tiger" [4.403]) ready to devour every morsel of their state as nourishment for his nefarious purposes. Narrative persona introduces what he overhears with a play on Catullus compounded with pronominal ambivalence. The introduction to the direct speech of these two innocents unsettles any auditor's confidence that they know which of the two is about to speak:

"when Adam first of men\ To first of women Eve thus moving speech\ Turn'd *him* all ear to hear new utterance flow" (4.408–410). Does "him" refer to Satan or to Adam? We might imagine that Satan could see who begins to speak. But for 28 lines "other auditors," that is, those of this poem, will listen to a speech devoid of any marks of gender in the speaker. All these devices serve, one might say, to "de-familiarize" the utterance overheard, that is, to invite an innocent appreciation of what *is heard* and, so-to-speak, *beheld*. More simply, if one cannot see who is talking and cannot hear whether that voice is male or female, one would not quite know what to make of these two—for the moment, at least beguiled by what hears and what one does not. The spell would be broken of course when narrative persona resumes: "To whom thus Eve replied," (4.440). What then is it that Satan and narrative persona are "actually seeing" that provides hints in their looks and bodily aspect for how to value right their words and deeds of these, their very first days?

Both see two who are two even before a gaze descends to "those mysterious parts." They are two of the same sort yet different—they could logically not be two otherwise. Their difference—though assigned to "sex"—seems for the moment mere corporeal differences absent their awareness as of yet of "those mysterious parts" of themselves: one's hair is longer than the other's. Their stature and locomotion appears obtained on two limbs rather than by four. Hence they are distinct from the other kinds; they require less to rise above what is below them. One fixes his gaze on no object before him; he looks off and "upward hither . . . among the trees" (cf. 8.313). He is not looking at the other, but there is both an openness to his gaze and a directness as if he questions his very questioning but yet is confident of a reply. The other looks at him. Her gaze is fixed on him because she deems him to have a grasp of matters beyond her present ken. She will soon speak of why she thinks so (see 4.475–491). There is something similar in the gaze of each and something different. She too looks up, but at him. She is shorter in stature. She leans slightly toward but not on him. For this moment there is distance, though remediable, in their relations. The moment is a pause for each to reflect. Soon they will clasp each other's hand and make their way to "a tuft of shade that on a green\ Stood whispering soft" (4.325–326), and sit down, and talk.

How they *really* look at this moment, that is, distinct from how narrative persona has cast his or Satan's sight of them, is a glimpse into the innocent drama of their relations with each other and their Creator in the past few days and a harbinger of a future they are never to have. This moment has a history. It is a direct result of the events of the past few days which they soon will relate to each other and have in mind when they converse with each other. To repeat, according to Plato's Socrates, "to converse is to use reason." There are four conversations (4.411–491; 4.610–689; 5.25–128 & 8.250–520) of

Adam and Eve in *Paradise Lost*. The first three, as illuminated by an innocent glimpse of those "Two of far nobler shape erect and tall," will be the focus of this study of Milton's Socratic rationalism. The fourth, that occurs after the Fall, must be reserved for another occasion, for reasons that belong to the conclusion of this study.

NOTES

1. The description of the Garden (4.205–285) as Satan looks down from the Tree of Life perhaps provides an answer by an analogical comparison. Satan surveys the Garden with "new wonder" (4.205); narrative persona, first attempts to geographically locate Eden with reference to details from Biblical and Ancient history (4.208–222). But as he comes to describe the beauties of the Garden itself, his own poetic art and memory of such gardens are unable ("if art could tell\ How . . ." (4.236ff) to convey what he sees; all poetic memorials of fabled gardens are discovered as falsehoods except in this place (Hesperian fables true\If true, here only (4.250–251); nothing else compares: "Not the far field\ Of Enna, where Prosérpin gathering flowers . . ." (4.267–268); Nor that sweet grove\ Of Daphne by Orontes, and the inspir'd\Castalian spring . . . "(4.275–279); nor that Nyseian isle . . ."; Nor where Abassin kings their issue guard\ Mount Amara . . ." (4.280–284). In short he has no resource to which to make comparison. These sights are "new to sight and strange"; they have no "rhyme" to them, but they do have a reason.

2. God, of course, would be free of this fault, and therefore value right, because he would have no need to recall anything "from his prospect high,\ Wherein past, present, future he beholds, . . ." (3.77–78)

3. Cf. 4.33–39, esp. 4.37–39: "O Sun, to tell thee how I hate thy beams\ That bring to my remembrance from what state \ I fell, . . ."

4. See the translation and note of Alter, 18n.26, on the Hebrew word, "*adam.*"

5. For discussion of the principle which is probably as old as Homer and surely the reason why Plato and Xenophon wrote dialogues, see Klein, 17–20.

6. Cf. THE ARGUMENT of Book 4: "Satan's first sight of Adam and Eve; his wonder at their excellence form and happy state, but with resolution to work their fall; overhears their discourse."

7. See esp. 3.14–21.

Chapter 3

Eve's First Words

A poetically crafted illusion of overheard conversation permits direct scrutiny of Milton's materials and methods relieved of the burden of moral judgments of good and bad resident in the poem's narrative persona. Otherwise, that fallen creature would, like a god knowing of good and evil, inevitably impose his judgments on these innocents by his imagined rhymes with texts literary, philosophic and theological within his vast experience. As a Euthydemean collector of wise sayings of the well-reputed, he will know what he imagines he sees: Eve gazes at her reflection in a limpid pool of water; Ah!, Ovid's Narcissus!; "vanity thy name is woman!" So too has the voluminous criticism on this passage and this poem, once again, "like gods knowing of good and evil" known what they were looking at.

Milton, however, by the ruse of overheard conversations invites a "fit audience . . . though few" (7.31) to simply investigate why this poet places Eve's waking moments at that limpid pool—there is no such detail in Genesis—and if the resonances with Ovid are, as they are, irresistible, why take that risk to occlude Eve's first moments of consciousness under such a cloud of associations? The vast majority of the poem's audience will, of course, have some sense of Ovid's tale and yet find little if anything amiss. After all, Eve in the end did not suffer the fate of Narcissus—but then again, this might begin to explain that big mistake to come. Be that as it may, Satan and narrative persona would seem to share with the audience of the poem one fundamental opinion about the pair: "in their looks divine\ The image of their glorious maker shone" (4.291–292).

To begin with this opinion about these looks—how they look to each other and to themselves—since these looks are central to the words and deeds of Book 4, in the first of the conversations of Adam and Eve in *Paradise Lost* Milton borrows Ovid's mischievous wit at the expense of the Delphic oracle and Socrates to translate Platonic self-knowledge into Eve's first words in *Paradise Lost* as her first words in Paradise.

Milton paid close attention to the structure, the poetic figures and the very words of Ovid's tale of Narcissus. At the crucial moment in Eve's account of her recovery from a fascination with an image at the pool, in five lines Milton employs both a surprise entrance of an admonitory voice and a tricolon of verbs describing the image in the pool which replicate the precise diction and tense of those same features in the Narcissus tale in Ovid's *Metamorphoses* (3.432–436)[1]. Other familiar features of Ovid's style—frame narrative, apostrophe, paradox and amphiboly—are also revised and re-deployed. Milton thereby signals to those who know Ovid that Ovid's Narcissus and Ovid's way of telling the tale is very much on his mind.

To varying degrees this has been obvious to Milton's audience almost from the beginning.[2] The popularity by Milton's time of Ovid's tales no less than their moral-allegorical retellings is well known.[3] But the question has always been why did the author of *Paradise Lost* risk associating the mother of mankind at the moment of her birth into consciousness with the fatal self-sufficiency, self-absorption and vain admiration of Narcissus. Such nascent inclinations in Eve would surely evince a flawed creation and a prelapsarian predisposition to the Fall. How then could the poet "justify the ways of God to men" (1.26) when he has his Satan—no stranger to self-admiration (see 2.763–765)—overhear Eve's account of her first moments to Adam (4.440–491) and thereafter (9.532–48; 606–612) orchestrate his temptation on that fatal day upon this theme? Satan did not need to read Ovid to recognize that beyond the Interdict there was an ancillary "fair foundation laid whereon to build\ Their ruin!" (4.521–522), but Milton's audience would.

The risks an author takes depend upon his notion of audience. Narrative voice in *Paradise Lost* mentions several. In the proem of Book 1 he is expansive: "men" (1.26) will stand in judgment of what he says about God and man; but later he hopes to "fit audience find, . . . though few" (7.31).[4] The "Preface" and the account of "Preliminaries" to *Paradise Lost* of this study argue that Milton invites this "fit audience" to consider the practice of Socrates. He, Xenophon thought, was always able to converse with his close associates though in earshot of whoever wished to listen.[5] Nevertheless, the terms of engagement for those "few" are considerable.[6]

The present chapter offers a rationale for the troubling association of Eve with Narcissus in a common but disguised referent for both: Plato's *1st Alcibiades*. Eve's account (4.440–491) of herself to Adam, of her rise into consciousness and of their first encounter displays an extraordinary depth of self-knowledge. Ovid frames his tale of Narcissus with a barb at the Delphic dictum, "Know thyself": his Tiresias had prophesied that the youth would live a long life, *si non se noverit* (3.348), "if he does not know himself." Both narratives shadow the drama of the *1st Alcibiades* in which the need for, the obstacles to, and the nature of a self-knowledge urged by the oracle is enacted in the conversation of Socrates and Alcibiades. A sign of the close kinship of these texts is the near identity of the initial and concluding states of mind of the three protagonists: Narcissus, Eve and Alcibiades. Each begins as a naïvely self-absorbed and self-sufficient being and each comes to understand their own absolute need of another to whom they will declare their devotion. Each discovers that their own happiness depends upon and can only occur through conversation with that other. There are obvious differences in the "poetic" circumstances and fates of Narcissus and Eve, but these differences too are anticipated by the *1st Alcibiades*. Ovid crafted a mischievous parody of the Socratic "teaching" on the Delphic dictum. The possibility of such was suggested by none other than Socrates himself (see 129a2–4). Moreover, Ovid's parodic premise—the analogic relation of 'looking into' (εἰσβλέπειν) something that reflects oneself—was proposed by Socrates and then distinguished from the way the soul 'looks into' itself (132d1–133b10). In short, Ovid's mischievous wit comes to life in 'playing dumb' while reading from a Platonic script. Milton, however, rescues Plato's account of Socratic self-knowledge from Ovid's wit as the rational ground for the conversation of Adam and Eve. The *1st Alcibiades* thereby informs Milton's optimal sense of a "joyning to it self in conjugall fellowship a fit conversing soul,"[7] and of the domestic "helpe meet" as "another self."[8]

FRAMING THE NARRATIVE

"Well then, does 'to know oneself' happen to be an easy matter after all, and was the one who put up this saying in the temple at Dephi some dimwit?" (*1st Alcibiades* 129a2–4)

Milton was as aware of Ovid's framing narrative (3.318–350 & 511–512) as of its pathetic subject—the self-absorbed Narcissus. Following Ovid's original, Milton frames his translation of Ovid's Narcissus into Eve's narrative of her first moments at the pool with his own theme of self-knowledge. Eve's first words in Paradise and *Paradise Lost* declare her remarkable self-understanding in the causal relations of Aristotle and Milton's own *Logic*[9]: "O thou for whom\ And from whom I was form'd flesh of thy flesh,\ And without whom I am to no end, my guide\ And head, . . ." (4.440–443). Sharing Adam's sense that they both owe praise to that Power "that rais'd us from the dust and plac't us here\ In all this happiness . . ." (4.416–417), she passes on to speak of her own contentment, but she has noticed that Adam is less happy than she: "I chiefly who enjoy\ So far the happier Lot, enjoying thee\. . .

while thou\ Like consort to thyself canst nowhere find" (4.446–469). For this reason she recalls for Adam's sake her first moments of consciousness when she too had lacked self-understanding: "That day I oft remember, when from sleep\I first awak't, . . .\. . . *much wond'ring where\And what I was, whence thither brought, and how*" (4.449–453, italics added). When she concludes her account of "that day" (4.449) her present contentment will be as manifest as her considerable self-knowledge. She knows *now* what she learned *then*, on "that day" when they first met.

"That day" beneath the platan tree where they first met she had said nothing to Adam. Adam would do all the talking. But Adam also in a panic moment had done something. Eve, therefore, recalls for his benefit that event which gave rise to all her present insight into herself and him. When she had found Adam by comparison "less fair, less winning soft, less amiably mild" (4.478–9) than the "shape" in the pool, Eve had started back for that pool deaf to his pleas. But as she tells him now, she only understood herself, her experience at the pool and him, when,

> thy gentle hand
> Seized mine, I yielded, and from that time see
> How beauty is excelled by manly grace
> And wisdom, which alone is truly fair. (4.487–491)

At the pool she says she had heard as she gazed at "a shape in the watery gleam" (4.461) a voice which had told her, "What thou seest\ What there thou seest fair Creature is *thyself*" (4.467–468, italics added). *That* 'self' she *now* knows is a "watery image." Some find Eve at this moment slender in self-appreciation. It is worth noting, however, that the "self" that renders this account (4.440–491) of herself to Adam as they converse is no "watery image." The depth of her declared devotion to Adam, however, appears and is in a sense completely selfless.

How this devotion is a sign of genuine self-knowledge is enacted in the *1st Alcibiades*. For the moment, however, I note apropos of Eve's "watery image" that only now, after Adam's touch of her hand, does she call her initially naïve interest in that image a "vain desire" (4.466). No less did Alcibiades's own progress to self-knowledge lead him to distinguish "the things of the self" (τῶν αὐτοῦ) from "each itself" (αὐτοῦ ἑκάστου) (e.g., 128d3–4, *sed passim* 127e9–130e7): his body and face (τὸ σὸν πρόσωπον 130e4) and his "looks" no less than all his other possessions (132c5–12, cf. 104a2-c1) came to be seen as all "things of the body," but "not the self." The soul as the genuine "self" was understood as the referent for the Delphic dictum only by this distinction:

ΣΩ: ψυχὴν ἄρα ἡμᾶς κελεύει γνωρίσαι ὁ ἐπιτάττων γνῶναι ἑαυτόν.
ΑΛ: ἔοικεν.
ΣΩ: ὅστις ἄρα τῶν τοῦ σώματός τι γιγνώσκει, τὰ αὑτοῦ ἀλλ᾽ οὐχ αὑτὸν ἔγνωκεν.
ΑΛ: οὕτως.

(*SO*: "Therefore, the one who gives the command to know oneself orders us to
    acquire knowledge of the soul."
AL: "Probably so."
SO: "Then whoever comes to know something that belongs to the things of the
    body, knows the things of the self, but not the self."
AL: "That is so.") (130e8–131a3)

In one essential respect, however, Eve's framed narrative of her experience
at the pool is quite different from Ovid's framed narrative of Narcissus. There
is nothing comic about it. Ovid introduced his tale of Narcissus with a comic
episode among the gods that turns serious. Ovid thereby created a context—a
'dumb joke' with a bad outcome—for the parody to come.

Jupiter in his cups (*diffusum nectare*) had "put aside his weighty troubles"
(*curas \sepossuisse graves*), and "stirred up a little harmless fun with Juno"
(*vacuaque agitasse remissos\ cum Iunone iocos*) (3.318–320). He announced
that women surely (*profecto*) have greater pleasure (*maior . . . \. . . voluptas*
3.320–321) in sexual congress than men. Juno, he knew, was in a cold fury
at his recent indiscretions with Europa and Semele (3.253–272). The tacit
premise of his wit was to justify his indiscretions at her expense. Since she
"gets it" less, she must enjoy it more, whereas since he needs to "get it"
more, he surely must enjoy it less. (Ha! Ha! Ha!) Juno got it alright, but was
not amused. When Tiresias summoned as fit arbiter sided with Jupiter, Juno
blinded him. Evidently Tiresias's prior experience as both man and woman
had not taught him very much about either. One almost wants to say he lacked
self-knowledge. Jupiter then took pity on his unwitting accomplice and "in
recompense for his loss of sight gave him the ability to know the future"
(*pro lumine adempto\scire futura dedit* [3.347–348]). The tale of Narcissus,
thus, will be the first demonstration of Tiresias's new powers. Jupiter's coarse
wit is a prelude to the parody. Parody, however, is not the same as mockery.
Ovid's Tiresias will mock the Delphic dictum for his own vulgar gain. Ovid,
however, may have played dumb, but like Juno, he knew better.

Within Ovid's narrative frame the tale of Narcissus is the means by which
a seer of modest renown first began to enhance his reputation. When asked
about the boy (*de quo consultus*), "whether he would have a long life"—
literally, "if he was going to see the lengthy intervals of mature old-age" (*an
esset\ tempora maturae visurus longa senectae*), Tiresias had sententiously

replied, *si se non noverit* ("if he does not know himself" [3.347–348]). The seer was courting scandal. Possessed of a local reputation throughout the cities of Boeotia (*per Aonias . . . urbes*) for *inreprehensa . . . responsa,*[10] ("faultless replies" [3.341]), Tiresias's prediction mocked that other renowned source for *inreprehensa responsa*, the neighboring oracle at Delphi. When Narcissus then perished at the pool Ovid appears to make common cause with Tiresias. Ovid has his pathetic subject assert that he knows to his ruin what he is: *Iste ego sum. sensi; nec me mea fallit imago* ("I am *that one*; I'm sure of it! nor does my likeness deceive me" [3.463]). But as some have noted,[11] the tales of both Echo and Narcissus are laced with Socratic associations. Is Ovid also mocking Socrates?

Nevertheless, in the end, Tiresias's gibe at the local competition succeeds. The boy's predicted demise seems to follow from his "self-understanding." The sensational affair then becomes known beyond the neighborhood: *Cognita res meritam vati per Achaidas urbes\ attulerat famam nomenque erat auguris ingens* ("the affair once known brought well-deserved repute [or, 'justly deserved scandal']^[12] to the prophet throughout the cities of Greece and the renown of the seer was enormous" [3.511–512]). An apparent pleonasm (*meritam vati . . . attulerat famam nomenque erat auguris ingens*) in the envoi mimics that growth. While *nomenque . . . auguris ingens* can only refer to Tiresias, the phrase, *meritam vati . . . attuleret famam* may also refer to Ovid: "the affair once known brought a well-deserved fame [or scandal] to the poet (*vates*)." One wonders then about Ovid's motive for his tale. Perhaps he reawakens the ancient quarrel between philosophy and poetry. If so, he like Tiresias has only courted scandal to gain a vulgar notoriety: this poet teaches that self-knowledge through philosophic introspection can be fatal.

One can imagine that unreflective lovers of Ovid's poetry might be delighted. But the tale of Narcissus like its Olympian prologue does not quite end the way one expects. Pace vulgar opinion in the cities of Greece, Ovid himself suggests the seer's prophesy was not fulfilled. When Lirope had asked about her child's future, *an esset\ tempora maturae visurus longa senectae* ("will he see the *lengthy intervals* of advanced age?" (3.346–348), Tiresias had replied, "if he does not know himself." But as Narcissus lanquishes at the pool after his putative insight into himself, as "his sorrows rob his strength" (*iamque dolor vires adimit*), he does see that 'lengthy intervals' of his life do not lie ahead (*nec tempora vitae\ longa meae superant* 3.468–469). He sees what he will not have. Ovid thereby 'drops a hint.' Yet if Narcissus did not know himself, what is Ovid doing?

Ovid's tale of Narcissus presents a dilemma not unlike Milton's translation of that tale into *Paradise Lost*. What motive could either poet have had for undermining the integrity of their poetic narratives? With all due respect to hypotheses of 'self-consuming artifacts' and the like, both poets compel their audiences to reconsider their assumptions about these narratives. Milton's Eve demands close attention to the way in which she may be like or unlike Narcissus.[13] We are obliged to return to Ovid. Ovid's tale of Tiresias and Narcissus also compels us to think again. Here, the dictum "know thyself" becomes a silly not to say vain injunction—'look at yourself in a mirror'—and the tale of Narcissus pointless mischief unless it asks anew, notwithstanding vulgar opinion "in cities," what γνῶθι σαυτόν, "Know thyself," really means. This is just what Socrates was always doing, and does do in Plato's *1st Alcibiades*: "Well then, does 'to know oneself' happen to be an easy matter after all, and was the one who put up this saying in the temple at Delphi some dimwit?" (129a2–4). The question—a Platonic instance of a query of Socratic rationalism—poses as a vulgar challenge to the dignity of a "generally accepted opinion." For a few it will prove to be something quite different.

Similarity of subject and narrative framing in the tales of Milton and Ovid—to say nothing as yet of Milton's precise translation of Ovid's Narcissus into Eve's birth into consciousness—appear to point to the Platonic Socrates. But what evidence is there that Milton was even thinking of Plato? The first sign of his intention to shelter Eve's discourse in the shade of such authority can be seen in his poetic theft of a Platonic pun.

"UNDER A PLATAN"

As they sit, "Under a tuft of shade that on a green\ Stood whispering soft, by a fresh Fountain side" (4.325–326), Eve tells Adam that when she had followed the voice "that day" (4.448) that led her from the pool, and its "smooth watery image" (4.480), "I espied thee, fair and tall,\ Under a platan . . ." (4.477–478). Some[14] have noted a similar setting in the *Phaedrus*, but have underestimated Milton's penchant for translating the linguistic wit of his sources. At the beginning of this dialog, Phaedrus has suggested to Socrates that they sit down under a "very lofty platan tree" (τὴν ὑψηλοτάτην πλάτανον *Phaedrus* 229a6). In the midday heat of the sun they need such a sheltered place of repose for the conversation that Socrates hopes will occur. Socrates is quite pleased with Phaedrus's choice and praises the charms of the locale: "By Hera," he says, "the place is indeed beautiful, and moreover, this (tree), the platan, is quite shady and impressive . . . " (νὴ τὴν Ἥραν, καλή γε ἡ καταγωγή. ἥ τε γὰρ πλάτανος[15] αὕτη μάλ' ἀμφιλαφής τε καὶ ὑψηλή *Phaedrus* 230b2). The two will converse for the rest of the dialog beneath this remarkable tree.[16] Here Plato plays quiet tribute to his own role in the subsequent conversation by punning on his own name: πλάτανος , cf. Πλάτωνος. His play on his own name testifies to the peculiar shelter that his own art of λογοποιεῖν, "making speeches," as in "prose writing"—the very activity discussed at length in the *Phaedrus*—offers to this and every dialog. Speech (λόγοι) in conversation (διαλέγεσθαι), and its shadow-like likeness in the Platonic dialogs mediate and shade the 'erotic' endeavor to see from the scorching, blinding, omnipresent brilliance of what makes all seeing possible, the "good" which in the *Republic* Socrates had likened to the sun. Milton borrows this Platonic pun, then, to identify the author who looms over and shelters Eve's account of the events of "that day." The "leaves,"[17] so-to-speak, which cast those shadows that shelter these events, however, belong not to the *Phaedrus*, but to the *1st Alcibiades*. A synopsis of the dramatic action of this dialog with close commentary on 129a2–133c15 will facilitate a return to Milton's translation of Ovid.

There can be no doubt that Milton was familiar with the Greek text of the dialog and, in particular, this crucial passage since in chapter 1 of his *Artis Logicae Plenior Institutio Ad Petri Rami Methodum Concinnata* (*Patterson*, ed., [*WJM* vol 11, 11.20])[18] he quotes Socrates's definition of διαλέγεσθαι: *Et Plato in Alcibiades primo idem vult esse* τὸ διαλέγεσθαι *quod ratione uti* ("And Plato in the *1st Alcibiades* asserts that 'to converse' is the same as 'to use reason'"), rendering 129c2: Τὸ δὲ διαλέγεσθαι καὶ τὸ λόγῳ χρῆσθαι ταὐτόν που καλεῖς ("I think you call 'to converse' the same as 'to use reason'."). The conversation (διαλέγεσθαι) of Socrates and Alcibiades at 129a2–133c15 will illustrate in word and deed the difference of τὸ γνῶναι ἑαυτόν ("to know oneself") from the source of the "dumb joke" that Ovid played on his Narcissus. Only a dimwit would have taken Socrates's example (παράδειγμα 1132d3) of "knowing oneself"—looking into something, that is, a reflecting medium,[19] in which one can see oneself—as the thing exemplified. In other words, Milton's Eve will turn out to be more like Alcibiades than Ovid's Narcissus.

SOCRATIC SELF-KNOWLEDGE

At first sight Alcibiades appears to be an Athenian Narcissus. Extraordinarily beautiful, wealthy, possessing all the advantages of powerful family connections, he once was pursued by countless claimants to his attention, including—albeit at some greater distance—Socrates, but he has repulsed them all. Now only Socrates, known for his irritating garrulousness, silently continues to shadow and watch his every move. Socrates seems a snub-nosed Echo. But just as Alcibiades is about to present himself to the Athenian Assembly as the new Pericles, supremely confident in his own mind that he alone knows better how to govern their affairs, Socrates arrests him with a quite extraordinary and unsettling (ἀτοπώτερος 106a3) assertion: Alcibiades will be unable to obtain what he desires without Socrates. From Socrates's account (103a1–106a2) of his long observation of this young man, one can see why Alcibiades is at once aloof, cautious, disdainful, vaguely interested and soon to be nonplussed. With all of his advantages and living in the greatest city in Greece, Socrates tells him, "you think that you are in need of no one for anything" (οὐδενὸς φὴς ἀνθρώπων ἐνδεὴς εἶναι εἰς οὐδέν [104a2]). Yet here is this annoying man suggesting otherwise. Nevertheless, with a measure of bemused curiosity and hauteur he agrees to allow Socrates to make his case (106a2–8).

Socrates will not give a long speech of the sort that Alcibiades has been accustomed to hear from his other admirers. Rather he asks whether he is willing to answer questions. Alcibiades anticipates no difficulty (οὐ χαλεπόν 106b8), but difficulties will arise: he soon becomes aware that he cannot explain both what he knows better—and wishes to display in the assembly—and how he acquired that knowledge. With Alcibiades's assent they will initially consider only two possible sources for such knowledge: ΣΩ: οὐκοῦν ταῦτα μόνον οἶσθα, ἃ παρ' ἄλλων ἔμαθες ἢ αὐτὸς ἐξηῦρες; ΑΛ: ποῖα γὰρ ἄλλα; ("SO: Well then, do you know only these things, namely, those which you learned from others, or which you discovered yourself? AL: What else is there?" 106d4–5). He soon finds, however, that he is repeatedly embarrassed by his own words. He says one thing and later another. To account for this wavering back and forth (πλανᾶσθαι 112d8; 117a10; 118a13 & cf. 113b8–10; 116e2–4), he tries in various ways to shift responsibility for his difficulties to Socrates, but his attempts are signs of how little he understands his own state of mind. At first he thinks that Socrates is "mocking him" (σκώπτεις, ὦ Σώκρατες 109d6) when Socrates wonders, "didn't you notice yourself that you don't know this?" (σαυτὸν λέληθας ὅτι οὐκ ἐπίστασαι τοῦτο; 109d1). When Socrates doubts that he could have learned what he thinks he knows from other teachers, Alcibiades wonders if Socrates will grant that he could know what he does in some other way (με ἄλλως εἰδέναι 109e10). Socrates agrees he might, "if at least you discovered it" (εἴ γε εὕροις 109e3). Although Alcibiades is only trying to rescue his claim to know political things, in a brief exchange he unwittingly reveals the dilemma his self-sufficiency poses for his present difficulties:

ΑΛ: ἀλλ' οὐκ ἂν εὑρεῖν με ἡγῇ;
ΣΩ: καὶ μάλα γε, εἰ ζητήσαις.
ΑΛ: εἶτα ζητῆσαι οὐκ ἂν οἴει με;
ΣΩ: ἔγωγε, εἰ οἰηθείης γε μὴ εἰδέναι.

(*AL*: But you don't think I could find out?
SO: Of course I do, if you searched.
AL: Then, you don't think I could search?
SO: I do indeed, if you thought you didn't know.) (109e4–8)

In his assumed self-sufficiency how could he think that he could learn what *he* did not know from another, but if *he* did not know what he lacked, why would he search (see 106d10–12) for it? In the subsequent conversation Alcibiades gradually becomes aware not just of his lack of knowledge of political things, but of his own disgraceful condition in his own eyes. He begins to acquire a measure of self-understanding (see, e.g., 114b4; 116e2–4; 117a5–7; 118a15–b2 & esp. 127d6–8) as his initial lofty indifference to Socrates's questions fades before his growing interest in answering them. It is not, however, familiar aspects of a Socratic elenchus that deserve notice in regard to Milton's Eve and Ovid's Narcissus, but rather the drama of Alcibiades's progress to self-knowledge.

Over the course of the first half of the dialog, Alcibiades tacitly loses his confidence that he needs no one for anything. Persuaded by a long speech of Socrates and a passing mention of the Dephic dictum (124a9) that his political hopes are in jeopardy, he agrees to join with Socrates in a common endeavor (κοινὴ βουλὴ 124b10) to remedy their common need: if they are to become as good as possible, they will need to care for themselves. But they soon realize that they do not understand what this care for oneself is (127e9), or how they would do it (128d11–12). When they realize they do not even know what this "oneself" is, Socrates is reminded of the Delphic dictum and now they are both at a loss:

ΣΩ: πότερον οὖν δὴ ῥᾴδιον τυγχάνει τὸ γνῶναι ἑαυτόν, καί τις ἦν φαῦλος ὁ
    τοῦτο ἀναθεὶς εἰς τὸν ἐν Πυθοῖ νεών, ἢ χαλεπόν τι καὶ οὐχὶ παντός;
ΑΛ: ἐμοὶ μέν, ὦ Σώκρατες, πολλάκις μὲν ἔδοξε παντὸς εἶναι, πολλάκις δὲ
    παγχάλεπον.

(SO: "Well then, does 'to know oneself' happen to be an easy matter after all,
    and was the one who put up this saying in the temple at Dephi some dim-
    wit, or is it something difficult and not at all a commonplace?"
AL: If you ask me, Socrates, it seems a commonplace as often as it seems
    impossibly difficult.) (129a2–6)

Just as earlier (117d7–9) Alcibiades's wavering back and forth had revealed to him his ignorance of what he thought he knew, so here both men come face to face with their ignorance. At this very moment of their greatest confusion in the dialog—they do not even know how they will proceed—Socrates has a sudden insight about what they both are doing: ἔχε οὖν πρὸς Διός. τῷ διαλέγῃ σὺ νῦν; ἄλλο τι ἢ ἐμοί; ("By Zeus, wait a minute! With whom are you conversing right now? Is it anything other than *with me?*" 129b5–6). In the end, their understanding of γνῶθι σαυτόν will depend upon this insight, although for the moment it appears anything but perspicuous. Socrates shortly thereafter offers to give a παράδειγμα αὐτοῦ ("a instructive example of it [i.e., to know oneself] 132d3)," lit. "something that *is shown* [or 'something *that shows*'] alongside of it"). Their "conversing with each other" (διαλεγεῖσθαι) throughout the dialog will come to show itself beside Socrates's "paradeigmatic" account (132d1–133c7) "of the Delphic inscription" (τοῦ Δελφικοῦ γράμματος 132c10). The παράδειγμα, however, at first appears as only one instance among others of "seeing oneself in a reflecting medium." As Alcibiades says, this happens "in both mirrors *and in things of this sort*" (εἰς κάτοπτρά τε καὶ τὰ τοιαῦτα 132e1, italics added for emphasis). Their conversation will turn out to be another such medium.[20] "Know thyself," then, will be what can happen in conversation. What can happen, however—as Socrates will carefully explain—is only *like* what occasionally happens, "but solely with regard to visible sight" (ἀλλὰ κατὰ τὴν ὄψιν μόνον 132d3), when looking in a mirror and some other things.

Socrates now considers an unusual hypothetical case and urges Alcibiades to examine it as well (σκόπει καὶ σύ). "If it (i.e., the Delphic dictum) in giving advice to our eye just as it does to a man, said 'see yourself,' how would we grasp what it recommends? Isn't it to look into this, into which the eye looks when going to see itself?" (εἰ ἡμῶν τῷ ὄμματι ὥσπερ ἀνθρώπῳ συμβουλεῦον εἶπεν "ἰδὲ σαυτόν," πῶς ἂν ὑπελάβομεν τί παραινεῖν; ἆρα οὐχὶ εἰς τοῦτο βλέπειν, εἰς ὃ βλέπων ὁ ὀφθαλμὸς ἔμελλε αὐτὸν ἰδεῖν; [132d5–8]). Alcibiades agrees. Socrates now asks, "Do we both *have in mind* (ἐννοῶμεν δὴ) into *what* of the extant things as we look, we would see both 'that' (ἐκεῖνό) and at the same time ourselves?" (ἐννοῶμεν δὴ εἰς τί βλέποντες τῶν ὄντων ἐκεῖνό τε ὁρῶμεν ἅμα ἂν καὶ ἡμᾶς αὐτούς; 132-d10-e1). Alcibiades confidently replies, "into *both* mirrors *and* things of this sort" (εἰς κάτοπτρά τε καὶ τὰ τοιαῦτα. [132e3]). The question, however, is not quite as obvious as it seems because the participial phrase εἰς τί βλέποντες τῶν ὄντων ("looking into *what* of the extant things") bears a dual allegiance. If, as Alcibiades has naturally assumed, it refers to seeing with the eyes (ὁρῶμεν), then Alcibiades was quite right to answer as he did. But the phrase could equally depend upon their activity of mind (ἐννοῶμεν δὴ) as they are "looking into *what* of extant things," that is, among all the things that exist, do we see both 'that' (ἐκεῖνό), [namely, "the eye"] and ourselves. Simply stated, Alcibiades thought of mirrors, because he had seen them with his eyes. But when he had in mind the question Socrates was asking, and his mind surveyed all extant things, he did not see "*both* mirrors *and* other such things" by looking in a mirror. Quite to the contrary, he was looking into that place *in himself* that recalls things that he had seen and could bring to mind a class of things of a such particular sort from among the manifold of all beings. It is just this different kind of "seeing"[21] which Socrates will go on to describe: ἆρ' οὖν, ὦ φίλε Ἀλκιβιάδη, καὶ ψυχὴ εἰ μέλλει γνώσεσθαι αὑτήν, εἰς ψυχὴν αὐτῇ βλεπτέον, καὶ μάλιστ' εἰς τοῦτον αὐτῆς τὸν τόπον ἐν ᾧ ἐγγίγνεται ἡ ψυχῆς ἀρετή, σοφία, καὶ εἰς ἄλλο ᾧ τοῦτο τυγχάνει ὅμοιον ὄν; ("Therefore, is it the case that, my dear Alcibiades, *the soul too*, if it is going to know itself, it must look into the soul, and above all, into this place of it in which the virtue of the soul, wisdom, arises, *and* into anything else with which this happens to be similar?" [133b7–10]).

Just prior to this clarification of the purport of the παράδειγμα, Socrates has displayed the two possibilities. First he had stated what Alcibiades originally "*had* in mind" (ἐννενόηκας οὖν 132e7), and then an alternative, εἰ δέ γ᾽ εἰς ἄλλο τῶν τοῦ ἀνθρώπου βλέποι ἤ τι τῶν ὄντων . . . . ("*But if* [he] looked into some other thing of those things that belong to a man, or something of extant things . . . ." 133a9–11). What Alcibiades had had in mind at first when Socrates had asked his question was seeing with his corporeal eye and this, as Socrates tells him, was correct in a sense:

ΣΩ: ὀρθῶς λέγεις. οὐκοῦν καὶ τῷ ὀφθαλμῷ ᾧ ὁρῶμεν ἔνεστί <τι> τῶν τοιούτων;
ΑΛ: πάνυ γε.
ΣΩ: ἐννενόηκας οὖν ὅτι τοῦ ἐμβλέποντος εἰς τὸν [133a] ὀφθαλμὸν τὸ πρόσωπον ἐμφαίνεται ἐν τῇ τοῦ καταντικρὺ ὄψει ὥσπερ ἐν κατόπτρῳ, ὃ δὴ καὶ κόρην καλοῦμεν, εἴδωλον ὄν τι τοῦ ἐμβλέποντος;
ΑΛ: ἀληθῆ λέγεις.
ΣΩ: ὀφθαλμὸς ἄρα ὀφθαλμὸν θεώμενος, καὶ ἐμβλέπων εἰς τοῦτο ὅπερ βέλτιστον αὐτοῦ καὶ ᾧ ὁρᾷ, οὕτως ἂν αὐτὸν ἴδοι.
ΑΛ: φαίνεται.

(SO: You're right. Isn't there also in the eye with which we see some such thing?"
AL: Sure.
SO: You had in mind, therefore, that when someone looks into the eye, his face appears in the sight of the one right in front of him just as if in a mirror—that which we also call 'the pupil,' since it is a phantom image of the one who is looking.
AL: That's true.
SO: Therefore, when the eye is seeing the eye, and is looking into this, the very best part of it, and that by which it sees, in this way it might see itself.
AL: It *appears* [that it does].) (132e4–133a8, italics & brackets added)

This original "Alcibiadian" notion of Socrates's paradeigmatic analogy will be the germ of Ovid's parody of self-knowledge—a beautiful boy gazing in a reflecting pool was looking into another of "those things of this sort."[22] But Socrates, and even Alcibiades, and much later Milton, had something else *only like that* in mind.

There is reason to doubt that either Socrates or Alcibiades place much stock in this first notion of the "paradeigmatic analogy." Alcibiades's reply, "it appears (φαίνεται) [that it does]," was weak. Socrates himself had been cautious: "thus it *might see* itself," (οὕτως ἂν αὐτὸν ἴδοι). It was weak not because Alcibiades doubted that the eye could see itself in this way. He had agreed to that: "That's true" (133a4). Rather, his muted disappointment—"it appears"—here must stem from his present awareness of what both he and Socrates had previously said and agreed to. They had agreed (129c5–131c8) to distinguish the "things of the self" (τὰ αὐτοῦ) from the "self" (αὐτὸν) and further, they identified the "self" with the soul. All parts of the body they had agreed were among "things of the self," and therefore, "whoever knows some thing of the body, knows the *things* of himself, but not himself" (131a2–3). Alcibiades's days of wavering back and forth (πλανᾶσθαι) are over. Here he knows what he had said previously and what he is saying now.

Socrates now considers an alternative (εἰ δέ γ') to what they have been saying. This alternative contains an ambiguous proviso which would allow one to think that either they both were still speaking about the eye as before, or perhaps, *now* about something else: εἰ δέ γ' εἰς ἄλλο τῶν τοῦ ἀνθρώπου βλέποι ἤ τι τῶν ὄντων, πλὴν εἰς ἐκεῖνο ᾧ τοῦτο τυγχάνει ὅμοιον, οὐκ ὄψεται ἑαυτόν. ("*But if* he [or "it," referring to "the eye," see 133a5] should look into some other thing of those things that belong to a man or some thing of extant things, *unless* [he (or it) is looking] *into that to which this happens to be similar*, he [or, "it"] will not see himself" 133a9–11, brackets and italics added for emphasis). Socrates might seem to still be talking only about the corporeal eye. But the subject for βλέποι and ὄψεται is unspecified. "The eye" has just been mentioned, but here he asks about "the things that belong to a man" (τῶν τοῦ ἀνθρώπου) and the proviso requires that unless the "thing that looks" is similar to "what it looks at," it will not see itself. Thus, "the things that belong to a man" must be looked into *by a man*. That Socrates is considering both the eye and a man is manifest by what he says next. He speaks first of the eye. "The eye if it is going to see itself must look into itself and into that place of the eye in which the virtue of the eye arises. This, I suppose, is sight" (133b2–5). Now at 133b7–10 (as noted above) he mentions the soul: "Therefore, is it that, my dear Alcibiades, *the soul too*, if it is going to know itself, it must look into the soul?" He does not mention the soul solely because, on analogy with the pupil of the eye, the soul of a man also is "the best part of 'it'" (see also 130a3) and by means of which 'it' sees (cf. 133a6), but because if a man wants to look at and 'know' himself—which is the issue—he will not see into himself, *unless* [he is looking] *into that thing to which this happens to be similar.* Socrates speaks of the soul rather than the man because the man too, like the eye, must look into the best part of himself (see 129e3–c7). He therefore asks as he must, Ἆρ' οὖν . . . καὶ ψυχὴ εἰ μέλλει γνώσεσθαι αὐτήν, εἰς ψυχὴν αὐτῇ βλεπτέον, καὶ μάλιστ' εἰς τοῦτον αὐτῆς τὸν τόπον ἐν ᾧ ἐγγίγνεται ἡ ψυχῆς ἀρετή, σοφία, καὶ εἰς ἄλλο ᾧ τοῦτο τυγχάνει ὅμοιον ὄν; ("Is it that . . . *the soul too*, if it is going to know itself, it must look into the soul, and above all, into this place of it in which the virtue of the soul, wisdom, arises, *and* into anything else with which it happens to be similar?" 133b7–10, italics added). The opportunity for such looking into the soul is provided by the conversation (διαλέγεσθαι) of Socrates and Alcibiades. In Plato's art of "prose writing," λογοποιεῖν, their speech shadows their deeds.

In the drama of the *1st Alcibiades* Alcibiades comes to a better sense of himself through becoming aware of and owning to a *likeness to himself* in what he himself says in response to Socrates's questioning. Once he abandoned his hauteur, he gradually began to see those questions neither as mockery nor as entrapment, but as Socrates's honest attempt to understand just what he means by what he says. At first he tried to claim that it was Socrates who was saying these things. Socrates, therefore, had to draw his attention to what he was saying now and what he had said before. At first Alcibiades accused him of "putting words in his mouth." Socrates was saying these things and Socrates was responsible for his wavering back and forth, not him (see 112e1–113b7). Later he said he felt "inexplicably *like* someone in a very odd condition" (ἀτεχνῶς ἔοικα ἀτόπως ἔχοντι 116e3). Still later he was ashamed to admit that he did not know what he thought he did (118a15–c2), but he knew he was in a bad way. As this awareness grew he came to have a sense of himself, and as he did, his attachment for Socrates grew; he became willing to join him in a common search for that understanding which he admitted they both needed. By the end of dialog he promises to be Socrates's constant companion. He is unalterably convinced that he needs Socrates and no other. He knows that he cannot "go it alone"; he knows that he was a fool to think that "he does not need anyone for anything." He "knows himself"; he knows, in Milton's phrase, the value of "fellowship [of] a fit conversing soul." To speak more precisely, in the best case of conversation (διαλέγεσθαι), Alcibiades came to see, in *the effort* of Socrates to understand what he, Alcibiades, has just said in reply to Socrates's question, a *likeness* of *his own effort* to answer that question in the first place. To see *this effort* would be to see his soul, himself, in its best possible condition in the best place of his own soul at work in the endeavor of Socrates. In this sense "looking into something else that happens to be similar" would be—when talking with Socrates—looking at "one's other self." This insight would be, as Socrates says (133b9–10) "the virtue of the soul, wisdom" (ἡ ψυχῆς ἀρετή, σοφία). And as he goes on to add, "Can we say, then, that there is a more divine thing belonging to the soul than this, about which there is knowing and thinking?" (ἔχομεν οὖν εἰπεῖν ὅτι ἐστὶ τῆς ψυχῆς θειότερον ἢ τοῦτο, περὶ ὃ τὸ εἰδέναι τε καὶ φρονεῖν ἐστιν; 133c1–2). Alcibiades does not think they could. Milton did.

Milton's Adam does converse with "a more divine thing belonging to the soul than this":

supreme of things;
Thou in thyself art perfet, and in thee
Is no deficience found; not so is man,
But in degree, the cause of his desire
By conversation with his like to help,
Or solace his defects. (8.414–419)

In his conversation with "th' Almighty" following upon the Naming of the Beasts (8.311–356) Adam discovers his single imperfection, and thus his need of "conversation with his like" by conversing with a being not like Him—self-sufficient, "perfect in [whom] . . . no deficience is found." "His single imperfection" (8.423) is his need for a 'like consort.' Now he knows he is not self-sufficient. He is not like that being. He had sensed his imperfection ("I found not what methought I wanted still" [8.355]) in his knowing survey of the beasts, but he did not yet understand what he lacked—"fellowship . . . fit to participate\ All rational delight" (8.389–391) until in discourse with that other—like himself only *in so far* as he was made in his image—he discerns through that other the perfection he would always lack. This being, whom he could not name (8.357–358) as he had the beasts, cannot, he knows, provide the lasting fellowship he desires. For so much the "gracious voice divine" was pleased and found him "knowing not of beasts alone, . . . but of *thyself*" (8.448–449 italics added). He therefore promises to create for him a being whom Adam will name "fair Eve" (4.481), who will answer to his desire for such fellowship, and to whom he will declare his lasting, if yet not fully knowing, devotion. (8.491–499). These dramas of Adam's self-knowing through conversation, first with his Maker, and as I shall now show, with Eve, suggest that Milton was translating the *1ˢᵗ Alcibiades*.

OVID'S PARODY AND MILTON'S
PLATONIC TRANSLATION

"What there thou seest fair Creature is thyself" (4.468).

The tacit premise of Ovid's parody of Socratic self-knowledge is the "dumb joke" that his character Tiresias perpetrates on the Delphic oracle. Ovid's wit plays along, plumping the pretentiousness of the prophesy with Socratic associations. But Ovid is more like his Juno; he gets the joke, but he is not amused. He will break in on his Narcissus at the pool not just to rebuke him but to punish his credulity. In a sense the respect due a source of Ovid's own generative powers was being debased. One can be sure Ovid knew well what his Tiresias mocked. The specious self-knowledge of his own

Narcissus—*iste ego sum! sensi; nec me mea fallit imago* ("I am that one! I'm sure of it!; my likeness does not deceive me" [3.463])—will be exposed by the hallmark of extreme ignorance of self in the *1st Alcibiades*.

Right after Narcissus proclaims his supposed self-knowledge, he wavers: "What am I doing? Am I wooed, or do I woo? What then will I be wooing?" (*quid faciam? roger, anne rogem? quid deinde rogabo?* [3.465]). He wants to converse with the one he sees, but his wandering in mind and in speech (πλανᾶσθαι) was, for Socrates at least, the sign of "the most extreme ignorance" (ἀμαθίᾳ [...] τῇ ἐσχάτῃ 118b5) in Alcibiades. From that ignorance Alcibiades began to grow in devotion to Socrates. From this ignorance Narcissus's devotion to what he cannot bear to leave will lead to his death. In his decline Ovid displays Narcissus's failure to grasp the fundamental premise of Socrates's revealing παράδειγμα of self-knowledge: he never would understand the difference between the things of the self (τὰ ἑαυτοῦ)—his eyes, his looks, his body—and his self (ἑαυτόν).[23]

The following account of Milton's translation of Ovid's Narcissus into *Paradise Lost* depends upon two arguable assumptions that entail an apparently fatal objection to the thesis of this chapter: Eve's initial insight into herself and Adam's worth to her as a companion (4.489–491) will come without her saying a word. Eve's first words (4.440–491) in *Paradise Lost* are, thus, her first words in Paradise. Milton hints at Eve's stately silence until this moment in several ways. Her demeanor has been paradoxical. Narrative voice from the Tree of Life spoke in oxymorons of her "coy submission, modest pride" (4.310), and Adam will later gush to tell Raphael of her "obsequious majesty" in approval of his "Pleaded Reason" as he led her to the nuptial bower (8.509–511) after their encounter beneath the platan (see 8.500ff). Adam, we shall say, does not quite know what to make of her. Moreover, in Book 4 Milton twice teases an anticipatory desire in his audience to hear these two talking. First, he flirts with amphibologia in describing the place where they choose to have this conversation:

So hand in hand they passed . . .
. . .
Adam the goodliest man of men since born
His sons, the fairest of her daughters Eve.
Under a tuft of shade that on a green
Stood whispering soft, by a fresh fountain side
They sat them down . . . (4.321; 324–327 italics added).[24]

One almost thinks *they* are standing on a green whispering "sweet nothings" to each other. Then, just as the human pair *are* about to speak for the first time in the poem, Milton flirts again, as previously noted (chapter 2), with amphiboly in an *imitatio* of Catullus 13.14, the locus classicus of anticipatory pleasures: "when Adam, first of men,\ To first of women, Eve, thus moving speech,*Turned him all ear* to hear new utterance flow" (4.408–410 italics added).[25] Is it Eve who is about to speak and Adam who is "all ear"? At the very least, Adam would have been quite eager to hear Eve if she had been silent to this point, and moreover, her silence would account for a discontent—so foreign to her own feelings—which she has noticed in him: "I chiefly who enjoy\So far the happier lot, enjoying thee\Preëminent by so much odds, while thou\ Like consort to thyself canst nowhere find" (4–445–448).[26]

With less need of argument, it is assumed that from that moment when Adam seized her hand until she finally does speak to him (4.440ff) she has been thinking a good deal. In short, her evident understanding of herself and Adam and a "wisdom which alone is truly fair" appears to profit from a certain distance from the events of "that day." Could her self-knowledge have arisen without her saying a word? Milton's negotiations with Ovid's parody will be conducted in the words both poets use, but the drama of the *1st Alcibiades* shapes both these tales, not the words. Together, words only now uttered and deeds several days done now begin to interpret anew that sight of these two which narrative persona had rendered in "Hee for God only, shee for God in him" (4.299).

In *Paradise Lost*, Eve relates to Adam that as she "[w]ith unexperience't thought" had come to gaze fixedly at a "shape" in the pool "and pined with vain desire" (4.466), a voice, speaking directly to her had gently warned her,

> What thou seest,
> What there thou seest fair creature is thyself,
> With thee it came and goes: but follow me,
> And I will bring thee where no shadow stays
> Thy coming, and thy soft embraces, hee
> Whose image thou art, him thou shalt enjoy
> Inseparably thine, to him thou shalt bear
> Multitudes like thyself, and thence be called
> Mother of human race . . . . (4.467–475)

Adam will later identify this voice when he describes to Raphael the first approach of Eve after her creation: "On she came,\ "Led by her heavenly maker, though unseen,\ And guided by his voice . . ." (8.484–6). But here in Book 4, the entrance of an authoritative voice to disabuse Eve of her fascination is unexplained. Eve does not wonder who might be speaking nor whence such a voice might come. She listens, heeds the advice and follows. New to consciousness—as she admits to Adam, "much wondering where and what I was, whence thither brought, and how . . ." (4.451–2)—and Paradise, and not expecting that a voice must issue from a body, Eve accepts this guidance without question. She is, after all, the original of innocence.

In the *Metamorphoses* Narcissus too was admonished by a voice:

credule, quid frustra simulacra fugacia captas?
quod petis, est nusquam; quod amas, avertere, perdes!
ista repercussae, quam cernis. imaginis umbra est:
nil habet ista sui; tecum venitque manetque;
tecum discedet, si tu discedere possis! (3.432–436)

(You gullible fool! why to no avail do you keep trying to grasp the fleeting likeness?
What you seek is nowhere; what you love—turn away!—you'll lose!
That which you see is a shade of a reflected image;
That has nothing of its own; with you it both came, and stays;
With you it will depart, if you can depart!)

The voice which rebukes Narcissus perhaps would be more striking, were it not for the frequency of apostrophe in the *Metamorphoses*. To speak too broadly perhaps, for some reason the poet cannot maintain the decorum of artistic distance on his subject. Here in Book 3 the poet[27] appears exasperated if not incensed at his subject. This direct address to Narcissus signals a moment of crisis. But the boy apparently cannot understand what the voice is saying. In a sense nor will Eve, but for a far different reason. With Eve there will be no crisis; her "Heavenly Maker" is speaking, but not knowing that voice, Eve hears *a* voice. There is no note of exasperation in it, no rebuke nor ominous prediction, but rather a gentle benevolence. This difference in tone however does not obscure the precision of Milton's imitation of Ovid, a practice which Ovid himself considered a kind of "lending" rather than "theft."[28]

In the voice's address to Eve Milton will precisely translate Ovid's verbal tricolon in the latter's address to Narcissus while remaining attentive to Ovid's penchant for paradox. Describing what the boy is looking at, Ovid had fashioned a concise triplet, *tecum venitque manetque;\tecum discedet . . . ,* ("with you it both came, and stays; with you it will depart . . . ." [3.436]), where the anaphora, *tecum*, works in concert with the connectives—*que* to join all three phrases in a tight temporal progress. The paradox resides in the center: *manetque*. Ovid teases the boy with a paradox of motion and rest: the image "remains in one place" (*manetque*) yet is capable of movement (*venitque . . . \. . . discedet*): it came and it will go; it "lasts" (*manetque*) so long as it does not move, yet the proof of its perdurability belongs to its movement from past (*venitque*) to future (*discedet*). Just this sort of paradox is Ovid's stock-in-trade in the *Metamorphoses*. Narcissus does not understand the way in which the image abides with him over time; *manetque* will hold him at the pool. He does not see that what "stays, endures, and lasts" only when he is motionless is that which he has *tecum*. It is "with him" (*tecum venitque . . . \ tecum discedet*) only when he moves from past to future. But when he moves, it will depart (*discedet*). Such might be the hard truth about the evanescence of youthful beauty in time.

When Milton translates Ovid into *Paradise Lost*, his "Heavenly Maker" exactly renders Ovid's verbal tricolon while undoing Ovid's web of paradox: "With thee it *came* and *goes*: but follow me,\ And I will bring thee where no shadow *stays*\ Thy coming [...]" (4.469–70, italics added). Milton translates *manetque* out of the web of conjunction and anaphora in Ovid's text, while continuing its predication of the image as "shadow." Ovid too had called the image in the pool a "shadow" but his Golden Line, *ista repercussae, quam cernis. imaginis umbra est* ("that which you see is a shade of a reflected image" 3.434), looks suspiciously like one more of Ovid's "borrowings"—in this case the proverbial and paradoxical description of man's estate, either in its Pindaric (σκιᾶς ὄναρ\ ἄνθρωπος ["a dream of a shadow\ (is) a man]" *Pyth.* 8.95–96) or, in its Aeschylean form (εἴδολον σκιᾶς, ["a shade of a shadow" *Ag.* 839]). No wonder Narcissus thought there was something there. But where Ovid had ensnared Narcissus in paradox, Eve's "Heavenly Maker" frees her from a shadow, even a verbal one. What the voice tells Eve about the image can have no paradoxical hold over her. The image merely comes and goes; it is a transient thing. But what awaits her will be something. Adam has substance.

Milton's translation of *manetque* by "stays" shows his fidelity to Ovid's text and Ovid's wit. Drawing upon a transitive sense available in *maneo, -ere*, "to await," or "to wait for [someone]," Milton could have employed the metrically suitable "waits" in the sense of, "to look forward (esp., with desire or apprehension) to (some future event or contingency)." That would have been the obvious choice. Instead he employs "stays" which offers an additional sense of "hinder." Thus, even as "stays" preserves *manetque* as a predication of "shadow," the verbal notion removed from paradox is repositioned in new doubled application to the circumstances of both Eve and Adam: "And I will bring thee where no shadow *stays* \Thy coming, and thy sweet embraces, hee\ Whose image thou art, him thou shalt enjoy" (4.470–472, italics added). No shadow at the pool "hinders" Eve's approach to Adam and no vain image but substantial Adam "awaits" her coming. Thus, even when Milton departs from Ovid's text, he remains faithful to his wit. Nevertheless, the shadow of Ovid's wit continues to hang over Milton's translation. Ovid had told his Narcissus what he was looking at; it was a "shadow of an image" (*imaginis umbra*). When Milton's voice speaks of Eve as Adam's image, Ovid's disparagement of that image seems by association to deprive Eve of any substance.

Both voices in apostrophe address an obvious lack of self-understanding. Both creatures do not know what they are doing. Both voices speak of what those creatures are seeing and what the future holds. Both Narcissus and Eve do not seem to know what they are drawn to, and what will follow from their present fascination. Nor did Alcibiades (see 104e1–105e5). Eve's "Heavenly Maker" tells Eve, "What thou seest,\ What there thou seest, fair creature, is thyself."[4.467–8]. It is hard to conceive of what this "thyself" could mean to Eve other than that it was something. Ovid was far less approving and far more confusing. Chiding his predicament, Ovid seemed vexed that Narcissus was so engaged: *credule, quid frustra simulacra fugacia captas?* ("You fool!, why do you keep trying to grasp the fleeting semblances to no avail?" [3.432]). Milton's "Heavenly Maker," however, addresses a "fair Creature," and thus grants a certain moral as well as aesthetic stature to what Eve sees. Since she is "fair," her interest in what shows "fair" cannot be entirely misplaced. But Narcissus is offered no insight into his present infatuation. Called a fool, he is rebuked by a rhetorical question with an obvious answer. To put the matter differently, Milton seems to have noticed that Ovid's voice never told Narcissus *what* he was seeing. Rather he tells him, *quod petis, est numquam* ("what you seek is nothing" 3.433). Surely he must have thought he was looking at *something*! Thus, Ovid hides from Narcissus the existence of and an identity for the one thing that could release him from his infatuation. Eve's "Heavenly Maker" preserves that thing with an as yet incomprehensible predication. Here Milton is no longer reading Ovid but Plato's *1st Alcibiades*. Alcibiades and Socrates too had become aware of something, αὐτὸ ταὐτό, "the self itself," as yet incomprehensible (see 129b1) which they had nearly dismissed as nothing (129a2–4). Their understanding of that thing through a likeness would only arise concomittent with Alcibiades's self-knowledge when he sees himself in and through another self. In Eve's case, she will have to wait until she encounters Adam.

But Ovid is aware of what his Narcissus is seeking and will lack. After telling him that what he seeks is nothing, he now confounds the boy with a succession of verbs: *quod amas, avertere, perdes* (3.433). Ovid's voice now speaks to the boy's future, but the remark cannot be univocally rendered. The voice may express, (1) pity for the boy's plight, "what you love, if you turn away,[29] you will lose!"—in rueful meditation on the boy's present infatuation, or, with the same syntax but a different sense implied by the afterthought, *si tu discedere possis* (". . . if you can leave"[3.436]); (2) in disdain for the boy's choice of beloved. If the imperative, *avertere*, is genuine, the voice (3) prophetically warns of the future ruin of his beloved, that thing (*quod*) that Narcissus now, and Echo formerly, loved[30]: "turn away!—what you love you will lose (*perdes*)." Or, once again, (4) the voice may anticipate the harm[31] he will do himself when he recognizes the object of his own yearnings: "turn away!—you'll destroy (*perdes*) what you love!" These variants of tone surely mystify Ovid's intent in apostrophe, but one and all address an utter lack of self-understanding in the boy. Whether in pity, or mockery, or warning, or prophesy, the voice tells Narcissus he neither knows what he does nor what he pursues. Here too with a similar panoply of expression Ovid's parody mimics its original.[32]

But when Milton's "Heavenly Maker" informs Eve of her future he summons her to leave behind her present fascination with a promise: "I will bring thee where no shadow stays \Thy coming, . . . , hee \Whose image thou art, him thou shalt enjoy \Inseparably thine . . ." (4.467–475). One apparently gratuitous addition in this passage, "[i]nseparably thine," reveals that poetic theft for Milton is more than mere imitation. There would be no reason for Milton to have added this prophetic characterization of Eve's future if not to illuminate the relations of Eve and Adam in comparison with Narcissus and his image. In Ovid, "inseparably thine" would have declared the awful truth about Narcissus's beloved. The phrase is the never stated secret behind the webs of paradox and ambiguity that Ovid's voice weaves around Narcissus. Had it been stated, it would have revealed to Narcissus the source of that image, shattering the spell of his infatuation. But in Milton that source is strangely now another; ". . . hee \ whose image thou art." This phrase in feminist readings has seemed to declare that Eve is as superficial and insubstantial as the image she gazes at. Reductive extremities aside, it has been more common to assume that Eve from the very moment of her creation has a natural predisposition to vanity. She is attracted to a visible beauty, to a "fair" she beholds in the pool; judging by the appearance of things, she rejects of Adam as "less fair" (4.478); and she describes herself as one who "pin'd with vain desire" (4.446). These predications, however, might very well all be true of Eve, but for a far different reason.

Attention to Ovid's Latin in Milton's translation suggests that Eve is never trapped in the paradoxical infatuation of Narcissus. If Eve now recalls that she once "pined with vain desire" (4.446) for *a* beautiful image in a pool, it is only because that day she came to know herself through Adam. She now knows what she felt then was a "vain desire" only by comparison with her present contentment. She has somehow obtained self-knowledge through contact with another who is truly other. She now sees, "[h]ow beauty is excelled by manly grace,\ And wisdom, which alone is truly fair" (4.490–91). But at the pool there was no vain desire for a mere beautiful form when she was attracted to what she saw. Even *that* had, in an as yet unfulfilled promise, substance. Once again, Eve's "Heavenly Maker" never called, as Ovid did, *that* thing an image, a shade or a semblance (cf. *imaginis umbra*, 3.343 & *simulacra* 3.342).

"[W]hat there thou seest . . . " did bear a resemblance to her, not in the appearance of her bodily form—She could have no knowledge of her own appearance—but "with answering looks \Of sympathy and love . . ." (4.464–5).

It was a *likeness* as a φαινόμενον is "something that shines through" from her own, not insubstantial, emotions:

> As I bent down to look, just opposite,
> A shape within the watery gleam appear'd
> Bending to look on me, I started back,
> It started back, but pleased I soon returned,
> Pleased it returned as soon, with answering looks
> Of sympathy and love; (4.460–5)

This is neither the vanity of self-admiration nor the infatuation with superficial beauty of physical form, as can be seen if, once again, we compare Eve with Narcissus. Narcissus seemed to be moved by "answering looks" (see 3.450–462). Curiously speaking to what he sees in the pool, Narcissus lamented, *cupit ipse teneri!* \ *nam quotiens liquidis porreximus oscula lymphis,*\ *hic totiens ad me resupino nititur ore;* ("He himself yearns to be held! \ As many times as I present my kisses to the waters \so does he strive towards me with upturned mouth\face" [3.450–52]). Yet where Eve reads "answering looks\ Of sympathy and love," Narcissus only recognized the aspects of body for which he knew he had been pursued. He spoke of lips, of mouth, of face (*ore* 3.452), of visage (*vultu* 3.457), of beauty of body (*forma* 3.457), of youthful aspect (*aetas* 3.457), of tears (*lacrimae* 3.459); he 'reads' only a desire to be held (*cupit . . . teneri* 3.457), signs with nod of the head (*nutu . . . signa* 3.460), and was mystified by what those motions might mean for him (*spem nescio quam mihi . . .* 3.457). The reason for his preternatural incapacity to 'read' emotion is not hard to find. Having never felt anything for another—to judge from his past history with Echo and the other nymphs[33]— he had nothing within to compare with what he saw. At best he could only sense a "friendly visage" (*vultu . . . amico* 3.457) in the image in the pool. But he did know of those beauties of body that he saw, for those beauties had long been the wonder of Echo and those nymphs.[34] This is vanity.

Eve's attraction to "looks" that answer to her own feelings is inadequate as an end but necessary to the beginning of her relations with Adam. At the moment of her birth into consciousness, those "looks" are where she begins her discovery of the other, who will be, "hee\ Whose image thou art." This curious phrase—so apt yet misleading in the case of Narcissus—can only imply that Eve is a likeness *of* and *for* Adam. This "image" the "Heavenly Maker" speaks of is neither superficial nor corporeal since he was describing what Eve was perceiving: "What thou seest\ what there thou seest," the "answering looks of sympathy and love," not the mere aspects of body that Narcissus saw. Eve is not a Narcissus and Adam will not look like Eve ("Not equal, as thir sex not equal seem'd" 4.296). *This* likeness is not visible in that way, but it is visible as "looks" are visible for those with the interior substance to recognize them. They are, as they will later be described, "peculiar graces" (5.15; cf. 8.43 & 59–63).

Eve's yearning after "sympathy and love" will become her referent for the likeness which Adam presents to her. Adam will show Eve herself through what he shows of himself. In his desperate entreaty to Eve as she turns back to the pool (4.480–488) Adam shows *his desire* for her creation. From the first he had shown "less fair\ less winning soft, less amiably mild" (4.488–489) beneath the platan, and his pleadings now are even less winsome. These entreaties will not be enough. Eve in the end for her part will show Adam, but only when those entreaties are animated by a touch. Then his Maker's promise will be fulfilled: "What next I bring shall please thee, be assur'd\ Thy likeness, thy fit help, thy other self,\ Thy wish, exactly to thy heart's desire" (8.449–451). Here will be a true *sympathia*—alike in what they suffer. From such *sympathia* they can begin their growth in love. So much did Adam divine in part when, as he later tells Raphael, he had pleaded his inferiority to God and his need for a fit mate: "Man by number is to manifest\His single imperfection, and begct \Like of his like, his image multiplied,\ In unity defective . . ." (8.422–26). This drama should be familiar: Socrates had asked Alcibiades, "the soul, if it is going to know itself, it must look into soul, and above all, into this place of it in which the virtue of the soul, wisdom, arises, *and into anything else with which this happens to be similar* ?" (133b7–10 italics added for emphasis).

"AND WISDOM, WHICH ALONE IS TRULY FAIR" (4.491)

The history of the relations of Adam and Eve begins with Eve's account of her birth into consciousness at the pool. Her story brings to light the very first moments of their story as a "Fair couple, linkt in happy nuptial league" (4.339). Milton's translation of Ovid's Narcissus into Eve's account of her first moments at the pool also translates the birth of that awareness to an encounter with Adam "[u]nder a platan." Here, not at the pool, in contact with Adam, not alone, "pining with vain desire," Eve comes to knowledge of herself and him. Eve is an innocent at birth and will remain so until the Fall. Her growth will be crippled by no predisposition to vanity or anything else. She will grow in the native capacity of her species to reason. What both Eve and Adam possess by the gift their creator at their creation is *a rational desire for the same*. They do not know it as such though it operates in them from the first. It will be the ground of their discoveries to come.

Eve begins from her own yearnings for "sympathy and love." By a native wit of the species she first reads "answering looks" in what she sees in the

pool. What she sees answers to what she feels. Yet when a voice guides her—
as a rational creature she understands speech by the gift of her Maker—she
will "follow straight." She has no reason to query its benevolent instruction
since she cannot compare what her Maker promises and what sight shows:
she is "invisibly led" (4.476). But when she first sees Adam, she now has a
basis for choice: more and less. Adam she says she thought was "less fair"
than "that smooth watery image" at the pool. She began to turn back. Adam
then pursued her, but what he said did not cause her to question her own judgment. Adam, she says, was "less amiably mild." She would have noted a difference in tone between the voice's benevolence and the desperate pleadings
of Adam. Her first choice, her return to the pool, therefore, is manifestly free.
Discounting the promise of that voice, "him thou shalt enjoy\ Inseperably
thine . . ." (4.472–3), she judges Adam "less" than what she has perceived
through sight and hearing. She turns back to the pool.

Eve's judgments are sensible, rational and free, yet incomplete. There
would be much in what the voice had said to her that she did not yet understand. To what could the predicate, "thyself" refer? The most immediate
among these imponderables, however, would have been the middle element
of Eve's tricolon (4.478–9) of Adam's insufficiencies: "less fair,\ Less winning soft, less amiably mild." The voice had spoken of "soft imbraces"
(4.471), but what could this "soft" mean? Knowing only what she sees
and what she hears, Eve knows nothing of "soft" in the realm of touch, or
of body. How would she even know she has one? She had no mother who
embraced her at birth. But when Adam cannot delay her flight, he follows
and takes her by the hand. This act partakes of no violence; implies no subjugation; and abridges no freedom of choice or will. Rather it will introduce
both Adam and Eve into the mysterious realm of an "other," of touch, of
body and of themselves.

When Adam takes her hand, Eve discovers that Adam is far more than "fair
indeed and tall"; Adam would be, as the voice had told her, "no shadow," but
what could a "shadow" have meant to Eve before now? It was a distinction
without a difference. But *now*, Adam has a body—and so does she! In an
instant she knows what is "no shadow," "what is a "watery image," and the
substantial object of her formerly vain desire. Such is the nature of touch, the
most immediate, most revealing, most directly comprehending reciprocity,
not just of sensation, but of rational understanding at the highest level[35]—as
Eve's account will show. This touch of the hand reveals to Eve what she is,
and what each are, one to another. Her first words in Paradise some days after
"that day" beneath the platan tree describe him and display her considerable
knowledge of herself: "O thou for whom\And from whom I was formed
flesh of thy flesh, \And without whom I am to no end . . ." (4.440–41). Her
first descriptor of what she is and shares with him, "flesh of thy flesh," is

corporeal. Taken together, the address and self-description declare unbeknownst to both the rationale of their creation by God: a new creation, distinct from God and the host of Heaven, a kind of two ("male and female he created them"), other to each other in fleshly body, yet related. Angels have no true other in substance, but are other only by relation to God. Touch entails relation in and of the body. Touch is the ground and foundation from which human discourse flows. There must be a "two." This is what God intended when he made beings of flesh. This communion in touch transforms in a flash Eve's understanding. As she now tells Adam, speaking of what she learned at that moment on "that day" when mere words failed: "thy gentle hand\ Seized mine, I yielded, and from that time see \. . ." (4.487–488). As a result of touch, what she, a "fair Creature," had seen in the pool, "the answering Looks\ Of sympathy and love," of a fair creature, is now a "watery image" of both the "vain desire" she once had felt and that Adam too had fruitlessly expressed ("Return fair *Eve,* . . ."). Both superficial appearances in the realm of the "more and less" are demoted by Adam's touch: "beauty is excelled by manly grace\And wisdom . . . alone is truly fair." Beauty (the "fair" in outward appearance) and the "amiably mild" (which she found lacking in his tone of address), both outward semblances of the fair, are now excelled by a manly grace, a nobility of manly speech and deed. This could not have occurred unless Eve had seen in Adam's yearning for sympathy and love a likeness of her own yearning for the same as she turned back to the pool. But how is this wisdom if not that Eve in the flash of self-understanding consequent upon Adam's touch had seen *in the effort of Adam* to understand what she, Eve, was doing ("Whom fliest thou? whom thou fliest . . . ") *a likeness of her own effort* to find sympathy and love? As Socrates had said to Alcibiades, " *soul too,* if it is going to know itself, it must look into soul, and above all, into this place of it in which the virtue of the soul, wisdom, arises, *and* into anything else with which it happens to be similar" (133b7–10, italics added).

One might think that Eve at that moment in the flood of insight consequent upon Adam's touch might have granted to Adam a certain wisdom to have done as he did. But Eve's first words in Paradise (4.440–491) declare the insights that she now has—and in a sense, that Adam yet lacks. Eve's first words, after all, respond to Adam's address to her:

Sole partner and sole part of all these joys,
Dearer thyself than all; needs must the power
That made us, and for us this ample world
Be infinitely good, and of his good
As liberal and free as infinite
That raised us from the dust and placed us here
In all this happiness . . . (4.411–417)

Although she affirms his ample praise of their Creator, "What thou hast said is just and right" (4.443), her words expand upon her "So far the happier Lot" (4.446), and thus inform his yet doubtful appreciation of that being, his Maker, that had created her for him (see 4.446–448). When Eve, therefore, speaks in fine of a "wisdom which alone is truly fair" she is not thinking of Adam, but rather *speaks to* a wisdom—of which they both are aware only now as they talk "beneath a tuft of shade"—that had made them for each other. As Socrates had said to Alcibiades, "Can we say, then, that there is a more divine thing belonging to the soul than this, about which there is knowing and thinking?" (133c1–2). Perhaps too, this is what Milton had in mind when he had his narrator anticipate their capacity to know that being: "Hee for God only, shee for God in him" (4.299). As Socrates would have said, it all depends on what one looks into. It must be similar. As beings who "worthy seem'd for in their looks Divine\ The image of their glorious maker shone" (4.291–292), they would have to be devoted to each other to find through each other that likeness of what they both yearned to see in order to know themselves.

In Plato's *1st Alcibiades* all the different questions Socrates asked Alcibiades—what do you know? and how did you acquire that knowledge? did you discover it yourself? or did you learn from an other?—turn out to have the one and the same answer: the recognition of the fatal error in self-sufficiency. In Ovid's *Metamorphoses*, Milton found both the error and, by looking into something else similar—Platonic self-knowledge, its correction in a devotion to a "fit conversing soul." Perhaps for a few, Milton's deft translation of Eve's first words in Paradise will seem to have been worth the risk.

NOTES

1. Citations to Ovid's *Metamorphoses*, W. S. Anderson, ed., *Ovidius: Metamorphoses* (Stuttgart: B. G. Teubner, 1998) with book in lower case roman numerals; to Plato from the text of the *1st Alcibiades* unless otherwise noted, Ioannes Burnet, ed., *Platonis Opera*, 1 ed., 5 vols., vol. 2 (Oxonii: Oxford University Press, 1973); to Aristotle, the texts of Rudolphus Kassel, ed., *Aristotelis De Arte Poetica Liber* (Oxford: Oxford University Press, 1965) and W.D. Ross, ed., *Aristotelis Physica* (Oxford: Oxford University Press, 1966).

2. Louis Martz, 219, traced the interest to Thomas Newton's edition of *Paradise Lost* (London, 1750), but noted "the reminiscence of Ovid's story has been felt by every reader." However, critical notice now has become tired—content with a myth or a psychopathology. Christine Froula, 149, speaks of narcissism never mentioning Ovid. Mary Nyquist, 122, nods to Ovid, but talks of "specular" and "female auto-eroticism" and a Narcissus myth. Appeals to a mythic tradition proliferate (See bibliography of Max Nelson, 384–89.) notwithstanding Anderson's dismissal, 372, of

a lost Hellenistic source. In either case, the relation of Ovid's text to *P.L.* 4.467–475 was receding from view. Richard DuRocher, 85–93, and Martz, 219–22, instanced close comparison of the tales until Heather James, 121–45, and Maggie Kilgour, 307–39. Both are invested in narcissism: for James, as a facet of the romance genre; for Kilgour, of *poesis*. DuRocher and Martz favored thematic considerations of epic structure and *metamorphosis*. Synoptic studies of Milton's appropriations from Classical sources read through Renaissance practice (See esp. Davis P. Harding, 73–77.) or operate between Le Comte's "Sly Milton" (*passim*) and L. P. Wilkerson's lofty dismissal, 437: "Milton would feel nothing incongruous in the association of 'our general mother' with Narcissus."

3. See Richard F. Hardin, 44–62.

4. Modern criticism has offered various candidates for those "few." Joseph Summers, 30–31, parenthesis in text, suspected that Milton in some measure cultivated a "guilty reader" compelled to reexamine his misplaced sympathies in moral dramas in and of the poem. Yet such a reader could grow into the challenge: "If we are to read *Paradise Lost* . . . we must not rule out the possibility that the poet may be more sensitive and more subtle, intellectually, morally and sensuously, than we ourselves." For Stanley Fish the "reader" was the focus of the poem's architecture; a mode of spiritual self-examination already familiar to Milton's contemporaries relentlessly would lead Milton's "fit audience" to be "Surprised by Sin." Milton created ", . . a reader who is fit because he knows and understands his limitations" (49). Historicist approaches (e.g., Marcia Landy, 322–323 & 326–330; Nyquist, 118–122) are less concerned with Milton's audience than their own contemporaries; they seek 'resistant' readers "fit" to recognize absolutisms of faith, politics and gender perceived in Milton's verse.

5. See," He, to be sure, was always in the open." (ἐκεῖνός γε ἀεὶ μέν ἦν ἐν τῷ φανερῷ [*Mem.* 1.1.10])

6. See once again, Jonathan Richardson (*Explanatory Notes and Remarks on Milton's Paradise Lost*, 1734,) cxliv–cxlv. In a similar vein, see Michael B. Sullivan, "Horatian Humor in Milton's *Tetrachordon* Sonnet," *Milton Quarterly* 38, no. 3 (2004): 129. Milton argues for philological attainments (*On Education* [2.369–374]) and a capacity for "reading of Books, whatever sort they be" (*Areopagitica* [2.507–521]).

7. *Doctrine and Discipline* (2.251).

8. Milton in *Tetrachordon* interpreting Gen. 2.18 ("I will make him a helpe meet for him.") had observed, "God as it were not satisfy'd with the naming of a help, goes on describing *another self, a second self, a very self it self*" (*CPW* 2.600, italics in text). In *Paradise Lost*, see esp. "Like consort to thyself" (4.449), and "my Self \ Before me" (8.495–496).

9. Pace Scriptural references (Gen. 2:23; 1 Cor. 11:3 & Eph. 5:23), see Aristotle *Physica* 194b16–195a3 & esp. 194b18–20 in re, "O thou for whom"(4.440): εἰδέναι δὲ οὐ πρότερον οἰόμεθα ἕκαστον πρὶν ἂν λάβωμεν τὸ διὰ τί περὶ ἕκαστον (τοῦτο δ' ἐστὶ τὸ λαβεῖν τὴν πρώτην αἰτίαν), ("we do not think, moreover, that we know each thing until we grasp the 'on account of what' in regard to each thing. [this is to grasp cause in the primary sense])," and Milton's *A Fuller Course of Logic Conformed to*

the Method of Peter Ramus (WJM vol. 11, 8.236–238). Following upon the primary sense of cause (τὸ διά τι), "O thou for whom." Eve (4.441–2) in naming Adam describes herself in the sequence of the chapter headings in Milton's *Logic* (WJM vol. 11, 2.222–238): the *material*, "from whom"; the *formal*, "I was form'd flesh of thy flesh"; and implied in the passive, "was form'd," the *efficient*, and concludes with the *final*, "without whom I am to no end."

10. For *inreprehensa* as a conspicuous neologism, see Anderson (above, note 1), 373n.340; *responsum* is oft an "official reply," thus, of an oracle. That Tiresias takes this pose is clear from *de quo consultu* (3.345–346).

11. See e.g., Kilgour (above, note 1), 323–324; Lee Jacobus ("Self Knowledge in *Paradise Lost*: Conscience and Contemplation," *Milton Studies* 3 [1971]: 112–16.) cites commentary of Milton's contemporaries. Anderson (above, note 1), 374n346–348, is more sensible in denial of "Socratic self-knowledge" to Narcissus. See also: "So may he himself love, and not gain what he loves" (3.405), which mimics the definition of philosophic eros (see *Symposium* 201b2); and, Echo's insufferable garrulousness reduced to mere repetitions of the last thing said by her unwilling interlocutor recalls unpleasant experience of Socrates's interlocuters when they find their own words repeated by Socrates with a new and unsettling intent.

12. The double sense of *famam* as "something said" and, by synecdoche, "reputation" is here paired with a doubled sense of *meritam*, as "well-deserved," and elsewhere in Ovid as pejorative, of scandalous speech or suggestion: cf., 3.325: *meritam . . . linguam*; and substantively at 9.589: *Et merito!*.

13. She is, of course, both, depending upon an audience's careful attention or not to details of Ovid's tale and those "generally accepted opinions" they presently hold about Eve, about the tale of Narcissus, and even, about self-knowledge.

14. Kilgour (above, note 1), 334 *et alii*, but Milton had noted this setting for the conversation of the *Phaedrus* in the *7th Prolusion* (2.295).

15. A rare instance in prose of a poetic appositive genitive.

16. For the significance of this tree and its relation to speech, λόγος, see Alfred Geier, *Plato's Erotic Thought: The Tree of the Unknown* (Rochester: University of Rochester Press, 2002), 151–56.: "the tree, and *everything* related to and of it . . . is an image, a very beautiful image, of the (very beautiful) *written* word . . . ." (154, parenthesis and italics in text).

17. On word play in the *Phaedrus* associating books and trees, see, once again, Geier (above, note 14), 153–154.

18. Although Milton's *Logic* was not published until 1672, critical opinion (see the preface of Walter J. Ong, S. J. in Hughes *CPW* [above, note 3], 8.144–147) has settled on composition within the period of 1641–1647, thus well before the first edition of *Paradise Lost* in 1667.

19. Albert W. Fields, "Milton and Self-Knowledge," *PMLA* 83, no. 2 (1968): 392, parenthesis added, remarks that, "in the *Alcibiades* he (i.e., Socrates) says that although one cannot apprehend the true self by introspection, he can attain self-awareness by mirroring himself in soul of another," but Fields "platonizes"—one sees

a generic self "by viewing himself mirrored in the world's stage." *Contra* Fields (394) this is not, "essentially the same method that Socrates suggested in *Alcibiades*."

20. Socrates seems to glimpse such a medium when he remarks just after his sudden insight, οὐκοῦν καλῶς ἔχει οὕτω νομίζειν, ἐμὲ καὶ σὲ προσομιλεῖν ἀλλήλοις τοῖς λόγοις χρωμένους τῇ ψυχῇ πρὸς τὴν ψυχήν; ("Then isn't it right to think that you and I *associate with each other* when we are *using speech* with the soul in relation to the soul?" (130d8–10 italics added for emphasis).

21. Alcibiades himself was somehow aware this different kind of seeing when he asked Socrates τὸ ποῖόν τι *διανοούμενος* λέγεις, ὦ Σώκρατες; ("What sort of thing *as you think about it* (lit. 'directing your mind towards it') do you mean, Socrates?" [132c11 italics added]). The participle (διανοούμενος) is otherwise pleonastic.

22. See *spectat positus humi geminum, sua lumina, sidus* ("he looks, lying on the turf, at a twin constellation, his own eyes" 3.420)—the first sight Ovid mentions after (3.415–420) the onset of his fascination.

23. See esp. 3.466–468, sed passim 466–492.

24. Unless one attends to the period close at 324, one is tempted to think that Adam and Eve "stood whispering soft," not as syntax and punctuation require, the "tuft of shade."

25. Cf. *quod tu cum olfacies, deos rogabis \totum ut te faciant, Fabulle, nasum.* ("which, when you smell it, you will beg the gods,\ that they make you, my dear Fabullus, all nose!"). Milton's amphibolous introduction blurs the referent for "him" (410): either Satan, who lurks near, "as a tiger," ravenous to hear, or Adam. The possibility that Eve might be speaking dissipates with the mention of the Interdict at 4.420ff and is resolved at 4.440, but Adam's entire speech (4.412–439) is conspicuously ungendered.

26. Adam later (see 8.499–520) gives no hint of conversation with Eve until he mentions "wisdom in discourse with her" (8.552), the very topic with which Eve will end her discourse with him beneath the platan: "And wisdom, which alone is truly fair" (4.491).

27. For consistency of the voice in apostrophe in *Metamorphoses* as a feature of the poetic persona of Ovid, see Joseph B. Solodow, 52–55. For the emotional weight of direct address in the *Metamorphoses*, see esp. 53, in re ix.666–797 & esp. ix.790–791.

28. Seneca the Elder in the *Suasoria* notes that Ovid defended his borrowing of lines from Virgil, *non subripiendi causa, sed palam mutuandi, hoc animo ut vellet agnosci*... ("not for the sake of underhanded thievery, but openly 'borrowing,' in this spirit—that he wished it to be recognized . . ."[3.7]).

29. See Galinsky (above, note 1), 57 & Anderson (above, note 1), 381–382 in re substitution *metri gratia* of an imperative, *avertere* for a conditional, *si averteris*, or a gerund, *avertendo*.

30. See 3.481ff and esp. 491–3, where *quod amaverat Echo* (3.493) echoes *quod amas* (3.433).

31. See 3.480–493 and esp. 480–1.

32. See Socrates's expressions of pity (113c5–7; 118b4); mockery (109d1–5); prophetic insight (124c8–10); and warning (105d2–4).

33. See esp. 3. 354–355.

34. See 3.420–423 and esp. 424: *cunctaque miratur, quibus est mirabilis ipse* ("and he wonders at all the things for which he himself is wonderous").

35. The association of intellectual insight with the sense of touch—and not coincidentally, concluding in an insight into the "truly fair"—is also Platonic: see *Symposium* 211b5–212a7 and the exceptional metaphoric use of ἐφάπτεσθαι.

Chapter 4

An Interlude

A Question of Ends

There is reason to think that Adam would have been both pleased and yet at a loss for what to say to Eve when, days after they first met, she now began to speak with him. Only now did it seem the promise of the Divine Presence—"What next I bring shall please thee, be assured\ Thy likeness, thy fit help, the other self,\ Thy wish, exactly to thy heart's desire" (8.449–451)—might be fulfilled. Adam, as he later told Raphael, had spoken to that Presence of his "single imperfection" that was "the cause of his desire\ By conversation with his like to help,\ Or solace his defects" (8.417–419). But when, after his dream-induced desire—seeing his own flesh and bone taken then rendered in such a lovely form—began to dissipate, he gradually began to think that *this* was not after all what he had asked for.[1] So Eve herself had occasion to note (4.447–448). But now she was talking, but *what* was she talking about? For the moment "in delight\ Both of her Beauty and submissive Charms" (4.497–498) he merely smiles.

With the touch of Adam's hand the day they met Eve had more reason to be pleased and grateful to that Power that Adam tells her made them both. But that granted, Eve's talk just now was all about Adam. Her talk of herself, and of "That day I oft remember" (4.449), was intended to offer solace to Adam by the example of her own brief experience of him several days before. She too had sought a "like consort" to herself. She as well had had her fair hopes raised by a voice at the pool only to be at first disappointed. But now, days later, she reminds him of the appeal he had made to her: "to have thee by my side\ Henceforth an individual solace dear;\ Part of my soul I seek thee" (4.485–487). And with that touch of his hand, she tells him, these words of his were fulfilled for her. The voice at the pool that day had spoken of, "he\

Whose image thou art" (4.471–472). Now several days later, Eve tries to show Adam a likeness of his yearning *in herself* which he that day had satisfied.

To judge, however, from the sense narrative persona imposes on these events Adam does not as yet grasp what Eve has told him. Adam surely understands her acceptance of him, but the mode of reasoning would be strange. Eve revalued the "fair" by the "truly fair." As she tells him, "and from that time [I] see\ How beauty is excelled by manly grace\ And wisdom, which alone is truly fair" (4.489–491). But as she now "half imbracing lean[s] \ On our first Father" (4.494)—her proffered analogue at this moment to Adam's clasp of her hand that day—narrative persona now reads this gesture as of amorous intent and thinks of Jupiter's "superior Love" (4. 499) of Juno.

Here Milton conveys Adam's confused appreciation of Eve through the lens of his narrator's confusion about Adam. Adam surely is pleased by what Eve has said. He smiles—but what is this "superior Love"? The pangs of desire vocalized—"Return fair Eve,\ Whom fly'st thou?" (4.481–482)— did not argue superiority. Rather, narrative persona reads Adam's aloof satisfaction—"hee in delight\Both of her Beauty and submissive Charms" (4.497–498)—as a fit response, as it might appear, to Eve's willing surrender to his assumed excellencies.[2] But, as chapter 5 will soon detail, Adam's own account to Raphael of the events of "that day" reveals a different source than a "manly grace" and "wisdom" for his impulse to grasp Eve's hand. Eve too is, if not confused, at least too quick to assign a virtuous origin to a motion which she nonetheless experiences as a virtue.

For the present, however, narrative persona now adds a poetic analogue to suggest the interest to which Adam's "superior Love" appears inclined:

> as *Jupiter*
> On *Juno* smiles, when he impregns the clouds
> That shed May flowers; and pressed her matron lip
> With kisses pure: (4.499–502)

Narrative persona seems to recall Virgil's personified rendering of the agent of fecundity in nature[3]:

> *tum pater omnipotens fecundis imbribus Aether*
> *coniugis in gremium laetae descendit, et omnis*
> *magnus alit magno commixtus corpore fetus.*

> then [Jupiter] the father omnipotent with fruitful showers
> to the lap of his joyous partner descends and, great now
> intermingled with her great substance nourishes all
> sort of offspring. (*Georgics* 2.325–327)

With the tag, "[t]hat shed May flowers" (4.501), however, Milton has his narrator overlay a Virgilian allusion with a Homeric one to complicate a premature bestowal of the garland of domestic bliss:

Ἦ ῥα, καὶ ἀγκὰς ἔμαρπτε Κρόνου παῖς ἧν παράκοιτιν
τοῖσι δ' ὑπὸ χθὼν δῖα φύεν νεοθηλέα ποίην,
λωτόν θ'ἑρσήεντα, ἰδὲ κρόκον ἠδ' ὑάκινθον
πυκνὸν καὶ μαλακόν, ὃς ἀπὸ χθονὸς ὑψόσ' ἔεργε.

And there, the son of Kronos clasped his wife in his arms
and under them the wondrous earth made grow new flourishing grass
and the tender lotus, and spring crocus, and hyacinth
thick and soft, to keep them off the solid ground. (*Iliados*, 14.346–349)

The tag, "[t]hat shed May flowers," unsettles an imagined moment of domestic bliss with a hint of the deception of Zeus\Jupiter by Hera\Juno with the girdle of Aphrodite. This Homeric source for the floral detail absent in Virgil does not implicate Eve in a Juno-like entrapment of Adam,[4] but that, all the same, is not to say that Adam is self-aware. Rather, Milton invites his fit audience to examine more closely the terms of marital bliss for these two. Satan, of course, immediately leaps to his own conclusion:

> aside the Devil turned
> For envy, yet with jealous leer malign
> Ey'd them askance, and thus to himself plained.
> Sight hateful, sight tormenting! thus these two
> Imparadised in one another's arms
> The happier Eden, shall enjoy thir fill
> Of bliss on bliss, (4.502–508)

HIS "PLEADED REASON[S]" (8.510)

As evening falls, however, the two now make their way to the wedding bower. Their recent talk has left Adam with an interest to renew those marital relations that followed upon their first meeting several days before—and perhaps have continued thereafter. But now that they have talked a new element has been introduced into those relations. Narrative persona sets the scene:

> Now came still evening on, and twilight grey
> Had in her sober livery all things clad;
> Silence accompanied, for beast and bird,
> They to their grassy couch, these to their nests

Were slunk, all but the wakeful nightengale;
She all night long her amorous descant sung; (4.598–603)

These preliminaries drawn from the viewpoint of narrative persona and Satan, Adam's pleased new appreciation of Eve, the wedding bower, its description (4.690–719), their evening devotions (4.720–735), narrative persona's extended coda of praise, "Hail wedded love" and blessing (4.750–775) would all seem to proclaim their marital bliss here in Book 4 as the peak of their existence in Paradise: "Blest pair; and O yet happiest if ye seek\ No happier state, and know to know no more" (4.774–775). But what of those imperfections of their talk when they do not quite understand what the other said or meant, and thus begin to converse?

Adam, as we later learn (8.449–450), had been promised by the "Presence divine" one who would be for him "thy likeness, thy fit help, thy other self\ Thy wish, exactly to thy heart's desire." Eve as they talked "under a tuft of shade" had offered him a glimpse of her own experience as a likeness for his, but Adam was yet to see her in that light. The following morning (chapter 5) he will. Rather, as it seems, the simple fact that she was talking now was enough for him. Her account of their first meeting (4.477–491), moreover, would have left him unsure of—as he later described it to Raphael—his "pleaded reason" (8.510). When they first had met Eve did change her mind about returning to the pool, but it was not what Adam said that changed her mind. Yet his Creator, so he once again later tells Raphael, had found that he did reason (8.412–452) appropriately of himself and of his own need of fit help and fellowship. He therefore now, as evening descends and they pass hand in hand to the wedding bower, attempts to give reasonable garb to those desires that follow from their creation in body.

Adam's awkwardness in reasoning on this occasion (4.610–633) is palpable. It is, perhaps, not hard to see why. He alone of all such creatures knows he needs to give her a reason—he knows from their talk she is his like in looking for one—for his desire for her which he had the moment he saw her. That she was "his flesh, his bone" was reason enough for him then. But what would be a reason for her? That he has not discerned that reason in her first words to him is a sign of how unsure he was of her, and still is. At this moment—and strange to say of the first Parent of humankind—he will offer a basket of the usual or generally accepted excuses for his desire: habit, nature, the design of a higher power, the example of other creatures, self-conceit, obligation, need, comfort, ease, and lastly, an intelligence of Nature.

He begins with an address to his "Fair consort" (4.610) that tries to assure her that his doubts about her, which Eve had noted (4.447–448), are at an end. He then points to a habit they share with other creatures: "the hour\ Of night, and all things now retired to rest\ Mind us of like repose" (4.610–612).

He adds a divine warrant for such conduct: "since God hath set\ Labor and rest, as day and night to men\ Successive" (4.612–614). But having cited other creatures as a likeness for their own conduct, he draws attention to an important difference:

> other creatures all day long
> Rove idle unemployed and less need of rest;
> Man hath his daily work of body or mind
> Appointed which declares his dignity,
> And *the regard of Heav'n on all his ways*;
> While other animals unactive range,
> And of their doings God takes no account. (4.616–622, italics added)

With this exaggeration (cf. 4.428–435) he begins to blend the obedience she knows is required by the Interdict with what might be called erotic imperatives of his corporeal nature as well as with a vague sense of their horticultural duties. He thereafter reminds her of the work that awaits them on the morrow, and only obliquely, insinuates his real motive with a note to paucity in the labor supply. "With first approach of light," he claims,

> we must be risen
> And at our pleasant labor, to reform
> Yon flowery arbours, yonder alleys green,
> Our walk at noon, with branches overgrown,
> That mock our scant manuring, and require,
> More hands than ours to lop their wanton growth (4.624–629).

Thus with a bashful urgency he declares his conjugal wish in imagined economies of labor under the constraints of necessity: "As nature wills," he says, "*night bids* us rest" (4.663, italics added).

"WITH THEE CONVERSING, I FORGET ALL TIME," (4.639)

Eve now in the interest of continuing their talk deftly parries Adam's both thesis and arguments with the very "beauty and submissive charms" that have already so captivated him. She calls him, "[Her] author and disposer" (4.633) but reminds him of to whom, not to what, she owes obeisance. "[W]hat *thou biddst\ Unargued* I obey; *so God ordains*" (4.634–636, italics added & cf. 4.470–476). Banishing the thought of Nature as her guide, she demonstrates her freedom in a declared obedience to him that needs no argument even as she argues for a different pastime for their evening repose: "God is thy law, thou mine: to know no more\ Is woman's happiest knowledge and her praise\ With thee conversing I forget all time" (4.637–639). So much for "the hour\ Of night." And leaving no time for Adam to reargue his embarrassed conjugal pleadings she declares the charming measure of her growth in love of him in an extended *epanalepsis*[5] of sixteen lines as prologue to a proposed topic for their continuing conversation:

All seasons[6] and their change, all please alike.
Sweet is the breath of morn, her rising sweet,
With charm of earliest birds; pleasant the sun
When first on this delightful Land he spreads
His orient beams, on herb, tree, fruit, and flower,
Glistering with dew; fragrant the fertile earth
After soft showers; and sweet the coming on
Of grateful evening mild, then silent night
With this her solemn bird and this fair moon,
And these the gems of heaven, her starry train:
But neither breath of morn when she ascends
With charm of earliest birds, nor rising sun
On this delightful land, nor herb, fruit, flower,
Glistering with dew, nor fragrance after showers,
Nor grateful evening mild, nor silent night
With this her solemn bird, nor walk by moon,
Or glittering star-light without thee is sweet. (4.640–656)

Eve's lovely confession of her affection for Adam gently reshapes his appeal to diurnal rhythms as arguments of necessity into an opportunity to talk. This present "walk by moon,\ Or glittering star-light" is *the* case in point. Eve redirects Adam's temporal imperative, "night bids us rest" into an occasion to stay up and talk: "Bút whérefore *áll níght lóng* shine thése, for whóm*Thís* glórious síght, when sléep hath shút all eyés?" (4.657–658, italics and scansion added).

Eve's question is not easy to fathom. She asks Adam to explain something that she is presently seeing and evidently points to: "Wherefore all night long shine *these*?" She after all can indicate what she is looking at. Nevertheless, her question asks about *that something* in a way that would exclude the testimony of all those who experience with open eyes that something in the way that she and Adam do: "when sleep has shut all eyes." That is, Adam asks when none of those like us are looking, "for whom\ This glorious sight?" One may well ask why she asks this question in this peculiar way. But perhaps it is not peculiar at all. Following immediately upon her charming declaration of affection for Adam and their talk together one might assume the question was simply rhetorical: 'Adam, whom else but *for us*? Let's not miss that sight, and stay awake, and talk.' Or, is she already thinking of those "spiritual creatures" singing "[w]hile they keep watch or nightly rounding walk," of whom Adam soon will remind her (4.677–685)? Does she attempt to have him talk about *them*? But that cannot be right because angels too have eyes—how else could they "keep watch?"—and they too sleep (see 5.673ff). Or could her question really not be about the stars at all, but her own lingering uncertainty about their relations. Confident in her own feelings for him she yet wonders about his feelings for her: "Adam, does this starlight have a reason beyond a delight in a good I would find only in our conversation about it?"—This would reaffirm her need of him to enjoy all things else in talk even as it obliquely queries whether he has such an exclusive need of her as she has just confessed to him. 'Do you think of things apart from our shared experience of them and will you talk about *them*?' Or is it merely a ruse to postpone their resort to the wedding bower? None of these possibilities, however, quite honor the simple limits and difficult challenge of the question she in all innocence poses: "wherefore all night long shine these, *for whom* This *glorious sight*, when sleep has shut *all eyes*?" (italics added).

"HIS OWN WORKS AND THEIR WORKS AT ONCE TO VIEW" (3.59)

The poem (3.56–69) itself has already brought to view one *for whom* this glorious sight remains ever present to his "unsleeping eyes" (5.647). With a new invocation to holy light narrative persona has opened consideration of events in Heaven and on Earth in Book 3 at the moment when,

> the almighty Father from above
> From the pure empyrean where he sits
> High throned above all highth, bent down his eye
> *His own works and their works at once to vie*w:
> About him all the sanctities of heaven
> Stood thick as stars, *and from his sight received*
> *Beatitude past utterance*; (3.56–62, italics added)

Eve's innocent query, it appears, delves into greater matters than she realizes. The best conversations often do. Neither Adam nor Eve, of course, is aware of things "invisible to mortal sight" (3.55), though in his reasoned invitation to the wedding bower Adam has surmised "the regard of heaven on all his ways" (4.620). But Eve's question wonders about an activity of an other or others which is in some way akin to their own wonder at such things. This likeness also is implied in a kinship among the objects of interest of the almighty

Father: "His own works and their works at once to view." At first, one might assume this phrase relates the Father's work at creation to those works of his creatures—here, chiefly if not exclusively, the horticultural labors of Adam and Eve.[7] Eve's question, however, has a different focus: she assumes a "glorious sight" for someone else *for whom* it is a good. She is thinking in her way of that decisive sense of cause, the end, or *finis,* or τέλος. This sense of a sight as a good for a spectator is also preserved in an ambiguity of reference in regard to the sight of the Almighty Father. As He looks down from his throne, "His own works and their works at once to view," the narrator adds, "and from his sight receiv'd\ Beatitude past utterance." Here one might assume the phrase refers to those creatures of the creator who, after the fashion of popular iconographies, receive blessings from the beam of his eye. But the phrase allows as well the sense wherein the Father in seeing receives a blessing in contemplation of that good that he beholds. In contemplation of "this glorious sight" he knows the good of what he sees.[8]

An emphasis on this delight in contemplation in preference to but not to the exclusion of a more familiar and conventional view of the creator blessing his creatures is, moreover, supported by the similarity of the occasion of Eve's wonder and her desire to talk with Adam to Aristotle's account of the birth of philosophic wonder (τὸ θαυμάζειν) and the search after the identity of the highest wisdom (σοφία) in *Metaphysics* 1.3. Speaking of *things above all knowable, the primary things and the causes* (μάλιστα δ' ἐπιστητὰ τὰ πρῶτα καὶ τὰ αἴτια), Aristotle observes that,

ἀρχικωτάτη δὲ τῶν ἐπιστημῶν . . . ἡ γνωρίζουσα τίνος ἕνεκέν ἐστι πρακτέον ἕκαστον· τοῦτο δ' ἐστὶ τἀγαθὸν ἑκάστου, ὅλως δὲ τὸ ἄριστον ἐν τῇ φύσει πάσῃ. ἐξ ἁπάντων οὖν τῶν εἰρημένων ἐπὶ τὴν αὐτὴν ἐπιστήμην πίπτει τὸ ζητούμενον ὄνομα· δεῖ γὰρ αὐἑήν τῶν πρώτων ἀρχῶν καὶ αἰτιῶν εἶναι θεωρητικήν· [10] καὶ γὰρ τἀγαθὸν καὶ τὸ οὗ ἕνεκα ἓν τῶν αἰτίων ἐστίν.

Ὅτι δ' οὐ ποιητική, δῆλον καὶ ἐκ τῶν πρώτων φιλοσοφησάντων· διὰ γὰρ τὸ θαυμάζειν οἱ ἄνθρωποι καὶ νῦν καὶ τὸ πρῶτον ἤρξαντο φιλοσοφεῖν, ἐξ ἀρχῆς μὲν τὰ πρόχειρα τῶν ἀτόπων θαυμάσαντες, εἶτα κατὰ μικρὸν οὕτω προϊόντες [15] καὶ περὶ τῶν μειζόνων διαπορήσαντες, οἷον περί τε τῶν τῆς σελήνης παθημάτων καὶ τῶν περὶ τὸν ἥλιον καὶ ἄστρα καὶ περὶ τῆς τοῦ παντὸς γενέσεως.

The most authoritative knowledge . . . is that *knowledge which knows 'the for the sake of what'* (ἡ γνωρίζουσα τίνος ἕνεκέν) each thing need be done: this is *the good of each thing* (τἀγαθὸν ἑκάστου), and generally speaking, the best in all nature. Of all those things that have been mentioned, then, the name under investigation [i.e., "wisdom (σοφία)] belongs to this same knowledge, because it is necessary that this be *capable of speculative insight* (θεωρητικήν) of the first principles and causes, *because one of the causes is the good and 'the for the sake of which'* (καὶ γὰρ τἀγαθὸν καὶ τὸ οὗ ἕνεκα ἓν τῶν αἰτίων ἐστίν).

But that it (i.e., wisdom) is *not involved with making* (οὐ ποιητική) is obvious even by the example of those who first philosophized. Human beings presently and at first began to philosophize *on account of wondering* (διὰ γὰρ τὸ θαυμάζειν). At the outset they wondered at strange things *within their reach* (πρόχειρα)[9] but little by little they came to be quite at a loss about greater things, for example about the changes of the moon and those of the sun and the stars and about the coming into being of the All. (982b4–17)[10]

Here several points deserve notice. Eve's question of Adam, *"for whom\ This glorious sight"* asks about a good for the sake of *whom* as opposed to a "for the sake of *what*" because the first touch of his hand—a "strange thing," for her at that time, yet "within her reach,"—was several days before the source of her insight into herself as a good for him. She so-to-speak now "personalizes" her interest in the end (τέλος) of what she sees and wonders if there are others who enjoy this good as well. Adam in his first response to her will not personalize, but for the very same reason as Eve: his own recent past experience.

Adam's initial response to Eve's question will follow the logic of the name he gives her at this very moment: "Daughter of God and man, accomplished Eve" (4.660). His name describes how he understands how she came to be what she is. He had, after all, been witness through a "cell\ Of fancy" (8.460–461) to her creation. He names her by those causes he had observed had a part in her making: the efficient and the material. But in adding "accomplished Eve," Milton has Adam ironize his own incomplete understanding of her. Adam has yet to apprehend that form in which she appears to him as the "good for the sake of which," or, as Eve said, "for whom . . . I was formed flesh of thy flesh." His first glimpse of *this good* will soon be presented to him as they hand in hand converse on their way to the wedding bower.

Adam in the midst of answering Eve will suddenly abandon his account of efficient and material causes, and for a very good reason: he has caught a glimpse of her face. His initial attempt to give an account had failed to honor her premise of a spectator present to the celestial events he would explain to her, a premise which his sight of her own bodily presence now in fact reveals to him. Simply stated his sight of her is a good for him. Nevertheless his distinct attempts both speak of goods—first, a "for the sake of what," then, a "for the of sake of whom"—tacitly introduce two distinct modes of naming a comprehensive good for them both: nature and creation. Here Milton points to a conversation about the good of what they behold that these two will never be allowed to have. Cut short this night by their arrival at the wedding bower, their talk beneath the stars is further postponed one may assume the following morning by Eve's dream and therein, Adam's own discovery of his own other self in Eve. Then, just at the point that these two could really begin to talk,

Raphael arrives from heaven as that "warning voice" (4.1) narrative persona had deemed was needed. The change this poetic "remedy" works in the conversational relations of Adam and Eve will facilitate the Fall.

Nevertheless, Milton provides some hints to the topics they might have addressed in seemingly casual remarks of narrative persona, Raphael and Adam. These remarks are designed by the poet to reveal to his "fit audience . . . though few" the challenge of Eve's question. A brief itinerary of the course of thought these remarks suggest may be of use. Adam's reply to Eve's question reveals their difficulty of giving an account of their own good. As they reach the wedding bower a casual aside in narrative voice proposes an understanding of that good with a poetic figure of speech. The narrator speaks of a "sovereign planter," who "framed\All things to man's delightful use" (4.691–692). The limits of this notion of an end Milton with the aid of Aristotle had carefully examined in his *Artis Logicae Plenior Instituto ad Petri Rami Methodum Concinnata* (hereafter, the *Art of Logic*). That examination[11] simultaneously posits a non-figurative understanding of a different good as an end—a knowledge of good achieved in contemplation, not in activity of making. In Raphael's account of the days of Creation, however, the figurative way of speaking of an end is restored as the assumed intent of the Father's creative acts to remedy the losses suffered in the War of Heaven. At the close of Raphael's account of the Days of Creation, however, Adam has a question about the good of that making. There is to his way of thinking a better way. He will offer a critique of the Ptolemaic cosmos of creation with Copernican economies based once again on the very philosophy of nature of which Eve's countenance had signaled her tacit disapproval. These scattered ruminations on a good for man taken together pose a further question. Adam's prologue to his critique, "When I behold this goodly Frame, this World\ Of Heav'n and Earth consisting" (8.15–16), recalls the Psalmist's wonder posed in the manner of a Socratic question: "O *what is man* that thou rememberest yet,\And think'st upon him? or of man begot\That him thou visit'st and of him art found?" (Psalm viii," 12–14).[12] In short, Eve's wonder at the heavens in their conversing might have brought them to wonder about themselves. Closer consideration of the course of these seemingly isolated remarks follows below.

ADAM: "NOR THINK, THOUGH MEN WERE NONE . . ." (4.675)

In the same terms as the name he gave her as they began to converse, Adam's initial attempt to answer Eve's question—"*wherefore* all night long shine these, *for whom*\ This glorious sight, when sleep has shut all eyes"

(4.657–658, italics added)—renders the "wherefore" by speaking of those efficient and material causes of this spectacle in Nature. With confidence he begins, we may assume, pointing at those lights in the evening sky:

Those have their course to finish, round the earth,
By morrow evening, and from land to land
In order, though to nations yet unborn,
Ministering light prepared, they set and rise;
Lest total darkness should by night regain
Her old possession, and extinguish life
In nature and all things, which *these soft fires*
Not only enlighten, but with kindly heat
Of various influence foment and warm,
Temper or nourish, or in part shed down
Their stellar virtue on *all kinds that grow*
On earth, made hereby apter to receive
Perfection from the sun's more potent ray.
These then, though unbeheld in deep of night
Shine not in vain, (4.661–675, italics added)

Of the end or final cause and the formal cause which Aristotle argues are identical in the completion of processes of Nature (see *Metaphysica* 4.24 [1023a34] & cf. *Artis Logicae* I.viii [*WJM* 11.66.20–24]) Adam can say little since the "for whom" of this glorious sight remains unspecified; he speaks merely of, "all kinds that grow on Earth." Nor does Adam appear to grasp that his attempt at natural philosophy will likely lead to an infinite regress since no term in his account is *an end* (τέλος), a term which *is not for the sake of* something else. And as Aristotle also noted, "those who fashion an infinite regress fail to notice that they have removed the nature of the good—for surely no one would attempt to do anything unless it was likely to come to a completion" (οἱ τὸ ἄπειρον ποιοῦντες λανθάνουσιν ἐξαιροῦντες τὴν τοῦ ἀγαθοῦ φύσιν [καίτοι οὐθεὶς ἂν ἐγχειρήσειεν οὐδὲν πράττειν μὴ μέλλων ἐπὶ πέρας ἥξειν) (*Metaphysica* 1 minor. 2 [994b12–14]).

At this point in his talk with Eve, however, Adam suddenly abandons his original line of argument. He seems to remember Eve's original qualification: "when sleep has shut all eyes." Looking directly at Eve, he offers in imperative mood a different way to consider her question: "*nor think*, though men were none\That heaven would want spectators, God want praise\. . . (4.675–676, italics added). Adam now recalls and expands upon their shared experience of the past few evenings. His remark is both a direct address to Eve *and* implied self-criticism for his attempt at natural philosophy. In this approach to Eve's question Adam now recognizes both a form—beholding those works of their great Creator—and a good for those spiritual creatures that is not for the sake of something else and thus, is an end in itself:

Millions of spiritual creatures walk the Earth
Unseen, both when we wake, and when we sleep:
All these with ceaseless praise his works behold
Both day and night: how often from the steep
Of echoing hill or thicket have we heard
Celestial voices to the midnight air,
Sole, or responsive each to other's note
Singing their great creator: oft in bands
While they keep their watch or nightly rounding walk,
With heavenly touch of instrumental sounds
In full harmonic number joined; their songs
Divide the night, and lift our thought to heaven. (4.676–688)

This resort to first person plural pronouns, the imperative mood and a shift in tone from lecture-hall didacticism of his initial reply to a delight in a shared recollection of singing voices and harmony all suggest that Adam is no longer looking at the stars but at Eve. In fact, the blunt interjection of an imperative, "Nor think, . . ." (4.675), suggests that Adam's sudden shift originates in a look of disappointment Adam has discerned in Eve's face as he lectured on those lights in the night sky. Eve would show such disappointment to Adam here because she at this moment lacks that "wisdom, which alone is truly fair" (4.491) about the good as an end she had found in Adam "that day" they met.

This proleptic surmise of disappointment in the face of Eve looks ahead to events the following morning when her distressed countenance receives its proper name among moments of marital epiphany. Adam awakes the following morning to the songs of birds, but,

            so much the more
His wonder was to find unwak'n'd Eve
With tresses discompos'd, and glowing cheek
As through unquiet rest: he on his side
Leaning half-raised, with looks of cordial love
Hung over her enamoured, and beheld
Beauty, which whether waking or asleep,
Shot forth *peculiar graces*: . . . (5.8–15, italics added)

As to the character and import of these "peculiar graces" it suffices to observe that narrative perspective in the passage just quoted unwittingly inscribes a sequence: a wonder at the presence of the strange in the beautiful that gives rise to conversation.

NARRATIVE PRESENCE: "ALL THINGS TO
MAN'S DELIGHTFUL USE" (4.692)

When these two in their starlit stroll now arrive at the bower, Milton, with an aside positioned in narrative perspective, invites consideration of the scope of Eve's question of "for *whom?*," personified from her first experience of a "for the sake of *what*" in Adam. In either form she asks about an end as the decisive notion of cause as "the good" of anything. This casual aside (4.690–692) in narrative voice clarifies through complication the aim of Eve's question.

As Adam and Eve hand in hand approach their Bower, narrative persona notes, "it was a place\ Chosen by *the sovereign planter*, when he fram'd\ *All things to man's delightful use*" (4.690–692, italics added). The aside is of a piece with the Creation narrative with a brief poetic turn. Poets are granted license to speak in this way. A "sovereign planter," after all, is a metonym. The poetic figure here implies that Adam's "all kinds that grow\ On Earth" (4.671–672)—a phrase congenial to Aristotelian physics—were planned for, arranged, sown, and cultivated by the Creator for the sake of these two. Their delight, their good, was His end; they were those "for whom" all things were done by this Creator. The "sovereign Planter," then, has some end in mind for his making. And as the "sovereign Planter," so man can thereafter also make use of all these things for some further good for Man.

In Milton's discussion "*De Fine*" (I.viii) in his *Art of Logic*, however, the remark about things framed for man's use is equivocal. Following precisely Aristotle's discussion of "the for the sake of which" (τὸ οὗ ἕνεκα), Milton quotes *Physica* 2.2 (194a34–36)[13]: "We use things *as if* everything was for our sake: because we too are *in a certain sense* an end" (*rebus, . . . , utimur,* quasi *nostra causa essent omnia: nam & nos* quodammodo *finis sumus* ([*WJM* 11.66.12–16], emphases added). Milton has in mind with this remark a certain sense in which it would be appropriate to speak of ourselves as an end (τέλος or *finis*) for physical things *in other than* a figurative sense.

Several points deserve notice. In the first place, the figurative sense of speaking of an end is explained in Aristotle's account (*Physica* 2.8 [199a8–20]) of the close relation between the processes of nature and those of art. Aristotle notes that, "on the whole, art brings to fulfillment some things which Nature is unable to bring to pass; with regard to other things, she (i.e., art) imitates [Nature]" (ὅλως δὲ ἡ τέχνη τὰ μὲν ἐπιτέλει ἃ ἡ φύσις ἀδυνατεῖ ἀπεργάσασθαι, τὰ δὲ μιμεῖται [199α15–17]). Thus he observes that a "for the sake of which" or an "end" is appropriate to both art and nature. This is all well and good. Since men for their own sake make use of the things of nature in the exercise of some art, these things seem to have been suited to our ends, because, as these remarks seem to assume, they were created for our sake. But since Milton in the *Art of Logic* shares Aristotle's qualification, "*as if*," the aside on the "sovereign Planter" (4.690–692) in narrative voice in *Paradise Lost* is thereby placed in doubt.

In the *Art of Logic* just prior to his indication of a tacit agreement with Aristotle about a qualified sense of a figurative "end" and a "for the sake of which," Milton asserts that Aristotle says, "in the way in which man is proposed as an end for physical things, so God is for man" (*Sic Physicis rebus finis homo propositus est, homini Deus* [*WJM* 11.66.12–13]). Then, citing the authority of Aristotle, he adds, "[something] of which Aristotle, *Physics* 2.2, was not unaware" (*Quod nec ignoravit Aristoteles*, Phys. 2.2) and continues as we noted above, "We use things *as if* everything was for our sake: because we too are *in a certain sense* an end." Having given the distinct impression that Aristotle holds that as man is an end of physical things, so God is for man, now Milton strangely adds, "The wise Hebrew, Proverbs 16:4, teaches that God is the end of everything" and supplies the text, "God made everything for himself." (*Deum esse omnium finem docet sapiens* Hebraeus, Proverb. 16.4. *Deus propter se fecit omnia.*) For some reason Milton has gone to considerable lengths to conflate two different senses, the figurative and the literal, of an "end" on the assumed authority of Aristotle while pointing to a Biblical passage that reveals the fundamental difference of those two senses. Milton's logical treatise, one may note, points to Aristotle's *Physics* for an explanation.

In *Physics* 2.2 Aristotle begins speaking of the arts, and of our relation to those things as an end since we use them, but then, parenthetically, he points to another sense of an end, but *qualified in some unspecified way* (πως): we are also an end for things,

> since the arts as well work on their material—some arts simply, others, to make it more pliant, we too make use of existing things *as though* they were for our sake (because *in some sense* we too are an end, because 'the for the sake of which' is meant in two ways, but *that* has been discussed in [my writings] concerning philosophy [i.e., in the *Metaphysics*].
>
> ἐπεὶ καὶ ποιοῦσιν αἱ τέχναι τὴν ὕλην αἱ μὲν ἁπλῶς αἱ δὲ εὐεργόν, καὶ χρώμεθα ὡς ἡμῶν ἕνεκα πάντων ὑπαρχόντων (ἐσμεν γάρ πως καὶ ἡμεῖς τέλος· διχῶς γὰρ τὸ οὗ ἕνεκα· εἴρηται δ' ἐν τοῖς περὶ φιλοσοφίας). (194a33–36)

Having turned to the *Physics* to account for the apparent qualification to the aside in *Paradise Lost* with the remark in *Artis Logicae,* it would appear our confusion can be resolved by this other way of speaking of ourselves as an end of things. Perhaps in that other sense things *are* "delightful for man's use" not in a merely figurative sense. But for some reason Aristotle does not explain in the *Physics* this other sense of ourselves as an end. But *Artis Logiae* goes even further.

Milton, as we noted above, adds, as it appears, support for this claim about God as an end for man, on the testimony of "[t]he wise Hebrew," citing Proverbs 16:4: "The Lord has made all things for himself" (*Deus propter se fecit omnia* [11.66.15–17]). But when one examines the *Physics* one finds that Aristotle explicitly only affirms the first part of Milton's proposition, "We too are *somehow* an end" (τέλος [194a35]), and then directs attention to the *Metaphysics* for that different sense of an "end": "[which] *has been discussed in my* [writings] *'concerning philosophy'*" (εἴρηται δ' ἐν τοῖς περὶ φιλοσοφίας). One obvious reason for this redirection might be that this different sense of end is not a fit topic for the *Physics*.

In the *Metaphysics* in the passage already noted above, speaking of origin of philosophy in wonder Aristotle now makes clear—as he did not in the *Physics*—the twofold sense (διχῶς [194a35]) of "end" that he nevertheless did mention in passing when speaking of an "end" in the *Physics*. In the *Metaphysics*, however, he distinguishes (982a21–982b10) two kinds of knowledge of an "end." There is a *wisdom* (σοφία), that is *contemplative* (θεωρητική) that aims to obtain the highest understanding of things *that knows the 'for the sake of what' of things* (ἡ γνωρίζουσα τίνος ἕνεκα), that is, the good of each thing. This knowledge is *not concerned with making or production* (οὐ ποιητική) *and* there is a knowledge of lesser rank that does guide making since it knows the material. The matter of this latter knowledge does not belong to first philosophy.

Putting these various strands of argument together it is clear that the aside of narrative persona in *Paradise Lost*, "all things delightful to men's use," in a figure, that is, "as if," seems to identify that sense of end with a knowledge of making or production. One may imagine with the assistance of the figurative sense a maker in his mind's eye seeing the flowers and other verdure of the wedding bower as a good for man's use. The poetic precedent, of course, for this way of thinking, is not coincidently Homer's account of Zeus's complicity in fashioning the bed of his own seduction by Hera in the *Iliad* (14.346–349) with which this chapter began. With the aside Milton carefully[14] positions a figurative support for the Creation narrative in the "sovereign planter," while quietly pointing to another sense of end, a wisdom that is contemplative of the good of those things that has nothing to do with their use in making or production. This contemplative sense is exemplified, as also noted above, in the first sight of the Almighty Father in the poem:

Now had th' almighty Father from above
From the pure empyrean where he sits
High throned above all highth, bent down his eye
His own works and their works at once to view:
About him all the sanctities of heaven

Stood think as stars, and from his sight received
Beatitude past utterance. (3.56–62)

In what must also be described as a figurative sense of use, the Father might
be said to 'use' "His own works and their works" as that 'material' of his
thoughts. Milton in his *Artis Logicae* citing Aristotle's *Metaphysics* moreover
observes, "in the way in which man is proposed as an end for physical things,
so God is for man" (*WJM* 11.66.12–13). God is the good of such contemplation. His knowledge in contemplation is the end, the good, attainable or not,
of man's endeavor to think about these things for himself.

Adam, however, the following day will propose an improvement to the
Ptolemaic design of Creation Raphael has described. His mistake will be to
assume that the wisdom that is an end for man is a knowledge of making and
production in Nature. He thereby conflates the two distinct senses of man as
end for physical things: the figurative and the contemplative. Eve's question
(4.657–658) as they strolled to the Bower had invited him to think about
what he was seeing. With Adam's error, however, and thereby his "Entering
on studious thoughts abstruse" (8.40), Eve unobserved withdraws from the
discourse. Narrative persona notes the departure with regret:

                                    Eve
Perceiving where she sat retired in sight,
With lowliness majestic from her seat,
And grace that won who saw to wish her stay,
Rose, and went forth among her fruits and flow'rs,
To visit how they prosper'd, bud and bloom,
Her nursery; they at her coming sprung,
And touched by her fair tendance glādher grew. (8.40–47)

For these flowers, one may note, Eve has no designs upon their use. Her unnoticed departure on this occasion and the fatal events that will follow thereupon
bears mute testimony to the "peculiar graces" that Adam, as argued above,
had the night before first discovered in the disappointment in her face. There
was a wisdom in those looks he did not yet fully appreciate.[15]

RAPHAEL: "THE END\OF ALL YET DONE" (7.505–506)

The day following their conversation beneath the stars, Raphael has arrived to
inform the pair of their happy state and their peril. When Adam in his present
state finds disobedience inconceivable, Raphael supplies the "War in Heaven"
as a likeness for an event that Adam will be no less at a loss to comprehend:

"Great things, and full of wonder to our ears,\ Far differing from this World" (7.70–71). But eager to detain in talk such a fascinating guest, Adam asks Raphael to speak of,

How first began this heaven we behold
Distant so high, with moving fires adorned
Innumberable, and this which yields or fills
All space, the ambient air wide interfused
Imbracing this round this florid earth, what cause
Moved the creator in his holy rest
Through all eternity to build
In *chaos*, . . . (7.86–93).

Eve's question, notwithstanding imponderables of angelic misbehavior, yet lingers for Adam. Narrative persona as well points to Adam's lingering interest in, "how this world\ Of heaven and earth conspicuous first began,\When and *whereof created and for what cause,*\What within Eden or without was donc"(7.61–67, italics added). His version of that interest, however, seems less aware—though not exclusive of—Eve's contemplative formula, *"for whom* this glorious sight?"

In Raphael's account of the days of Creation the poetic figure in the narrator's casual aside at the Bower will now be rendered, if not as a tenet of belief, yet as suggestive of such. Speaking in prologue to the sixth day of Creation Raphael declares,

There wanted yet the master-work, *the end*
Of all yet done: a creature who not prone
And brute as other creatures, but endued
With sancity of reason, might erect
His stature, and upright with front serene
Govern the rest, *self knowing, and from thence*
Magnanimous to correspond with heaven,
But grateful to acknowledge whence his good
Descends, thither with heart and voice and eyes
Directed to devotion, to adore
And worship God supreme who made him chief
Of all his works: (7.505–516, italics added)

Raphael's statement now appears to provide an authoritative answer for Eve's question of "for whom" with a sense of an end (*finis*) as "the good of the thing" (*bonum rei* [*Art of Logic* I.viii. {*WJM* 11.62.20}]). All has been created for the sake of Man. This is no longer merely a way of speaking but that decisive sense of cause, "first in the mind of the efficient agent, and last in act and effect" (*Idémque finis in animo efficientis primus, in opere atque effecto est postremus* [*WJM* 11.64.13–14]). In this sense, appropriate only to the intent of a Creator, Man would be "the end of all yet done"; Man was the good He aimed at. And so in Raphael's narrative of the sixth day, the angel announces the good the Son intends prior to the account of His deeds on that day. Raphael's proem predicts, moreover, poetically speaking at least, that which *Paradise Lost* has already in some measure displayed. Books IV and V therein exhibit the stature and gifts accorded these creatures—as this study argues, their rational nature, that image and similitude of their Creator. And with those gifts, it would appear, these two thereafter show themselves "grateful to acknowledge whence [their] good\ Descends, thither with heart and voice and eyes\ Directed to devotion, to adore\ And worship God supreme" (7.512–515). This prediction is confirmed by the devotions of these two during these days in Paradise.

Eve herself, immediately following her first words, had confessed to Adam, "For wee to him indeed all praises owe,\ And daily thanks . . . " (4.444–445). That evening, when in their talk,

Thus at their shady lodge arrived, both stood,
Both turned and under open sky adored
The God that made both sky, air, earth and heav'n
Which they beheld, the moon's respendent Globe
And starry pole: "Thou mad'st the night,
Maker omnipotent, and thou the day,
Which we in our appointed work employed
Have finished happy in our mutual help
And mutual love, . . . (4.720–728)

They will do so again (5.144–208) the following morning after Adam consoles Eve in her distress at her most recent dream. In this display of their gratitude to their Creator, narrative persona stresses their untutored spontaneity:

Lowly they bowed adoring, and began
Their orisons, each morning duly paid
In various style, for neither various style
Nor holy rapture wanted they to praise
Their maker, in fit strains pronounced or sung
Unmeditated, such prompt eloquence
Flowed from their lips, . . . (5.144–151)

These two by their own lights are finding their own way to understand themselves and their stature in the world they inhabit. And gradually they are approaching Eve's question, "for whom\ This glorious sight":

These are thy glorious works, parent of good,
Almighty, thine this universal frame,
Thus wondrous fair; thyself how wondrous then!
Unspeakable, who sitst above these heavens
To us invisible or dimly seen
In these thy lowest works, yet these declare
Thy goodness beyond thought, and power divine (5.153–159).

As of yet, they do not understand themselves as "end[s] of all yet done," nor even of the means by which such a sense of themselves might be obtained. In brief they are not yet in their conversation aware of the wonder of themselves. The frequency and prominence of such devotions in the poem, however, perhaps explains why little if any notice has been paid to certain latent equivocations in Raphael's proem to the sixth day.

Raphael derives their gratitude from a *"self-knowing"*: "from thence*Magnanimous to correspond with heaven*" (7.511–512, italics added). "Self-knowing" would seem to follow from their admission, as Eve averred, that they "all praises owe\\And daily thanks" to their Creator. Adam later tells Raphael that in his very first moments of consciousness he asked all things he saw, "how came I thus, how here?\\ Not of myself; by some great maker then" (8.277–278). And with that sense that he was not the source of his own existence, Adam then immediately asked, "Tell me, how may I know him, how adore\\ From whom I have that thus I move and live" (8.280–281). *"Magnanimous* to correspond with heav'n,*" then, appears a synonym for a generosity manifested in a spirit of gratitude. What then is this *"good"* of their own they are to acknowledge? Is it that good they enjoy in this place fashioned for them by the Creator (see, e.g., 4.411–419) or is it the good the Creator had in mind at their creation? Both are "[their] *good*," but only the latter would, if enjoyed, constitute a *"self-knowing"* worthy of the name.[16] But how, even if possible, would it be known? In Eve's particular case her first knowledge of herself as a good for Adam proceeded from the touch of Adam's hand. But Raphael in prologue to the sixth day now speaks in generic terms. In these terms they would make the object of their inquiry—their work—the contemplation of "[their] *good*" as that end or good that their Creator had in mind at Creation. This, after all, was what Eve sought to know without yet knowing it.

Perhaps this is why in the first glimpse of the Father Almighty in *Paradise Lost* narrative persona implied a kinship between the respective works of the Father and of these creatures when, "[He] bent down his eye,\\ *His own works and their works at once to view*" (3.58–59, italics added). This "good" as a work of contemplation might have been anticipated in a conversation they would have expected to flow from Eve's question. It was presumably enjoyed in that glimpse (3.56ff) of the Father Almighty.

In the *Metaphysics* of Aristotle that good found in contemplation of these creatures is given the name of wisdom (σοφία [A.2]). It is so named because it is more choiceworthy than other sciences, and is valued for its own sake and solely in the interest of knowing. In short it comes to have this name, Aristotle states, "because there is need to contemplate first principles and causes, since the good and 'the for the sake of which' are one of the causes" (δεῖ γὰρ αὐτὴν τῶν πρώτων ἀρχῶν καὶ αἰτιῶν εἶναι θεωρητικήν· καὶ γὰρ τἀγαθὸν καὶ τὸ οὗ ἕνεκα ἓν τῶν αἰτίων ἐστίν. [982b9–10]).

Aristotle, however, concedes (982b28–983a11) that there is a question whether this wisdom could be properly thought to be a human attainment. Many readers of the Bible, were they but aware of Aristotle's remarks on this otherwise useless knowledge, would doubtless agree. But Aristotle goes on to observe that the poets—he cites Simonides: "god alone could have this privilege" (θεὸς ἂν μόνος τοῦτ' ἔχοι γέρας [982a30a].[17])—are of the view that "the divine" (τὸ θεῖον) would naturally be loath to grant this attainment to such a slavish nature as man possesses. But noting as well that poets are proverbial tellers of falsehoods, Aristotle grants an oblique and vague concession to a nameless few: "It is *not fit*," he says, "that a man *not make inquiry* into that knowledge suited to himself." (ἄνδρα δ' οὐκ ἄξιον μὴ οὐ ζητεῖν τὴν καθ' αὑτὸν ἐπιστήμην. [982a31–32].) Some readers of the *Metaphysics* would likely be aware that this bland pronouncement also succinctly describes the self-scrutiny which animates *a certain ordering principle* (κόσμος τις)[18] of the moral virtues in Book IV.3 of the *Nicomachean Ethics*, μεγαλοψυχία, or, as rendered in the anglicized version of its Latin translation, "magnanimity." In the *Ethics* Aristotle observes, "The *magnanimous* (lit. "great-souled") man seems to be he who deems himself fit for great things *since he is fit*" (δοκεῖ δὴ μεγαλόψυχος εἶναι ὁ μεγάλων αὐτὸν ἀξιῶν ἄξιος ὤν [1123b1–2]).

Adam and Eve will not be granted occasion to make their own inquiry into their suitability for such knowledge hereafter in Paradise. But at the moment that occasion eludes them Milton permits his fit audience a glimpse of the contemplative question that awaited that inquiry. It was the question that Eve did not quite realize she was asking as she and Adam were walking beneath the stars.

ADAM: "SOMETHING YET OF DOUBT REMAINS . . ." (8.13)

At the end of his account of the days of Creation and the Creator's joyous reception in Heaven upon his return, Raphael wonders if Adam thinks, as he does, that Adam's request for knowledge of these matters now has been fulfilled: "if else thou seek'st\Aught, not surpassing human measure, say"

(7.639–640). In keeping with the angel's original nutritional metaphor, "knowledge is a food" (7.126), Adam does offer a measured reply: "[thou] hast *largely allay'd* The thirst I had of knowledge, and vouchsafed\ This friendly condescension to relate\ *Things else by me unsearchable, . . .*" (8.7–10, italics added). He does have a matter that deserves further explanation. Yet what he has been told, he admits, has already surpassed his own "human measure." Here Adam concedes more than he in fact knows. His standard of measure in the peculiar graces of Eve's countenance, first recognized in that office during their evening starlight walk, have been absent in Adam's view since Raphael's brief ceremonious greeting to Eve (5.385–391) when the angel entered their Sylvan Lodge. Only when Adam broaches his doubts about the economies of the creator's Ptolemaic cosmos will Milton's narrative persona draw attention to Adam's oversight and Raphael's utter neglect.

Raphael's genial offer for further clarifications of his creation narrative encourages Adam to speak of, "something yet of doubt remains\ Which only thy solutions can resolve" (8.13–14). Here Adam once again returns to principles of that natural philosophy, of bodies in motion and material and efficient causation thereof that he had first applied to "this glorious sight" the previous evening. He begins from the same celestial phenomena that prompted Eve's question:

When I behold this goodly frame, this world
Of heaven and earth consisting, and compute
Their magnitudes, this earth a spot, a grain,
An atom, with the firmament compared
And all her numbered stars, that seem to roll
Spaces incomprehensible (for such
Their distance argues and their swift return
Diurnal) merely to officiate light
Round this opacous earth, this punctual spot,
One day and night; in all their vast survey
Useless besides; reasoning I oft admire
How nature wise and frugal could commit
Such disproportions, with superfluous hand
So many nobler bodies to create,
Greater so manifold to this one use,
For ought appears, and on their orbs impose
Such restless revolution day by day
Repeated, while the sedentary earth,
That better might with far less compass move, (8.15–33)

Among the many remarkable aspects of Adam's expression of doubt not the least is his apparent indifference to the preeminent stature of his own species in the design of the creator as described in Raphael's account. Imagining the scale of the events of creation, physical magnitude and brightness for Adam has become the measures of nobility, and thereby, the determinant of place. A greater body as source of light and heat should move less and would, if placed at the center. His proposal for such a 'Copernican revolution' appears in the view of narrative persona to obtain Eve's disinterest no less than Raphael's measured rebuke:

So spake our Sire, and by his countenance seemed
Entering on studious thoughts abstruse, which *Eve*
Perceiving where she sat *retired from sight*
With lowliness majestic from her seat
And *grace that won who saw* to wish her stay
Rose, and went forth . . . (8.39–44, italics added)

But narrative persona assigns as an effect—Eve's departure from the conversation of Adam and the angel—that which better might be understood as the very cause of Adam's foray into "studious thoughts abstruse." Neither Adam nor Raphael has noted her presence to conversation subsequent to that brief ceremonious greeting by Raphael (5.388–391) any more than her departure now. Narrative persona in more than twenty lines remedies that neglect, noting especially of Eve that, "A pomp of winning graces waited still,\And from about her shot darts of desire\ Into all eyes to wish her still in sight" (8.61–63). That sight would have told Adam that magnitudes of body, speed and light hardly deserved the name let alone the stature of nobility in comparison with that "Goddess-like demeanor" of one narrative persona thought deserved the name of "queen" (8.60 & 8.61). Such a sight had jarred Adam's confidence in his unaided speculation at the wedding bower the previous night, and might have reminded him on this occasion of "the end\ Of all yet done" (7.505–506). Eve had certainly found her end and good in Adam on the day they first talked. But Adam had yet to digest the good he had observed in Eve at the bower and recognized as his own the next morning—as chapter 5 will show—when Raphael arrives in Paradise.

It is amid these misapprehensions, oversights, failures to notice, speculative presumptions and incomplete reflections that Milton permits Adam to intimate the question Eve posed in gaze of "this glorious sight" in an echo of the Psalmist, and thus, as well, of Xenophon's Socrates. When Adam proposes his 'Copernican revolution' to Raphael, "When I behold this goodly frame, this world\ Of heaven and earth consisting" (8.15–16), a few contemplatives, perhaps "magnanimous to correspond with heaven," will also hear—as Milton once had rendered the Hebrew—

When I behold thy heavens, thy fingers' art,
The moon, and stars, which thou so bright has set
In the pure firmament, then saith my heart,
O what is man that thou rememb'rest yet,
And think'st upon him; or of man begot
That him thou visit'st and of him art found? (Psalm VIII, 9–14, italics added)[19]

The contemplative question, one might say, of the Psalmist queries the contemplative activity of Deity in regard to man both as a species and as individual. According to Xenophon, Socrates was constantly engaged in a kindred activity: "He himself was always trying to converse about the human things when he investigated what is pious, what is impious, . . . etc" (αὐτὸς δὲ περὶ τῶν ἀνθρωπείων ἀεὶ διελέγετο σκοπῶν τί εὐσεβές, τί ἀσεβές, . . . κτλ. [*Memorabilia*, 1.116]. Milton would have his fit audience consider if Eve's question invited them both to wonder what the Father observes as he gazes down "From the pure empyrean."

NOTES

1. The tone and substance of Adam's address to her (4.411–439) tries hard to conceal his growing concerns: "Sole partner and Sole part of all these joys" (4.411) would seem a lovely tender of exclusive affection if uttered in a gathering of other amiable objects, but in the binary solitude of Paradise it is reminiscent of the roving eye's disappointment at an almost empty room. "Dearer thyself than all" seems a lovely comparison, yet it hints at aloof self-possession. Adam speaks solely in first person plural speaking of their shared fate. He thereby would allow that she too may have her disappointments with him, because he seems to feel the need to make an argument for the goodness of God on grounds that they both have done nothing to deserve what they have, and they have nothing He needs. This does not sound like thanksgiving or a song of praise.

2. In this, narrative persona merely recognizes a "generally accepted opinion" (ἔνδοξόν τι) about the proper relations of men and women. Eve's acceptance of Adam "rhymes" with what he thinks he knows already.

3. So Fowler noted (249n497–501) but seems unconcerned with the "floral tag." Milton's familiarity with the Homeric alternative is visible in *Paradise Regain'd* 2.213–215 when Satan rejects the advice of Belial.

4. That point will come for Adam after he eats of the Tree (see 9.1029–1033):

> For never did thy Beauty since the day
> I saw thee first and wedded thee, adorned
> With all perfections, so inflame my sense
> With ardor to enjoy thee, fairer now
> Than ever (.)

So Hughes (402n1037–1045) noted of the resonances with *Iliad* 14.292–353..

5. Fowler, 258n639–56, admired more Milton's technique—"Magnificent rhetoric"—than Eve's charming redirection, for the moment at least, of Adam's domestic interests.

6. Hughes, 293n640, found reason to gloss "seasons" as "times, periods of day" since there could be no seasons of the year before the Fall.

7. "Works" of those other creatures would seem a poetic extravagance: see especially 4.340–351.

8. Narrative persona's rendering on this occasion of this sight (3.56–69) gives no notice to the Son's creative act in description of objects seen by the Father. This is consistent with Aristotle's account of two knowledges, one theoretical, of the "for the sake of what," that is, the good, that is not a knowledge of making, and another of material and thus of making, as discussed in *Metaphysics* 982a4–b17.

9. This is another example of Milton's "literalism" in rendering his Classical sources: what could be more "at hand" for Eve, literally, "before the hand," (πρόχειρα) than Adam's hand that seizes hers when she turns back to the pool?

10. There can be no question of Milton's familiarity with this passage, since he illuminates the intentional complexity of this passage in *De Fine* (I.vii) of *the Art of Logic*. (*WJM* 11.62–68)

11. Once again, *Art of Logic* in *WJM* 11.62–68.

12. Milton's translation from the Hebrew in Carell, ed. *Shorter Poems*, 340.

13. Cf. *Physica* 194a34–35: καὶ χρώμεθα ὡς ἡμῶν ἕνεκα πάντων ὑπαρχόντων (ἐσμὲν γάρ πως καὶ ἡμεῖς τέλος· . . .) "And we make use of it all *as though* everything that exists for our own sake (because we too in some way are an end; . . .)." In Greek, ὡς with the participle "sets for the grounds of a belief, thought, assertion or presumed intention in the mind of the subject of the main verb . . . without implicating the speaker or writer." See Smyth *Greek Grammar*, §2086.

14. In the this regard as well it bears notice that Milton in the cited passage of *The Art of Logic,* although he refers to a passage in the *Physics* which in turn obliquely directs interest to a passage in the *Metaphysics* (1.2) where Aristotle (982b1ff) *does speak of an distinct notion* of τέλος or end that is theoretic and not pertaining to making or production. Milton's assertion—i.e., "in the way man is proposed as an end for things, so God for man"—replaces with a citation from "Proverbs" the sense of "God as an end for man" which Aristotle tacitly identifies with "the knowledge we are seeking after" of Book A of the *Metaphysics*.

This citation to "Proverbs" unmistakably revives a notion of an end for the act of making. Thus he restores the poetic\figurative sense in place of the theoretical wisdom of the *Metaphysics*. One imagines he does so for two reasons: first, a theoretical wisdom of the *Metaphysics* A is of human attainment, but in *Paradise Lost*, as it would appear, the activity of God alone, and second, he wishes to affirm, as "Proverbs" clearly does, the act of Creation.

15. Adam will come to that fuller sense of "peculiar graces" after the Fall (see 10.909–946).

16. Eve's first words (4.440–443) which begin with that preeminent sense of cause as the good or "for the sake of whom" would be the obvious sense of "self-knowing."

17. A Platonic source (*Protagoras* 341e3) for Aristotle's quotation (982b30a) of Simonides has bearing on the ambiguous reference of "*Magnanimous* to correspond with Heav'n" in *Paradise Lost* (7.511, italics added). The very same passage from Simonides—"God alone can have this privilege."—is offered in both Plato and Aristotle to resolve on opposed grounds the identical problem that vexes the passage in Milton's poem: an ambiguity of poetic utterance that leads to apparent self-contradiction. The problem is stated by Protagorus in the dialog of that name when he reluctantly agrees to proceed by question and answer rather than long speeches:

Ηγοῦμαι, ἔφη, ὦ Σώκρατες, ἐγὼ ἀνδρὶ παιδείας μέγιστον μέρος εἶναι περὶ ἐπῶν δεινὸν εἶναι· ἔστιν δὲ τοῦτο τὰ ὑπὸ τῶν ποιητῶν λεγόμενα οἷον τ' εἶναι συνιέναι ἅ τε ὀρθῶς πεποίηται καὶ ἃ μή, καὶ ἐπίστασθαι διελεῖν τε καὶ ἐρωτώμενον λόγον δοῦναι.

"I suppose," he said, "Socrates, that the greatest part of education for a man is to be terribly clever about poetic utterances. This is to be able to understand the things said by poets, both those that are properly composed as well as those that are not, and to know how to make the distinction and to give an account [of it] when one is asked." (338e6–339a3)

Aristotle quotes Simonides to question a human attainment of a "divine wisdom" (θεῖα σοφία) of first principles and causes. Simonides as a spokesman for poets would, as it appears, begrudge such wisdom to mortals. Aristotle then dismisses the judgment with another poetic commonplace (παροιμίαν): "singers (ἀοιδοί) tell many falsehoods." But Aristotle seems to be aware that Plato's Socrates under questioning by Protagorus (*Protagorus* 338e6–342a3) as he defended both himself and Prodicus, cited the same saying of Simonides to an opposite effect.

Protagorus had attempted to have Socrates defend a lyric of Simonides in which Protagorus claimed that Simonides had contradicted himself. Socrates would therefore be ignorant of the greatest part of education for a man: to distinguish proper from improper poetic compositions. But when Socrates argued with the assistance of Prodicus that Simonides had not in fact contradicted himself in one way, Protagorus shifted his ground to argue Socrates had failed to notice an even more serious contradiction, one that even seems to rely on the testimony of Socrates's own ally, Prodicus. Socrates will by steps—and relying on Hesiod's comment in the *Works and Days* (ll. 289–292) that the road for a man to become virtuous is, "when one reaches the top, easy, though it remains hard" (ἐπὴν δ' εἰς ἄκρον ἵκηται\ ῥηιδίη δὴ ἔπειτα πέλει, χαλεπὴ περ ἐοῦσα.)—show that if Simonides says that becoming virtuous or good is "hard," (χαλεπή) he is not saying that becoming virtuous is "bad" (κακή). He argues that Simonides surely thought such an attainment was a good because otherwise he would not have claimed that, "God alone can have this privilege."

These details, only summarized here, of Aristotle's and Plato's citation of the same passage to diametrically opposite effect display the obvious: that poets often do seem to state contradictory things and that the discriminate understanding of those contradictories in spite of their difficulty is of human attainment. So much one may say Milton understood was involved for one "magnanimous to correspond with Heaven." The operation of both, contemplative inquiry and full-hearted gratitude in praise, for example may also be observed in the opening of the *Confessiones* of Augustine: *da mihi, domine, scire et intelligere, utrum sit prius invocare te an laudare te et scire te prius sit an invocare te.* ("Grant me, Lord, to know and to understand whether it is better to call upon you first, or to praise you first, and to know you first or to call on you first" [1.1.]).

18. "It is reasonable to assume that magnanimity is, so-to-speak, a certain ordering principle of the virtues." (ἔοικε μὲν οὖν ἡ μεγαλοψυχία οἷον κόσμος τις εἶναι τῶν ἀρετῶν [1124a1–2].)

19. Hughes, 363n19, had noted the fact ("The entire speech [of Adam, 8.15–38] is colored by Psalm viii.") without further comment. Fowler (429n15–38) notes the relation to Eve's question: "Adam poses more abstractly the same question posed to him by Eve (iv.657f)," but then calls it "a topic of Schools," citing Milton's *Prolusion VII.*

Chapter 5

Becoming Dear

Aristotle in *De Arte Poetica* stresses the value of talk in poetic story-telling:

It is necessary *to arrange the speech and work out with talk as much as possible* (τοὺς μύθους συνιστάναι καὶ τῇ λέξει συναπεργάζεσθαι ὅτι μάλιστα) that which is placed before the eyes. For in this way *most vividly* (ἐναργέστατα) one who looks—as though present to the very things done—could discover what is fitting and would least of all fail to notice *the contrasts* (τὰ ὑπεναντία)). (1455a22–25)

Hearing such talk makes us realize why novels, plays and dramatic poems have a larger audience than treatises on ethics. In stories with talk we learn through imitation and thus, take delight (see *De Arte Poetica* 1448b4–12) because in comparing what is said with what is done characters come to life for us in the very way our own character (ἦθος) is ever present to ourselves in the finding of fit (τὸ πρέπον) words for deeds and deeds for thoughts, and no less, sometimes in that dim awareness of contrasts or discrepancies (τὰ ὑπεναντία) between our words, our thoughts and our actions, and in our relations with others. "There will be character," Aristotle says, "if [. . .] the speech or the action makes manifest some choice, <whatever it is>, then [the character is] good, if [the choice is] good" (ἕξει δὲ ἦθος μὲν ἐὰν . . . ποιῇ φανερὸν ὁ λόγος ἢ ἡ πρᾶξις προαίρεσίν τινα ⟨ἥ τις ἄν⟩ ᾖ, χρηστὸν δὲ ἐὰν χρηστήν. [*De Arte Poetica* 1454a16–18]). When a poet presents characters talking to one another he displays their choice as a likeness of ours, and thus, the nature of beings both rational and free. The voluntary and will and reason in particular, Aquinas observes,[1] exist as rational potencies (*potestates rationales*) only in relation to opposites (*ad opposita*) that present a choice. Thus Satan left his perch in the Tree of Life and crept closer to the human pair, "To mark what of their state he more might learn\ By word or action marked" (4.400–401).

NATURE

Close attention to the first conversations of Adam with Eve (4.411–5.210) and Adam with a "Presence Divine" (8.250–520) offers this perspective on a so-called "state of innocence" of the human pair before the Fall. From such vantage one finds not a "state" at all, but rather a process of growth and development[2] in the innate faculties as *potestates rationales* granted to the pair by their Creator. Their individual choices and the character that each thereby attains will in every case be "good in its way," that is, "of use" (χρηστόν) to them in their growth. There is no defect in their creation nor reason to read a "fall before the fall" into their early days together though each has erred in judgments of each other, and of the promises their Maker made to them. A voice at the pool told Eve that it would bring her to one that she would enjoy "Inseparably thine" (4.473). The Presence Divine told Adam that one whom he next would meet "shall please thee, be assured" (8.449). Both initially would think otherwise. Their initial and subsequent choices, all rational, reveal nascent developments in their characters. In spite of what their Maker told them both, they did not begin in knowing affection for each other. They begin in ignorance of themselves (see 4.451–452 & 8.270–271) and each other, but are possessed of the gift of a human nature. They have a "nature" in the primary sense; they are rational and therefore free. What they make of that "nature" by their own lights is told in the poet's story of their "becoming dear." This is "nature" in another Aristotelian sense of φύσις, the activity of growth in living things from the causal "roots" in "nature" in the first sense. Milton in *De Doctrina Christiana* (*WJM* 15.92.13–19) following the lead of Augustine in *De Genesi Ad Litteram*[3] calls this growth the "ordinary providence of God."

This growth explains two episodes in Adam's first days wherein the intellectual powers he displays appear to surpass what might be assumed the original gift of a rational nature at creation. Adam himself appears astonished at his own ability to name the beasts: as he tells Raphael as the creatures were brought to him in pairs, he thought that he "understood \ Their nature, with such knowledge God endued \ My sudden apprehension" (8.352–354). Something similar appears to occur thereafter when he provides Eve with a comprehensive psychology of dreams after her own of the interdicted tree the morning following the day they first talked.

Early commentary on Genesis had queried the scope of that gift in Adam's naming of the beasts. Augustine was sure Adam "was endowed with sensation and a mind" (*certe sensu ac mente praeditum* [*Ad Litteram* 8.18,37]). In *Contra Secundum Iuliani Responsum* 5.1 he allowed "Adam's intellect" would have "far surpassed in swiftness" (*illius ingenio . . distare longe . . . celeritate*)[4] that of "the very best intellects" (*ingeniosissimi*) of all of Adam's subsequent fallen progeny. Aquinas, however, seemed to imply that beyond the grant of a rational nature Adam was given something more, a grant of knowledge "through specific kinds 'infused' by God" (*per species ab Deo infusas* [*S.T.* Ia. qu.94 a.3 ad 1]). If so, this would be a very different sort of providence, a special gift either at or after[5] the original gift and distinct from those two senses of nature—that primary sense of "what a thing is," and the other, a process of growth originating in that "thing." Such a gift would not be a cause in either sense.[6] When Milton thereafter added a dreaming Eve and Adam's ready analysis of that dream to his re-telling of events in Paradise he appeared to repeat the difficulty. As Samuel Johnson had blandly noted, "Adam's discourse of dreams seems not to be the speculation of a new-created being."[7] It was one thing for Adam to name things he saw. As a rational being he had speech from the first; he had a facility to give individual things names though he even surprised himself (8.271–273). But for a being who began not knowing "who I was, or where, or from what cause" (8.270) several days later to render a psychology that rivaled the concision of Aristotle, this was a bit much.

C.S. Lewis at least was aware of a humorous aspect to this psychology but dismissive: Adam's "lectures' to his wife," he said, "sometimes excite the smiles of the modern reader, but the joke is a shallow one" (119). His Adam was "the sum of all human knowledge and wisdom." In pursuit of a "state of innocence" wherein Adam and Eve were the "Lords of all" of Creation, Lewis, had no need to query the limits of Adam's gift. The two events were of a piece: "[w]hen he received the homage of the beasts he instantaneously 'understood their Nature' and assigned their name (8.352). He has complete insight into the mysteries of the soul and can give Eve a full explanation of the phenomena of dreams" (5. 100 *et seq.*). One consequence, then, of speaking of a "state" of existence of these two rather than their nature will be to speculate upon what Adam can be assumed to know rather than to carefully consider how he comes to say what he seems confident he knows. This shift from investigating a gift of nature and its growth to speculating about Adam's "knowledge set" was already well in evidence among Milton's contemporaries[8] and perhaps explains Lewis's sense of Milton's "shallow" joke. If Milton's own contemporaries were now eager to know the language God or Adam spoke and whether the propriety of names Adam gave the animals was given to him by God or of his own invention and in what sense, how better could Milton revive the interests of Augustine and Aquinas in the extent of that gift? He would fashion an analogue to the naming of the beasts in Genesis that revealed that gift at work. Lewis after all was right to expect smiles. He just did not see the question behind the smile: *How* in the world could Adam have known *that*?

That was a question one may assume Milton knew both Augustine and Aquinas had asked of Genesis 2:19–20. Milton would have known as well that such inquiries in both authors led to still more fundamental questions: for example, What did Genesis really mean by "in the image of God He made him"; and what is the theological cost for such a being if one assumes a special providence is at work? Present-day commentary[9] has had little interest in these questions, preferring instead to reference popular controversies of Milton's contemporaries regarding a language of Paradise and notions of inherent correctness of names agreeing with particular natures. In Stanley Fish's account, for example, the issue was now uncontroversial: "Adam's knowledge is infused into him directly from God, and the names he imposes, like God's, are accurate, intensively, and extensively" (114). It may be of use, therefore, to recover the occasion of Augustine's reticence and Aquinas's cautious ambivalence.[10]

AUGUSTINE AND AQUINAS: ON PROVIDENCE
AND THE GIFT OF NATURE

In Book 8 of *De Genesi Ad Litteram libri duodecim* Augustine considers in what way God spoke to Adam when he delivered the Interdict, a human being whom he was quite sure was "endowed with sensation and a mind (*certe sensu ac mente praeditum*)." In this passage he is inclined (8.18.37) to dismiss the notion that God spoke "internally in the mind in a manner suited to the intellect (*intus in mente secundum intellectum*)," that is, without the mediation of body. He suggests rather that He spoke "in the same fashion as He did to Abraham and to Moses, that is, in some sort of bodily aspect (*sicut Abrahae, sicut Moysi, id est, in aliqua specie corporalia*)," citing, moreover, Genesis 3:8, "and they heard His voice when He was walking in the evening in Paradise."

This observation (8.19.38), he notes, is also an opportunity to examine closely a great matter and one not to be overlooked (*Locus atque magnus neque praetereundus*), a twofold operation of divine providence (*opus divinae providentiae biperititum*) which he says will be of the greatest value to avoid thinking something unworthy of God himself. He does not explain here what indignity his earlier discussion of providence (8.8.15–9.18) avoids, but with a doctrinal recital of the names and offices of the Trinitarian God together with a citation of 1 Timothy 6:16 he seems to imply that he is concerned that this understanding of the way God spoke to Adam together with Genesis 3:8 might lead some to think that God himself, not just the means his voice was conveyed, was corporeal. No doubt that would be an unfortunate conclusion to draw, but it is hardly a possible inference from that earlier discussion of providence.

In that earlier discussion (8.9.17–18) there was a "two-fold operation of providence, in part natural, in part voluntary" (*gemina operatio providentiae . . . , partim naturalis, partim voluntaria).* Augustine argued for this distinction because it made no sense that Adam before the Fall was condemned to agricultural labors before he had sinned. Thus he interpreted, "And the Lord God took the human and set him down in the garden of Eden to till it and watch it" (Gen 2:15) to suggest that before the Fall Adam did willingly participate in what was already occurring naturally "by the hidden management of God" (*per occultam Dei administrationem*). And citing 1 Cor 3:7, "'neither he who plants is anything, nor he who waters, but the God who grants growth,' he concludes, "because even that part of the work which is applied externally, is applied by him whom nevertheless God created, and whom God governs, and even invisibly directs" (8.8.16). One may gather from these remarks that Augustine was inclined to the view that human beings are endowed with a rational intelligence based on sensation and mind whose development and growth is natural result of a gift of ordinary providence at Creation.

Aquinas appears to say and is usually taken to say something quite different[11]: he will assert that "the first man had knowledge of everything by means of forms (or notions) that were infused by God" (*primus homo habuit scientiam omnium per species a Deo infusas* [*S.T.*I[a] q.94.a.3 ad 2]). Milton appropriates this expression for Adam's astonished explanation to Raphael of his own ability to name the beasts: "with such knowledge God endued\ My sudden apprehension" [8.353–354, italics added].[12] Both passages, therefore, would assume that Adam's capacity to name the beasts was a gift of knowledge distinct from the gift of his nature at Creation: a gift of a God who attends to the special needs of individuals. Why Aquinas spoke of Adam's endowment in this manner and Milton was drawn to borrow the phrase becomes clear in Aquinas's studied ambiguity of description in this passage.

In the first place Aquinas uses the term Augustine had used, *species,* for the matters with which the mind operates. The range of available meanings allows it to refer to the activity of sight, "a seeing, a sight, vision, or view," an abstraction from such activity, "a form, shape, or outward appearance," or a mental representation of that abstraction, "a likeness, image, a notion" or even an aesthetic judgment of the same, "a beauty or splendor."

In *Quaestio 94 in Prima Parte Summa Theologicae* as part of his address to the state and condition of the first man, Aquinas is considering whether the first man had knowledge of all things. It would seem, he says, that he did not, because if he did it would be either by means of "acquired forms [or semblances]" (*acquisitas species*), or by "forms or semblances that arise at the same moment" as man does (*species connaturales*)—one might say, that were "innate" to us as men—or "infused forms [or semblances] by God (*species ab Deo infusas*)"—literally, "poured into man by God" at a time distinct from the gift at Creation. He rules out (*S.T.*I[a] q.94.a.3 arg. 1) the first two categories, of "acquired" and "co-natural or innate forms." The first is proper only to knowledge from experience, and he cites the beginning of the *Metaphysics* 1 of Aristotle (980b29–981b9) wherein experience is inferior to knowledge of first principles. As to the second, he argues, citing Book 3 of *De Anima*, that we are at birth "as tablet on which nothing is written." As for the third possibility for our "knowledge of everything" there are two ways of understanding what he means and both ways are instanced in his choice of a Scriptural explanation of what he means:

> *primus homo habuit scientiam omnium per species a Deo infusas. Nec tamen scientia illa fuit alterius rationis a scientia nostra; sicut nec oculi quos caeco nato Christus dedit, fuerunt alterius rationis ab oculis quos natura produxit.*

> The first man had knowledge of everything by means of forms poured into him by [the agency of] God. Nor, nevertheless, was that knowledge by a way of reasoning different from our knowledge: just as neither were the eyes which Christ gave to the man born blind by a way of reasoning different from the eyes which nature has produced. (Iᵃ q. 94 a. 3 ad 1)

The Scriptural story which exemplifies the identity of Adam's way of knowing with our way of knowing is a story (Jn 9:1–34) of Christ as the agent of a special providence. But one cannot but note that this statement which declares this example denies that there is, anything at all special about both the manner in which the blind man now sees and thus, the way in which we now and Adam once upon a time came to know things we see and then name them. Aquinas, one may say, wanted by means of an ambiguity of expression to preserve a way of understanding the way of our reasoning which would not be lost in the Fall and no less, to preserve as well a salubrious example of the providence, be it special or not, of God

That Aquinas thereby in a veiled manner can refer to the flood of sense perceptions, *species*, in rational deliberation as a gift of ordinary providence, that is, nature, however, is clear. No less, the phrase, *per species a Deo infusas,* accords with Augustine's own veiled comments on Adam's grant of nature—as noted above, *certe sensu ac mente praeditum* (*Ad Litteram* 8.18,37).

In the "naming of the beasts" Adam will use but does not yet understand his own nature and its powers.[13] When he says of the animals, "I nam'd them as they pass'd and understood\ *Their nature*" (8.353–354, italics added) he would not yet be used to using, and thereby having some awareness of his own nature. His explanation of the event to Raphael, "*such knowledge God endued*\ My sudden apprehension" (8.353–354 italics added), is Milton's 'englished' borrowing of an ambiguous phrase in Aquinas, *per species ab Deo infusas*, with the ambiguity muted but not removed. Milton's phrase would be an appropriate rendering of a gift by either special or general providence.

That Adam was not "endued by God" "with a knowledge" of names or natures but rather with the gift of a native *ingenium*, a *dispositio dianoetica* in a nature capable of dialectical reasoning,[14] becomes visible in his conversation with the "Presence Divine." In *Paradise Lost*, to the dumb show of Gen. 2:20, Milton added talk. This "Presence" was speaking to Adam as he presented those kinds to his view (see 8.349–350). Adam's account of the event to Raphael shows he had no need of any special favors.

"MY SUDDEN APPREHENSION"

Adam's "sudden apprehension" is a sign of the gift of a nature, by a grant of his Creator when "that mysterious force and efficacy of the divine voice was first declared" (*mirifica illa vis et efficacia divinae vocis primitus emissae* (Milton, *De Doctrina Christina* I. viii (15.92.17–18). Adam uses that nature in the naming of the beasts. He said he "understood\ their Nature" by virtue of a "knowledge God endued," but he did not quite grasp what he had done, so-to-speak, on his own. If he knew their nature, he did not yet know his own, at least to give it a name. Immediately thereafter he asked the "Presence Divine" for something like himself, something he could not find among the beasts. He knew what he wanted even though he did not quite know what to call it, so he described it at some length (8.385–391 & 416–433). Only then, however, did the "Presence Divine" find him knowing of himself. Having names for things and understanding the nature of a thing to which a name may be applied are distinct operations.

It is generally agreed that Adam's naming of the beasts in Milton's re-telling of Gen. 2:19–20 preserves the Scripture's threefold emphasis: God tests Adam; Adam demonstrates his dominion over the animals and in naming he discovers of his need of an Eve.[15] Milton's additions and borrowings recur to the interest of the Church Fathers in Adam's intellectual gifts. Both Augustine and Aquinas had surmised that Adam must have been very smart, but they appeared reluctant to say more. Milton, however, displays how smart Adam is when he shifts the focus and alters the terms by which that intelligence is judged with two modest additions. He first translates God's creative acts by fiat on the Fifth and Sixth day (Gen. 1:20–30) now into instructions for Adam as he names:

Not only these fair bounds, but all the earth
To thee and to thy race I give; as lords
Possess it, and all things that therein live,

Or live in sea or air, beast, fish and fowl.
In sign whereof each bird and beast behold
After their kinds; I bring them to receive
From thee their names; and thee fealty
With low subjection; understand the same
Of fish within thir watery residence
Not hither summoned, since they cannot change
Their element to draw the thinner air. (8.338–348)

These instructions raise a new but unobtrusive challenge. Whereas Genesis
2:19–20 only required Adam to name individual kinds or *species*, these
instructions in the tenor of Genesis 1 now invite Adam to identify as well the
participation of the species in three *genera*: "beast, fish and fowl." Logically
speaking,[16] Adam will be unable to discover the nature appropriate to each of
these three names until after he sees and names each of the individual species.
But the Presence is surely generous in this test. He gives Adam the names.
God in Genesis 1 had stressed the element in which these *genera* would live
in his grant (1:26) of man's dominion: "the fish of the sea and the fowl of
the heavens and the cattle and the wild beasts and all the crawling things that
crawl upon the earth." And in Gen. 2:19 "And the Lord God fashioned from
the soil each beast of the field and each fowl of the heavens and brought each
to the human to see what he would call it, and whatever the human called a
living creature, that was its name." Since he cannot bring fish into Adam's
presence, he does not mention either them or their element. Milton's "Presence Divine" also suggests correlation of these *genera* with the elements by
order of mention: "earth" (8.338), "sea or air" (8.341) parallels "beast, fish
and fowl." He adds further weight to his suggestion by means of the absent
third genus: "fish" *does* seem to have a nature defined by an element, "their
wat'ry residence." As he says, "they cannot change\ Their element to draw
the thinner air" (8.347–348). How much clearer could he be? Things that have
a nature cannot change what they are. This "Presence Divine" seems to be
giving Adam several hints on how to distinguish the *genera*. Last of all, one
might think his "Divine" authority would be beyond question for an Adam so
recently startled by "The rigid interdiction, which resounds\ Yet dreadful in
mine ear" (8.334–335).[17]

In Genesis 2:19 Adam was presented with individuals. God had "fashioned . . . each beast of the field and each fowl of the heaven . . . and brought
each to the human to see." Milton's second addition has Adam report as it
appears the same: "As thus he [i.e., the "Presence"] spake, each bird and
beast behold\Approaching two and two, These cowering low\With blandishment, each bird *stoop'd on his wing*" (8. 349–351, brackets and italics added).
Here, however, Milton borrows from the Noahic gathering of the animals

(Gen. 7:2). The "Presence" leads the animals to Adam "two by two." At first sight, this would seem to make Adam's task easier. Naming the "sun" and "earth" had been by the mere application of a proper name to an individual thing (8.272ff)—child's play, perhaps—but to see pairs demands the discrimination of "another such of the same sort." Adam as a being with sense and reason can count, and therein he displays the quintessentially human faculty of the διάνοια—as noted above, that *discursus mentis ac rationis quo aliud ex alio rationando colligitur.* One!—ah, another one—Ah ha! Two![18]

At this moment, however, Adam encounters two possible sources of confusion in his task. First, he will see "each bird and beast" all engaged in the very same activity: "pay[ing] fealty \ With low subjection." Thus, at the same time he discovers in counting their difference as individual *species*, he would appear to lose sight of a communality as members in particular *genus*. The stress on "each" in the instructions strongly suggests the species are intermingled. Second, one genus might in fact be two 'kinds.' The "Presence" had used two names for possibly the same thing, "bird" or "fowl," but "fowl" is both a generic synonym for "bird," and a *subalternum genus* designation for some game and domesticated birds. The latter sense complicates Adam's designation of a genus, if he follows the hints of a "residence" and "element" as the sign of a class. In short, one might think that Adam would be confused. Yet this is only as Milton himself had stressed in *Artis Logicae* 1.27, quoting Aristotle on the superiority of knowledge of universals over particulars in the *Analytica Posteriora* 1.24 (see 85b4–86a30): *Distributio generis in species valde quidem excellit, sed difficilis & rara inventu* ("The apportionment of a genus to the species stands out, indeed, to an extraordinary degree, but is difficult and remarkable to find" [11.244.24–24 & 252.15–16]).

This extraordinary intelligence in Adam as a gift of Nature at Creation—not a "knowledge God endued," nor *per species ab Deo infusas*—is clear in the sign Adam uses to distinguish the *genera*: "each bird and beast behold\. . . these cowering low\With blandishment, each bird *stoop'd on his wing.*" Rejecting the tempting suggestions of a relation of a *genus* to the elements of Air, Earth or Land from a voice of authority—as a rational being he was free to do so—Adam discerns the essential difference in the manifold he sees: *all* Birds *and* Fowl have wings. The acuity of his intellectual vision becomes clearer in the confusing array of alternatives he tacitly rejects: while all birds having left the air now comport themselves as if terrestrial fowl Adam silently must dismiss other hypothetical signs of a potential community: for example, claws, feet.

This episode is the demonstration in act of his dominion over the animals. Their obeisance was not mere ceremonial but rather in speechless submissive awe of his active intellect in use as they passed: *genus tractatur per species.* Adam, to be sure, as yet understood little of his nature and these faculties, but he used them in the elegant simplicity of, as he will later say, the "joining and disjoining" (cf. 5.106ff) in judging things as same and different. Then too it was surely his "mis-take" to believe his use of them was a "knowledge endued."[19] Yet it was in his nature to do so. He will grasp the remedy for such imperfections when he talks with Eve.

Milton's re-telling of the "Naming of the Beasts" in Genesis locates the gift of a nature in Adam in the primary sense of "what a thing is." Aided chiefly by the cautious inquiries of Aquinas (I^a qu. 75–102) about what man is (qu. 75–89) and what he was in his original condition at creation (qu. 90–102), Milton positions Adam's display of that nature at a point in his drama where the capacities of that nature are most open to question. He will renew this inquiry into that nature, now in growth and development, in Adam's remarkable account of Eve's dream. The question of *how* could he know *that* returns. Eve's dream is prior in the order of the narrative of *Paradise Lost*. It comes after Adam's colloquy with the "Presence Divine" in a history of their relations before the Fall. In such a history, then, Adam's account of Eve's dream is a result of what has happened rather than a cause of what will happen. It has been common to find in Eve's dream a foreshadowing if not a precursor of their Fall. In the narrative of *Paradise Lost* that teaches the lesson of obedience it is surely that. But in the inquiry into the nature of these rational creatures before the Fall their conversation about this dream is a sign of what these two are becoming. It is a sign of their φύσις in the way that what a thing is becoming is the result of what it is by nature. In this inquiry Milton drew upon the Augustinian teaching on providence in *De Genesi Ad Litteram*.

PROVIDENCE

Augustine in Books 4 and 5 of *De Genesi Ad Litteram* tacitly develops an understanding of divine providence as the orderly processes of nature in growth. Originally created instantaneously in, by and of the Word individual natures will later be described (6.14,25) as *causales rationes in mundi* ("causal root principles in the world") when "sown" (*insitae*) at the moment of Creation in corporeal substance (*substantia corporealis*). As Augustine charmingly explains, these natures as 'events' belong in and are of God as artificer: *qui simul et consummaverat inchoata propter perfectionem causalium rationum, et inchoaverat consummanda propter ordinem temporum* ("who at the same time had completed perfectly those things that were begun through the perfection of the causal principles, and began those things to be perfectly finished by means of the orderly sequence of times" [6.15.26]).[20] Thus did he bring the Six-Day narrative with God's rest on the seventh of Genesis 1 in conformity with a reduction of those events to a single day in

Gen 2:5 ("On the day the LORD God made earth and the heavens . . ."), with the assistance of Sirach 18:1, *qui vivit in aeternum creavit omnia simul Deus* ("God who lives eternally created everything at the same time").[21] The conjectural hinge of transition from nature as a cause to nature as process was Augustine's account of the seventh day. Citing the reply of Jesus to the charge of violating the Sabbath (Jn. 5:7): *Iesus autem respondit eis Pater meus usque modo operatur et ego operor* ("But Jesus answered them: My Father is working up to this very moment as I am working"), Augustine argued there was a work that God's rest indicated he had completed and a work that God continues to work without intermission:

> *Claret igitur ne uno quidem die cessasse Deum ab opere regendi quae creavit, ne motus suos naturales quibus aguntur atque vegetantur, ut omnino naturae sint, et in eo quod sunt pro suo quaeque genere maneant, illico amitterent, et esse aliquid omnino desinerent, si eis subtraheretur motus ille Sapientiae Dei, quo disponit omnia suaviter. Quapropter sic accipimus Deum requievisse ab omnibus operibus suis quae fecit, ut iam novam naturam ulterius nullam conderet; non ut ea quae condiderat, continere et gubernare cessaret. Unde et illud verum est, quod* septimo die requievit Deus; *et illud, quod* usque nunc operatur.

Let it be clear, therefore, that not even for a single day did God cease from the work of governing those things he had created, lest they would lose their own natural movements by which they are excited and enlivened so that they are in every respect "natures" and they abide in that which each are in accord with its own kind—and they would entirely cease to be anything at all, if that movement of the Wisdom of God, by which "she manages everything delightfully" (Wis. 7:24) were withdrawn from them. For this reason we take it thus, that God rested from all his own works which he made so that from that point on he would fashion no new nature any more, but not that he would cease to maintain and govern those things that he had fashioned. Wherefore it is both true that "on the seventh day he rested" *and* that "*he is working all the way to the present.*" (*Ad Litt.*, 4.12,23, citation & italics added)

In Book 5 Augustine assigns this 'working all the way to the present' to God's providence (see *Ad Litt.*, 5.20,40–23,46). Milton speaks of ordinary providence in similar manner in *De Doctrina Christiana* 1.8:

> *Providentia Dei est ordinaria vel extraordinaria.*
>
> *Ordinaria, qua Deus constantem illum causarum ordinem qui ab ipso constitutus in principio est, retinat ac servat.*
>
> *Haec vulgo et nimis etiam frequenter Natura dicitur, neque enim aliud quicquam natura esse potest, nisi mirifica illa vis et efficacia dininae vocis primitus emissae, cui dehinc omnia veluti mandat perpetuo parent.* (15.92.13–19)

Providence is ordinary or extraordinary.

Ordinary providence is that by which God maintains and preserves that invariable ordered arrangement of the causes which was established by him in the beginning.

These things are by common parlance and too frequently called Nature, for nature is nothing else but that wonderous and efficacious power of the divine voice when it first came forth and which thereafter all things obey as if by an everlasting command.

Here Milton mischievously attributes to common parlance (*vulgo*) that which, save for ornamental trappings of God's creative act, would sound like the two senses of φύσις in Aristotle.[22]

Later Augustine further refines this notion of providence into two senses. Speaking of the world as a whole, he says, *in ipso quoque gemina operatio providentiae reperitur, partim naturalis, partim voluntaria. Et naturalis quidem per occultam Dei administrationem, qua etiam lignis et herbis dat incrementum; voluntaria vero, per Angelorum opera et hominum* ("in that very thing [i.e., the world], moreover, is found a two-fold work of providence, in part natural, in part voluntary. The natural is through the hidden management of God, by which trees and grass are granted growth; the voluntary is through the works of angels and men" [*Ad Litt.*, 8.9,17]). In man himself, thereafter, he finds "this same two-fold power of providence is vigorously active" (*eamdem geminam providentiae vigere potentiam* [ibidem]). In the human body, a natural [power of providence] is attributable to the impulse by which it grows and ages, while the provisions it makes for its own survival are assigned to the voluntary. "In a similar fashion," he notes, "with respect to the soul, [man] is naturally moved so that he lives and is sentient, but voluntarily moved so that he learns and gives his approval" (*Similiter erga animam naturaliter agitur ut vivat, ut sentiat; voluntarie vero ut discat, ut consentiat* [ibidem]). Here one notices the same elements of the gift of nature, *sensu ac mente praeditum*,[23] as noted above, now at work in the voluntary or free acts of intellect of a rational creature as described by Aristotle and Aquinas. In this context Augustine thereafter speaks at length (*Ad Litt.*, 8.15–12.25) of the work of Man. There is the work that God continues to work in preserving the order of causes he created, and there is the work of learning that Man does in his freedom—in Adam's words, "to approve the best" among those objects that sense presents to his judgment. For this reason, Augustine also considers it proper (*Ad Litt.*, 8.10,23) to construe Gen 2:15. (*Et sumpsit Dominus Deus hominem quem fecit, et posuit eum in paradiso operari eum et custodire*) as "And the Lord God took up the man he had made and placed him in Paradise to work *him*[24] and to guard." Providence then is the work that God continues to be working up to this very moment *and* the work that He is working in working Man. These works Milton places before our very eyes when Adam talks with Eve about her dream.

LEARNING "BY CONVERSATION WITH HIS LIKE"

Before Adam ever speaks with Raphael, Adam displays to Eve a remarkable precision and depth of understanding of his own discursive rationality. In a few brief lines (5.100–107) he confidently describes the critical role of reason in judgment and in approval of the "aery shapes" that "mimic fancy" represents in the imagination from sensation. He knows as well what can happen in dreams and of the peril of "resemblances" that deceive, "Ill matching words and deeds long past or late" (5.113). Above all, Adam understands the source of deception: when reason "retires\ Into her private cell when nature rests" and "in her absence mimic fancy wakes\To imitate her" (5.108–511). Dreams in dreaming seem to make sense. It is no small problem to explain how then they can be false. A sign of the problem for both Adam and Eve is their immediate confusion at the event. For Eve dreams up to this point have only represented the realities of her waking life:

> glad I see
> Thy face, and morn returned, for I this night,
> Such night till this I never passed, have dreamed,
> *If dreamed*, not as I oft have wont, of thee,
> Works of day past, or morrow's next design (5.29–33, italics added).

In her experience there are only two possibilities: dreams simply represent her waking life, or, if not—"If dreamed" as contrafactual—then she must have been awake. She fears, therefore, she has done what she dreamed. At the end of her account she exclaims, "but O how glad I waked \ To find this but a dream" (5.92–93). Now dreams are false. Adam immediately sees the problem: "This uncouth dream, of evil sprung I fear; Yet evil whence?" (5.98–99). Adam speaks of "evil" only by associating the tree in Eve's dream with the interdicted tree and some unknown "dreadful thing" they both did not want. Neither he, nor Eve, nor "Presence Divine" has used the word before (see 4.424–426 & 8.323–336). Nor does either know of Satan's presence in the garden; sense has represented no such thing to them. How can they then understand it? Yet, in an instant, he appears to have constructed an entire rational psychology of dreaming.

There are, however, resemblances between this conversation in Book 5 and Adam's later account to Raphael in recollection of his first moments in Paradise.[25] Twice (8.292–311 & 452–499) he tells Raphael he had lapsed into dreams. There was in Adam, then, more than perfunctory sympathy when he tells Eve, "The trouble of thy thoughts this night in sleep \Affects me *equally*" (5.96–97, italics added). The depth of insight Adam finds in their shared experience of dreams he will express in a new mode of address: "Best image of myself, and dearer half" (5.95).

Thus far, the argument has displayed the evidence for Adam's rational nature by gift at creation in his reasoning from the evidence of sense that must precede his application of names to things and kinds. This same capacity had been given to Eve (see 11.287). In "joining and disjoining," in judging and choosing, Adam and Eve, without knowing what they do and why, begin their life apart and, through choices they dimly if at all understand, are drawn to each other. Adam's self-description to Raphael, " I to thee disclose\ What inward thence I feel . . . \Who meet with various objects, from the sense\ Variously representing; yet still free\ Approve the best, and follow what I approve" (8.608–611), evinces his ascent to self-understanding. The discussion which follows now presents his discovery of the root principles of that understanding of himself and Eve in his conversation with her. The "psychology of dreams," as I have noted above, is almost a philosophical commonplace. Milton's "innovation" was to position the discovery of these root principles—in Augustine's phrase, the *causales rationes in mundi*—not through the instruction of a sociable angel, but in the relations of these two with each other. In *Paradise Lost* before the Fall "finding" and "not finding" are the motions of these principles in act. These same acts of reason mark the crises for their life together: in Adam of Eve, "I found not what methought I wanted still" (8.355) and, "I waked\ To find her" (8.478–479); in Eve of Adam, "while thou\ Like consort to thyself canst nowhere find" (4.447–448) and "O sole in whom my thoughts find all repose" (5.28). The first cause I will call the primal *rational* desire for "same"; second, a *rational* love for an "other" that is the "not same." With the necessary but provisional assistance of the Interdict as an hypothesis of difference, Adam will discover the second as a cause only in and with Eve.

DREAMING

In Book 8 Adam relates to Raphael his first moments of his life as they seemed to him at that time. When he first fell asleep and dreamed he thought he was passing into non-existence (8.290–291). When he awoke he thought that everything was "all real, as the dream \ Had lively shadowed" (8.310–311). When he awakes from his second dream he draws the same conclusion. The being he now sees approaching (8.484) is, he says, "[s]uch as I saw her in my dream" (8.482). Only later when he talks with Eve about her dream will he find reason to question this judgment. With Raphael Adam makes no mention of the sophisticated psychology of dreams he has detailed to Eve. He tells Raphael what he did, his wants, what happened and what he felt at the time. He shows himself to be a creature of vigorous impulses and rapid judgments. He is naïve and as yet unreflective. When he awoke from his first dream, he did not stop to think, "what was *that*?" since he assumed *that* was the same as *this* he saw.

Adam's first dream in Paradise is Milton's addition. In Genesis 2:8–15 God made Adam and then placed him in the Garden he had made in Eden. Genesis allows us to think that Adam was awake the entire time. Adam's second dream has some Scriptural support—"And the Lord God cast a deep slumber on the human" (2:21)—but Genesis said nothing of dreams. Milton, however, adds these dreams as preliminaries to the two determinants of Adam's existence in Paradise: the Interdict and Eve. In Genesis teaching the lessons of obedience and of God's benevolence in the creation of Eve did not require dreams as a preface. For Milton's purposes in their discovery of their own rational nature in both senses, they did.

Before his first dream Adam was alone and ignorantly happy. Since he felt no desires, he suffered no lack to unsettle his contentment. He did have a question, but it did not disturb his happiness (8.282). In rejecting self-generation he entertains the notion of a "great maker" as the source of his being. He asks the living creatures he sees to tell him of this maker. Waiting for an answer he wanders aimlessly until he sits down and falls asleep. He does not know what is happening to him. In retrospect he can describe this first dream to Raphael as a "dream" because soon he would have another somewhat like it. He speaks of "fancy," but he does not distinguish between that "fancy" and his own thinking ("methought"). The one allows him to believe he still has being, the other, that there is some other being, which he calls a "shape divine" (8.294–295). When he awakes from his dream Adam will find nothing strange in what he thinks he saw.

When suddenly stood at my head a dream,
Whose inward apparition gently moved
My fancy to believe I yet had being,
And lived: one came, methought, of shape divine,
And said, thy mansion wants thee, *Adam*, rise,
First man, of men innumerable ordained
First father, called by thee I come thy guide
To the garden of bliss, thy seat prepared.
So saying, by the hand he took me raised,
And over fields and waters, as in air
Smooth sliding without step, last led me up
A woody mountain; whose high top was plain,
A circuit wide, enclosed, with goodliest trees

Planted, with walks, and bowers, that what I saw
Of earth before scarce pleasant seemed. Each tree
Load'n with fairest fruit, that hung to the eye
Tempting, stirred in me sudden appetite
To pluck and eat; whereat I wak'd, and *found*
Before mine eyes all real, as the dream
Had lively shadowed: (8.292–31\1, italics added)

When Eve later tells of her dream in Book 5 Adam would surely have recalled three similar aspects to his own initial experience of a dream. In Eve's dream too there was a voice that she acknowledged as a guide (5.91) who led to her to a place where there was a fruit-laden tree. In Adam's dream there were many such trees. Second, her appetite too was quickened (5.85) by sense perception and she too was strongly moved by a desire to eat. Finally, when Adam awakes, he too is convinced by his dream—as Eve by all her prior dreams of Adam and of their work together (5.32–33)—that dreams represent, and thus, are a guide to waking life. One might have expected, therefore, Adam would say to Eve, "Don't worry, dear, I've had that dream too." He does not in Book 5 because both his and Eve's confidence in the verisimilitude of dreams to waking life has been shattered by their awareness of the Interdict.

In his account of his first day in Book 8, however, Adam knows nothing as yet of a "sole command," when he wakes from his first dream. He has no reason to doubt what he has seen. In the dream a "shape divine" appears to answer his query about a "great maker." Adam's trust in dreams must surely grow still more when upon waking, a "Presence Divine" now seems to reify Adam's impressions of the "shape" in his dream. The "shape" had said, "I come thy Guide\ To the garden of bliss" (8.298–299) Yet why did the "Presence" now add, "Whom thou sought'st I am" (8.316), if not to distinguish himself from that "shape"? Adam had asked about his "great maker"; the shape said nothing of that. Yet Adam surely thought the "shape" in the dream was a guide. It led him to a place where he is now speaking with this "Presence." When he awakes he finds *that* place, "the garden of bliss," is *this* place. But speaking in retrospect to Raphael Adam notes that when he awoke, "[h]ere had new begun\ My wandering, had not he who was my guide\ . . . among the trees appeared" (8.311–313). The contrafactual refers not to deeds of the "shape" in the dream, but to the words of "Presence Divine." This "Presence"—more real than a "shape" in a dream—Adam seems to think was a better guide; he put an end to his wandering.

The "Presence" identifies himself as the "Author of all this thou seest", and then grants Adam to "eat freely" of "every tree that in the garden grows" (8.322 & 321) save one: "But of the tree whose operation brings\ Knowledge of good and ill, . . . etc." (8.323–333). The "shape" had said nothing of this exception. Rather, Adam had opined that "[e]ach tree" in *that* place was good to eat, and would have assumed the same for *this* place but for that "Presence" among the trees. In his dream, moreover, Adam had felt corporeal desire for the first time. All the fruit of the trees in *that* place, he says, "to the eye\ Tempting, stirr'd in me sudden appetite\ To pluck and eat" (8.307–309). His dream had "lively shadow'd" his appetite no less than the fruit. The "Presence," then, was a better guide than the "shape," because Adam now knew there were a place and a tree he should avoid: "Amid the garden by the tree of life\Remember what I warn thee, shun to taste" (8.326–327). This much Adam surely understands; it is, he tells Raphael, in his choice to avoid *that* (8.333–336). However, nothing he says suggests that as yet he mistrusts the guidance of "shapes" in dreams. He does not stop to consider that *that* place might not be same as *this*. He does not see they are *different*. In *that* place there was no check upon his appetite. The "Presence" appears to have tried to instruct him in that difference—a difference not just of place, but of the guide he encounters therein. Here Milton has joined Adam's account of his entrance into a "garden of bliss" to the declaration of Interdict by a "Presence Divine" as it seems, as a gentle corrective for Adam's trust in "shapes" in his dreams. It might be expected that an Adam possessed of, in Lewis's paraphrase of Augustine, "mental powers [that] surpassed those of the most brilliant philosopher"(117), might have discerned an analogy between the place he saw in his dream and the place of fancy in dreams and waking life. Such an insight, however, would have required him to use something he thought he saw in a dream in relation to the Eden he now sees as he talks to the "Presence" as a likeness for something invisible—that vague sense he has of his own thinking as he thinks about what he thought he thought at the time: "methought" (8.295). This would have been an operation of a *dispositio dianoetica* of the first rank. He would have had to have seen not just the two places as similar but different—the ordinary operation of the διάνοια[26]—but then, see those relations now as a likeness of the difference between what he thought he saw in the dream and what he now in thinking sees. This second operation, a making a likeness of his ability to see a likeness, would be a work of the fancy in thinking that demands no less a "wrenching turn" (περιαγωγή [*Respublica* 518c8–9 et al.]) in thought than that required of Plato's prisoners in the Cave. Adam is not quite up to *that*—at least as yet.

Adam's failure, if it may called that, to learn the difference between a "garden of bliss" and Eden under the tutelage of the "presence" is not a sign of his incapacity, but of his aboriginal nature. At present for him these things are not quite the same yet not different. Both a "shape" and the "presence" spoke to him. Where was the difference? The "shape," after all, was surely the "presence." Perhaps he might have grasped through what the "presence" told him that the "inward apparition [that] gently mov'd\ [his] fancy to believe" (8.292–293) was itself a "shape divine" of his fancy, summoning his unquestioning belief. Yet how would that "inward apparition" be different from the impression he had through his sense of the "Presence Divine"? To Raphael Adam shows he was vaguely aware of some sort of difference; a "Presence" is surely more than a "shape," but Adam expresses no distrust in the "shape." When he awoke, he found "all real." Thus, for the moment, the "Presence" is "another such of the same sort." In Adam, as in Eve at the pool, this "natural desire for the similar" as a good is the primal inclination of their rational natures. As native to the faculty of judgment of the representations of sense, it will soon enable Adam to name the species by "counting."

In Milton's account of the intellectual growth of Adam before the creation of Eve the Interdict appears as a device to suggest a "difference" between the garden of bliss and the garden of Eden, and thus, of this "Presence" and that "shape." To be sure, Adam grasps the Interdict as a command—as it surely was—and thus, a test of obedience. As a hint to understand the difference of dreams from waking life, however, it fails. Nevertheless, it would and does serve as an external check upon an aspect of his rational nature, his rational desire of the same, while he is unaware of this difference. In Book 5, this command will jolt him to the awareness that something is really different about Eve's dream. Here, Adam is at a great remove from his psychology of dreams in Book 5. The declaration of the Interdict might have taught him to cautious about his notions about guides, shapes and desires which he fancies to be real. He might have learned his dreams are not a guide for living. That he did not—even when instructed by a "Presence Divine"—will be obvious in his second dream. But it might be noted in passing that the failure of the Interdict as a didactic principle to teach the difference between dreams and waking life makes clear why the Interdict must be a command.

DESIRING

Adam's second dream comes after he has named the animals and then speaks of his own need for fellowship with one "fit to participate\ All rational delight" (8.390–391). Exhausted by his conversation with his Maker, Adam lapses into a dreaming state and therein he observes through "the cell of fancy" the creation of Eve. What fancy shows Adam in that dream will not quite be what he asked for.

Naming the animals Adam had displayed his native capacity for ratiocination. He could count. His subsequent grasp of the *genera*, "bird and beast" (see 8.349–351) was a further advance in his thinking. The playful examination by the "Presence" of Adam's need for fellowship now invites Adam to distinguish his own species as rational animal from these very *genera* he has just discerned. In doing so he learns for the first time of his relation to this "Presence":

Thus far to try thee, *Adam*, I was pleased,
And find thee knowing not of beasts alone,
Which thou hast rightly named, but of thyself,
Expressing well the spirit within thee free,
My image, not imparted to the brute.
Whose fellowship therefore unmeet for thee
Good reason was thou freely shouldst dislike. (8.437–443)

At first Adam did not know what name to give this "Presence." He does not understand its nature since it does not have "another like" (8.357–358). His lavish praise of this nameless being is all prelude to expressing his quandary: "but with me\ I see not one who partakes" (8.363–364). He does not yet realize that his first impulse in praise of *that* being—"for thou above all these"— is in a sense the secret of his own dissatisfaction with all the individual species of this *genus* to which he himself belongs: though an animal, he too is "above all these" yet remains less than that one that he now praises. "Man," he says, "by number is to manifest\ His single imperfection" (8.422–423). In asking for an Eve Adam is naïvely searching for the nature of his own *species*. The one he asks for in "her" imperfection will be neither like the one he now addresses, nor like in their "complacence"—as he is not—like those he has named, and yet "she" will be similar to both. To express the request arithmetically, "she" like Adam cannot be a "one" as the "Presence" is one, but must be different from the "two" in the way the individual animal *species* are a "two." The being of *this two*—what they are by nature—must be one in nature in seeking "[s]ocial communication" (8.429), but as two who are each "[i]n unity defective" (8.425) when they converse.

This curious way of speaking about Milton's addition to Gen. 2:18 of a conversation between Adam with his Maker before the creation of Eve serves to epitomize the logical relations which Adam employs under the whimsical questioning of the "Presence" to express his lack. He reasons dialectically: not "those" (8.369–398), but also, not "this of yours" (8.399–436). The "Good reason" (8.443) Adam displays in the charming interplay of their conversation surely explains why the "Presence" is confident that, "What next I bring shall please thee, be assured" (8.449). Without at first having a name for it,[27] Adam has begun to grasp his own *species*. He knows that the "Presence" is not fit for his fellowship: "Thou in thyself art perfect, and in thee\ Is no deficience found" (8.415–416). The "Presence" does not need an "other"; Adam knows he does. Nor can he "raise" these animals "to what highth" he wishes "Of union or communion" as this "Presence" has done for him. He does not yet know that Eve will do this for him. Adam does expect, one must assume, one like himself, a being who enjoys talking, possessing a "free spirit," and thus capable of conversation with his like. He has a desire for a being like himself.

When Adam lapses into his second dream he knows what he wants. When he wakes from this dream he has forgotten completely about this request. He had lapsed into a dream, when his capacity to reason became fatigued by the "celestial colloquy sublime." He could not even say whether his Maker stopped speaking or he stopped understanding speech (8.452–459). Thus Adam's second dream resembles his first in that now a sleep of reason (cf. 5.104–109) mimics the prior lapse of his "drowsed sense" (8.289). Only in recounting these events to Raphael is he more mindful of the state he had entered:

> sleep, which instantly fell on me, called
> By nature as in aid, and closed mine eyes.
> Mine eyes he closed, but open left the cell
> Of fancy my internal sight, by which
> Abstract as in a trance methought I saw,
> Though sleeping, where I lay, and saw the shape
> Still glorious before whom awake I stood;
> Who stooping opend my left side, and took
> From thence a rib, with cordial spirits warm,
> And life-blood streaming fresh; wide was the wound,
> But suddenly with flesh filled up and healed:
> The rib he formed and fashioned with his hands;
> Under his forming hands a creature grew,
> Manlike, but different sex, so lovely fair,
> That what seemed fair in all the world, seemed now
> Mean, or in her summed up, in her contained
> And in her looks, which from that time infused
> Sweetness into my heart, unfelt before,
> And into all things from her air inspired
> The spirit of love and amorous delight.
> Shee disappeared, and left me dark, I waked
> To find her, or for ever to deplore
> Her loss, and other pleasures all abjure:
> When out of hope, behold her, not far off,
> Such as I saw her in my dream, (8.458–482)

In the second dream, the "Presence" though familiar is once again called a *"shape"*\ Still glorious before whom awake I stood" (8.463–464, italics added). Once again this dream responds to a request he made in waking life (cf. 8.280–281 & 389–391). In both, the requests are fulfilled by this "shape" (8.298 & 463–471). In both he experiences yearnings he has never felt before (8.308–309 & 474–477). It is not surprising, then, that the verisimilitude of first dream shapes his response to the second (cf. "I waked, and found\ Before mine eyes all real as the dream\ Had lively shadowed" [8.309–311] & "I waked\ To find her, . . . \. . . \Such as I saw her in my dream" [478–479 & 482]). Any difference between these dreams and wakeful life Adam would not understand until he talks with Eve.

Milton casts Adam's first dream as a pure product of fancy. Inexpressibly happy in the place he found himself at creation, in awe of a "shape divine," Adam fancied himself carried to an even finer place. In speaking of this event with Raphael Adam never implies that he "saw" through a "cell of fancy" an actual transport to Paradise, although Milton's audience would be predisposed by Genesis[28] to think that he had. In the second dream he is once again carried, so-to-speak, to a finer place. Once again Adam thinks ("methought" [8.462; & cf. 295]) that he is watching, now through "the cell of fancy," something actually happening. Here fancy represents to him the physical pain of loss of a rib and flesh as a sensation of "sweetness" and "amorous delight." His second dream thus did show him something real, but in the absence of reason, it represented that reality of lack and loss in the "language" of desire. Thereafter he saw his bone and his flesh under the forming hands of the "shape" become the one he had requested. When she disappeared in his dream he awoke, "[t]o find her, or for ever to deplore her loss" (8.478–479). He was looking for the same being he had seen in his dream in the way fancy had represented her to him. When he sees her approach, he cries out "Bone of my Bone, Flesh of my Flesh, myself\ Before me,. . . etc" (8.495–499).

Here one sees once again the Adam's fundamental *rational* desire of the same as a good. He calls to one, "[s]uch as I saw her in my dream." Eve rejects this appeal; she freely chooses to turn back to the pool. She rejects Adam because she, too, in her maker's wisdom by the gift of nature has a *rational* desire for the same. When she told Adam of this event on the day they began to converse, she says he looked, "less fair,\ Less winning soft, less amiably mild\ Than that smooth watery image" (4.478–480) in the pool. In him she saw no "answering looks \ Of sympathy and love" (4.464–465). Those "looks" did not answer to the feelings she felt as she looked (4.461–462) and read in the looks she saw in the pool. She had no idea she was looking at herself. She was only looking at something identical to[29] what she felt. But Adam did not look like *that*. He was in the throes of desire for bone and flesh when he called to her, "Return fair Eve, \ Whom flyst thou, whom thou flyst, of him thou art,\ His flesh, his bone; to give thee being I lent\ Out of my side to thee" (4.4.481–484).

Adam's request of the "Presence Divine," however, had arisen out of his *rational* desire of the same. When he spoke of Man's imperfection by comparison with God: "the cause of his *desire* By conversation with his like to help,\ Or solace his defects" (8.417–419, italics added). He yearned for an equality and mutuality in conversation impossible with his Maker. As his Maker also promised, Eve would be, "[t]hy likeness, thy fit help, the other self,\ Thy wish exactly to thy heart's *desire*" (8.450–451, italics added). Adam's request made perfect sense; he had reasoned his way to it. The most peculiar aspect of his account of these events to Raphael, however, is Adam's claim about himself. Saying nothing of seizing her hand (see 4.489) as she attempted to leave, he claims that Eve "with *obsequious majesty* approved\ My *pleaded reason* (8.509–510, italics added).

Milton announces Adam's confusion with "Ill-matching words" (5.113) that convey his "ill-matched" sense of Eve. Adam thought he was being rational. In fact—as he will later explain to Eve—he was only "misjoining [the] shapes" (5.111) of his dream with those that his sense now represented to him (see 5.102–105). This was the "Wild work" of "mimic fancy" imitating reason role in waking life. As he only realizes when he hears Eve speak about her dream, reason's office in "joining or disjoining," in "framing\ All what we affirm or deny" can be counterfeited (5.106–110). Thus, when Adam awoke from his second dream the name he called her was not her proper name—nor was it the proper understanding of himself. In her own rational desire for the same she did not answer to that name.

JUDGING "PECULIAR GRACES" (5.15)

Adam well may have wondered in the days after "that day" (4.449) they met why Eve had at first rebuffed him. Her disinterest in him only had lasted for a moment; he had grabbed her hand and then led her to the "nuptial bower" (8.510). But when the desire his impassioned plea revealed had dissipated in the mysteries of their first marital congress, a doubt eventually began to take precedence in his thoughts. This Eve was not the Eve he had asked for. She was not talking. Eve had her own reasons to be silent; she had a lot to think about. So did Adam. "Why does she look at me that way (4.299) and yet say nothing?" "Why did she turn from me?" "Was it something I said?" In two senses it was. In those words Eve did not find what she desired. They were, "Less winning soft, less amiably mild" and until he then touched her hand they made no sense of her predicament. This awkwardness on both their parts during these days, was, as previously noted (chapter 2), obliquely signed in their static portrait (4.288–311).

Eve eventually began to talk in her growing sense of Adam's discontent (4.447–448) with her. Adam in delight at her first words was yet to fully remember the tenor of his plea before the "Presence Divine": of "his desire\ By conversation with his like to help,\ or solace his defects"(8.8.417–419). Narrative persona's grant of jovial satisfactions to Adam (4.497–498) was surely premature. And Satan's envy as he watched (4.505ff) in the pangs of his own "fierce desire" was misplaced.

As evening comes, Adam's circumlocutious invitation (4.610–633) to retire to "their blissful bower" is a lame excuse for his resurgent fancy-fed desire. His added rationale for their need of rest from labors that "require\ More hands than ours to lop thir wanton growth" (4.638–639) hints at off-spring. He is not interested in talking, but Eve most certainly is (4.639). Eve will parry his invitation with her own charming circumlocution (4.640–655) to delay. When they do enter the bower "talking hand in hand" (4.689) narrative persona once again unsettles a second *mise-en-scène* of imagined "love and amorous delight" (see 8.477) with a second Jovian coda (4.714–719 & cf. 4.499–503). Eve's charms now are "O too like" those of Pandora if Adam is "the unwiser Son," "ensnar'd" solely by "her fair looks."[30] This event in the myth this time Milton ironizes in his narrative persona. The myth reminds one that the gift of Pandora's deceptive charms was in recompense for the theft of "Jove's authentic fire." Eve's authentic *rational* charms will show themselves the following morning. Here Adam in trying to solace Eve's distress will come to understand and therein find solace for his own.

On the morning after the evening of the day they first conversed with each other, Eve is awakened by Adam who finds that she has been deeply disturbed by a dream: "His wonder was to find unwakened Eve\ With tresses discomposed, and glowing cheek,\ As through unquiet rest" (5.9–11). The poet reveals Adam's natural aversion to see such distress by describing what he has been wont to see these past few mornings as if that was what he was yet seeing in the present: "he on his side\ Leaning half-raised, with looks of cordial love\ Hung over her enamoured, and beheld\ Beauty, which either waking or asleep, \ Shot forth peculiar graces" (5.11–15). This is the native disposition of the rational desire of the same.

Eve's account of her dream to Adam speaking as she does of the distress and disturbance in her thoughts—already evident in her face—will initiate a revolution in Adam's thinking about her and himself. In reply his manner of sympathetic address, "Best image of myself and dearer half\ The trouble of thy thoughts this night in sleep\ Affects me equally" (5.95–97), speaks the essential truth of the ground of their conversational accord at its peak at this moment in *Paradise Lost*.

"JOINING AND DISJOINING" (5.106)

Eve begins in her account of her dream where Adam had begun in his report
of his to Raphael: with first impressions. In his account of his first dream
Adam speaks of a "divine shape" that brought him into the Garden. That
"divine shape" in the dream had called the place the "garden of bliss." When
he then awoke in the Garden he said he "found\ Before mine eyes *all real, as
the dream\ Had lively shadowed*" (8.309–311, italics added). Eve too began
her account of the night past—"for this night,\ Such a night till this I never
passed, *have dreamed\ If dreamed*, not as I oft am wont, of thee" (5.30–32,
italics added)—unable to discern a difference between dreams and waking
life. The only difference she noted between this dream and those of previous
nights was one of subject, not of verisimilitude.

In Adam's case, on the day he spoke with the "Presence Divine" a challenge to his dream's veracity would be implicit but remain ignored. As he
later told Raphael, in his first dream of the "garden of bliss" he had said,
"*each tree* Loaden with fairest fruit, that hung to eye\ Tempting, stirred in me
sudden appetite to eat" (8.306–309, italics added). When he then awoke, he
adds, "here had new begun my wandering, had not *he*[31] who was *my guide*Up
hither, from among the trees appeared,\ *Presence divine*" (8.311–315, italics
added). Adam only now speaking to Raphael calls this "Presence Divine"—
not a "shape divine"—but "my guide" because that "Presence" told him, as he
only now discerns, that there was a tree not like any other in *this* garden. His
"guide" was attempting to teach him something without success about a dream
of a "garden of bliss": it was imaginary. Adam on that occasion had been
surely shaken by the lecture he received on this "tree whose operation brings\
Knowledge of good and ill," but it did not weaken his confidence at that time
in a verisimilitude of dreams. His second dream, of Eve's creation from his
flesh and blood, shows he had not learned anything about dreams from his first.

After further conversation with this "Presence Divine" following upon his
stern lecture on the "rigid interdiction," Adam eventually came to speak of
his own "desire\ By conversation with his like to help\ Or solace his defects."
Pleased with the signs of his "knowing" of himself (8.437ff), the Presence
promised, "What next I bring shall please thee, be assured\ Thy likeness, thy
fit help, thy other self\ Thy wish, exactly to thy heart's desire" (8.449–451).
Dazzled by the demands of conversation with this Presence, Adam then
lapsed into sleep again, but as he told Raphael, the Presence had "open left the
Cell\ Of fancy my internal sight, by which\ Abstract as in a trance methought
I saw\Though sleeping, where I lay, and saw a shape\ Still glorious before
whom awake I stood" (8.460–464). Observing then the creation of Eve out
of his own flesh and blood in his dream he experienced new sensations as he
looked at her,

And in her looks, which from that time infused
sweetness into my heart, unfelt before,
And into all things from her Air inspired
The spirit of love and amorous delight. (8.474–477)

At this moment she disappears, and Adam tells Raphael "I waked\ To find
her, or for ever to deplore\ Her loss, . . ." (8.478–480). And then he sees her,
"not far off\ *Such as I saw her in my dream*, adorned\ With what all earth or
Heaven could bestow\To make her amiable. (8.481–484, italics added). Once
again Adam suffering in the pangs of desire—then, of appetite for the "fairest
fruit," now in longings of the flesh occasioned by his own loss of the same, he
assumes that what he sees nearby is the same as what he recently lost—and
that is what he will call her when she rebuffs him: "Bone of my bone, flesh
of my flesh, my self\ Before me; Woman is her name, of man\ Extracted"
(8.495–497). In this passage Milton's compositional wit is in full display.
Adam in his desire-fed exuberant praise of her looks, "adorned with what all
Earth or heaven could bestow" is merely engaged in material self-admiration;
the Eve he asked for thus disappears from Adam's sight at the very moment
Adam thinks of her exclusively in "[t]he spirit of love and amorous delight."
Such a being was not what he had asked for from the Presence Divine. Nor
in that spirit did Eve find—as was argued earlier—those "answering looks of
sympathy and love" she had found at the pool.

All these events and mistaken judgments recur to Adam—one might say, in
his "sudden apprehension"—as Eve now speaks of her dream of the previous
night. The very same faculty, the rational desire of the same, that led him to
assume an identity between dreams and waking life, will now play a role in
his discovery of a difference between those two visions that only seem the
same—but only with the aid of something that his "other" can provide.

Eve's aspect, her "peculiar graces," the sign to Adam's view of her distinct
apprehension of the common facts of their brief but shared experience of their
life together, now signs to Adam an image of himself that he had yet to recognize in his own dreams of paradise and of her. "Best image of myself and
dearer half,\" he says, "The *trouble of thy thoughts* this night in sleep\ Affects
me equally" (5.95–97, italics added). He now knows whereof he speaks. In
his past two dreams it would have been remarkable if he had noticed the
trouble in his own thoughts, so violent and unexpected was the shock that he
received for judgments upon waking from his dreams so natural to his native
sense of "the same." He had thought he was now in the "garden of bliss" the
"shape divine" had named, only to hear the blistering declaration of a "rigid
interdiction" that as he tells Raphael some days later, "resounds\Yet dreadful in mine ear" (8.334–335). Nor could he have thought a being so lovely
to eye, "so man-like" like himself, would respond as she did to his earnest

entreaties. On impulse he had seized her hand, and then for reasons of which he was unaware, the terror of his rejection was forgotten. He had not given a further thought to the distress at either event, until this moment when Eve reveals to him "the other" in his own thoughts of himself and her. But now he understands:

Best image of myself and dear half,
The trouble of thy thoughts this night in sleep
Affect me equally; nor can I like
This uncouth dream, of evil sprung I fear;
Yet evil whence? in thee can harbour none,
Created pure. But know that in the soul
Are many lesser faculties that serve
Reason as chief; among these fancy next
Her office holds; of all external things,
Which the five watchful senses represent,
She forms imaginations, aery shapes,
Which reason joining or disjoining, frames
All what we affirm or what deny, and call
Our knowledge or opinion; then retires
Into her private cell when nature rests.
Oft in her absence mimic fancy wakes
To imitate her; but misjoining shapes,
Wild work produces oft, and most in dreams,
Ill matching words and deeds long past or late.
Some such resemblances methinks I find
Of our last evening's talk, in this thy dream,
But with addition strange; yet be not sad.
Evil into the mind of god or man
May come and go, so unapproved, and leave
No spot or blame behind: Which gives me hope
That what in sleep thou didst abhor to dream,
Waking thou never wilt consent to do. (5.95–121)

Until Eve speaks of her dream neither Adam nor Eve had reason to question the verisimilitude of dreams. Adam thought his dreams were a guide to his past and future waking life. Eve found the same in her dreams of him (5.33). But when Adam hears Eve's account of her dream he comes to understand his own dreams in the light of hers. Dreams he now finds are no guide to waking life. The resulting rational psychology of dreams rests on his simultaneous grasp of the operations of their discursive reasoning in choice, and thereby the ground of their freedom in their authorship of "what they judge and what they choose" (3.123). Only now does he discern the difference in fancy's mimic work in both thought and dreams, and thus is able to reflect upon the heretofore innocently errant choices that have troubled their first few days together. Adam sees that something like reasoning occurs in dreams and that a dream-like operation, the fancy, has shaped his judgments even in waking life. Both of these operations he will discover through reconsidering his prior relations with Eve.

The dream of her making had offered Adam a name—"of him thou art\ His flesh, his bone"—to call her when he awoke. She spurned this appeal. Later (4.492–503) his desire for social communication prematurely identifies the mere fact of Eve's speaking as the fulfillment of his maker's vague promise of, "Thy likeness, thy fit help, thy other self" (8.450). Of this threefold designation it must be allowed that Adam already grasps in some degree all but the middle term. His "likeness," "Manlike," he had observed in her making; his other self was in view when he called her, "myself\ Before me" (8.495–496); but his recognition of his "latest *found*," as he calls her on the morning after her dream (5.18, italics added), as his "fit help" does not well fit with his wordless appreciation, "Both of her beauty and submissive Charms" (4.497) after they first converse. Eve's just completed account of her own mistaken judgment of him beneath the platan, then corrected by the touch of his hand, had been expressly offered to help him understand his own unhappiness by her example (see 4.448–449). Her account of herself at the pool and then, the way she first saw him, had displayed her own judgments swayed by a rational desire of the same. Adam's dumb satisfaction, then, testifies to his own continuing subjugation to his own rational desire of the same in his as yet unexamined fancy-fed opinion that "what will please thee, be assured" was the same as this beautiful shape made of his flesh and bone, though even now possessed of articulate speech.

However, as Eve speaks of her dream, Adam realizes she *was* what he yearned for, but not in the way that he thought, or rather—as he now realizes—as he had fancied. That was just an notion he had affirmed which he now denies (5.107–108). Adam for the first time sees both *his* mistakes, one of naming, the other in recognition of their being as a *species*. This talk is more than mere "social communication." He begins to reason, "joining and disjoining" what he formerly framed and had affirmed. He realizes his errors in "misjoining shapes," and he recognizes the "[w]ild work" in his first call to Eve. The name he gave her "Ill-match[ed] words and deeds long past or late" (8.111–113). Here Adam is not yet thinking exclusively of their "late" conversation the previous evening (5.144–155) but of his own "words" in his request to his Maker that followed from his "deeds" in naming the beasts. In both he had used one rudimentary faculty of reason, his rational desire of the same, the source of "joining." Now he begins to use the other, by "disjoining" "shapes" that "look" the same. "Ah, there's one; there's another; ah, not the same!" As Adam looked at Eve that morning when she awoke from her dream, she looked the same but somehow different (5.9–15). She was word-lessly showing the defect in his "thoughts" of her. With an astonishing facility as he listens he begins to see her as she really is.

"Best Image of myself and dearer half" (5.95) is a summary of the inter-nal discourse[32] of the mind that arose in Adam as he listened, and thereafter grasped as rational psychology. Eve is no longer an individuated part of the whole creation (4.411); she is his "dearer half. "She is his "[b]est image."

During the days prior to this moment Adam had entertained other like-nesses of himself. At first, His maker had playfully suggested he look to the beasts (8.370–375); then, more mischievously still, to Himself, ("What thinkst thou then of me,[33] and this my State" [8.403]). But Adam's rational desire of the same preferred to posit a being like himself—like him in being able to converse and like him as an equal would be like, "[i]n unity defec-tive (8.425). Then too, there was his Maker's promise, "[t]hy likeness, thy fit help, thy other self" (8.450) which Adam at first assumed was what that "aery shape" has fashioned for him in his dream. Yet in the dream he was surely puzzled by something "Man-like but different sex" (8.471). But now, "best" and therefore "dearer" to him is *this* Eve, the one whose apparent difference from him, first hinted at in his dream awareness of her sex (8.471), then signed in her looks as she awoke, and now described in her dream, disjoins his naïve experience from hers only to make clear their deeper kinship in the gift of their rational nature. Adam has discovered in Eve a rational love of the "other."

Adam's psychology of the dreaming state exhibits Adam's working out in thought and then speaking to Eve about what he learned only through listen-ing to her. This is the essence of human conversation, the talk Milton added to Genesis. Adam's remarkable grasp of their common experience of dreams in contrast to waking life is not an imposition of theory on experience but a rea-soned derivation from his past experience now reexamined in opinions now found questionable. As he thinks and speaks he discovers the first principles of his own thinking, his *dispositio dianoetica*.

Adam's internal discourse originates in his musing on three events in their brief history together—Eve's initial rejection of him beneath the platan; his doubt about her and its seeming resolution; and Eve's account of her dream now joined with his recollection of those two dreams of his. With Eve Adam also shares a belief in the providence of their Maker. Both in their freedom had implicitly questioned Providence if only in their choice of the "same" over the advice of an authoritative voice (see 4.469–4.73 & 8.449–450). Nev-ertheless both yet observe a sincere though puzzled deference to the Interdict. In the argument from obedience in *Paradise Lost* a belief in providence sup-ports the Interdict (see 5.515–518). In the argument for the natural growth of discursive rationality in the pair, however, the Interdict is a preliminary hypothesis of difference for the discovery of works of providence signed by that command.

Adam and Eve find and know their happiness in each other in this work called providence—as Augustine said, *quod [deus] usque nunc operatur.* Milton places that work before our very eyes in conversation wherein each is and both are becoming dear.

NOTES

1. *S.T.* Ia qu. 83 [*de voluntate:*] art.1.

2. Summers's account of the "first vision of perfect man and woman" (95) and his stress on "grateful vicissitude" as "the divine ideal: [. . .] the result of multiplicity of wills and motions, truly free, yet moving either in unison or harmony" (72) is a congenial point of entry.

3. See esp. 5.20,40–23,46: the "work that God "is working up to the present" (*usque nunc operatur*).

4. Cf. Milton *De Doctrina* 1.7: *Sine permagna autem sapentia ita subito nomina animalibus dedisse non potuit* "Without very great wisdom he could not have given so suddenly names to the living creatures" [*WJM* 15.52.10–11]) .

5. Fiore wishes to have it both ways: "at the moment of creation" (26); "immediately after his creation"(27).

6. See *Artis Logicae* 1.3 *Nec male definiatur cause* quae dat esse rei. ("A cause would not be inadequately defined as *that which gives being to a thing*" (*WJM* 11.28.11–12).

7. *Lives of the English Poets* 1. 186.

8. Fish details at some length (107–116), in a section, "Language in Paradise" (of his discussion of his third chapter," Man's Polluting Sin,") raising the topic among Milton's contemporaries intertwined with the notion of a perfect or paradisical language which he carries back to Heraclitus and, with a straight face, Herodotus. He assumes (144) Milton accepts the doctrine of an "infused knowledge."

9. See again Fish, "Language in Paradise, "(107–130); Fowler, on the naming of the beasts (447n.343–56) and on the psychology of dreams (287n.100–113); Leonard, John (1989), "Language and Knowledge in *Paradise Lost*" in Danielson (97–100) and Leonard, *Naming, passim.*

10. For Aquinas's discussion of the need of ambiguity [*obscuritate verborum*] in veiling "divine things in the knowledge of the faith" [*divina in scientia fidei . . . velanda*], see *Super Boetium De Trinitate* pars 1 q.2 a.4, esp., co.2, and citing Augustine *De Doctrina* 4.9, 23; Augustine in turn, 4.10, 24, cites Cicero *Orator ad Brutum* 23, 78: *neglegentie . . . diligens,* "a careful sloppiness."

11. See, Fish, (cited above), Leonard, *Naming* (1990), 1–22. Fiore (26–27), strangely attributed the phrase to Augustine: "Augustine maintains that God at the moment of creation, infused into Adam's and Eve's minds the knowledge which, though they had no choice in acquiring it was necessary to lead a properly ordered

human life."(26). Augustine, however, said no such thing; the notion is pure Aquinas (see *S.T.* I^a q. 94 a. 3 co.).

12. Fowler has noted the congruence without comment, 447n.343–56.

13. The "Presence" does not acknowledge Adam's self-understanding (8.438–439) until after he asks for something he cannot even specify let alone give it a name (see 8.411–436).

14. See *Artis Logicae* 1. 9: in re *dianoia: est . . . discursus mentis ac rationis quo aliud ex alio rationando colligitur* ("'dianoia': it is a discourse of the mind and reason by which one thing is gathered by reasoning from another" [*WJM*11.364.19–20]); see also, 1.1: *Et tamen* Plato *in Alcibiade primo idem vult esse* τὸ διαλέγεσθαι, *quod uti ratione*. ("And moreover, Plato in the *1st Alicibiades* would have it that 'to converse' is the same as 'to use reason'" [*WJM* 11.20.3–4].

15. See Fowler, 447n*343–356*.

16. *Artis Logicae* 1.27: *genus tractatur per species* ("the genus is investigated through the species"(pl.) [*WJM* 11.248.13]).

17. But see *Artis Logicae* 1.22 *"De Testimonio divino,"* esp. *Et divinum quidem testimonium affirmat vel negat rem ita esse, facitque ut credam; non probat, non docet, non facit ut sciam aut intellegam cur ita sit, nisi rationes quoque adhibeat.* ("And indeed, divine testimony affirms or denies a thing is so, and makes me believe; it does not prove, it does not teach, it does not make me know or understand why it is so, unless it also employs reasons" [*WJM* 11.282.6–9]).

18. See also Augustine, *Ad Litteram* 4.3,7: *numerus omni rei speciem praebet* ("number furnishes the kind for every thing."

19. On the possibility of such "'mis-takes," see *S.T* I^a q. 94 a. 4 co.

20. So in Paradise Lost, 7.176–179 & cf. *Ad Litteram* 6.3.4.

21. As well as, Jn 1:1–3; 5.7; Acts 17:28; Rom. 11:36 & Col.1:16.

22. For similar ornamentation in Augustine see *Ad Litt.*, 5.20,40–23–44 with reference to the supplied example (23,44) of growth in a tree.

23. *Contra Secundiam Iuliani Responsionem Imperfectum* 5.1

24. In the Septuagint and in Augustine's Latin translation, the pronouns αὐτόν and *eum* (Jerome has *illum*.) are ambiguous; all refer to the masculine, either, *Paradisus* (ὁ Παραδεῖσος) or *homo* (ὁ ἄνθρωπος).

25. Hughes, 369n292 so noted without comment.

26. See Jacob Klein: the "simple business of our διάνοια [. . .] consists in comparing, that is, in separating and relating" (115). For his account in Plato of the turn of the διάνοια in thought to making likenesses, εἰκασία, see Ch. V "Digression: ἀνάμνησισ and μνήμη (108–172, esp. 115–125).

27. It is worth noting that Adam first deploys the *species* designation, "Man" in denial of its unity in imperfection (8.416) and thereafter, with pointed reference to "counting": "Man by number is to manifest\ His single imperfection" (8.422–423).

28. See, "And the LORD God planted a garden in Eden, to the east, and he placed there the human He had fashioned."(2:8) and, "And the LORD God took the human and set him down in the garden of Eden to till it and watch it" (2:15).

29. Once again, as in chapter 3. "Eve's First Words," she relies upon the gift of nature to read emotion in the looks of the human face.

30. As he assuredly still is (see 5.18, "My fairest") before she speaks, until she speaks of her dream the following morning.

31. The text of Hughes which represents Milton's spelling has the emphatic personal pronoun, "hee."

32. The character of this internal discourse, ὁ μὲν ἐντὸς τῆς ψυχῆς πρὸς αὑτὴν διάλογος ἄνευ φωνῆς γιγνόμενος, ("the discourse which arises within the soul with itself without sound" [263e3–4]), as the work of thought (διάνοια [264a9]), the identity of this discourse with spoken speech or talk (λόγος) as a flow from the mouth; the source of false opinion and its correction as the work of διάνοια; and, finally the place of affirmation and denial, and the "same" and "other" in that discourse are discussed in Plato's *Sophist* (263a2–264b8.)

33. Again the emphatic pronoun, "mee," preserved in the text of Hughes.

Chapter 6

"No More of Talk" (9.1)

Narrative persona begins his account of the fatal events in Book 9 of *Paradise Lost* with regret at a loss of further conversations of Adam with the inhabitants of Heaven. For him it might be said such loss of talk would be a paradise lost:

No more of talk where God or Angel Guest
With Man, as with his Friend, familiar used
To sit indulgent, and with him partake
Rural repast, permitting him the while
Venial discourse unblamed: I now must change
Those notes to Tragic; . . . (9.1–6)

This anticipation of a loss shadows and in fact obscures an earlier actual end of talk in Paradise between the human pair just when Adam has finally become aware of "[his] likeness,[his] fit help, [his] other self\ [His]wish, exactly to [his] heart's desire" (8.450–451, *re* 5.95ff.)—that counterpart, akin but different, of Eve's sense of him she obtained with the grasp of his hand. Now, just at the moment one might have expected Adam and Eve would really begin to talk, an angel arrives and interrupts their colloquy. Raphael will with ceremony acknowledge Eve's presence and then ignore her. For Adam, dazzled by the "glorious shape" of this heavenly visitor, prior professions of his heart's desire soon fade to inconsequence. Eve, forgotten and unseen by both, will remain as silent auditress until Adam "[e]ntering on studious thoughts abstruse" (8.40) presumes to improve in theory upon the cosmology of Raphael's Creation narrative. Eve leaves to tend her flowers. But narrative persona assures, "Yet went she not, as not with such discourse\ Delighted, or not capable her ear\ Of what was high" (8.48–50). Rather he

127

supposes it was an absence of affectionate accoutrements—to "intermix\
Grateful digressions and solve high dispute\With conjugal Caresses, from his
Lip\ Not words alone pleased her" (8.54–57). When she returns, therefore,
again unseen, at end of day as the angel is about to depart, she must to some
degree be taken by surprise to hear Raphael's rebuke (8.561–594) of passion
in Adam. She resolves to protect him from himself. As she tells him the following morning,

Offspring of heaven and earth, and all earth's lord,
That such an enemy we have, who seeks
Our ruin, both by thee informed I learn,
And from the parting angel over-heard[1]
As in a shady nook I stood behind,
Just then return'd at shut of evening Flowers. (9.273–278, italics added)

Their talk the morning of the fatal day will be no conversation worthy of the
name. Eve has something on her mind and she has made up her mind. For the
first time in their talk in Paradise she is first to speak: "And *Evé fírst* to her
*hús*band *thús* be*gán*" (9.204, scansion in italics). She has decided they must
each go their own way to their morning tasks. Initially she merely proposes
they divide their labors to avoid distraction:

For while so near each other thus all day
Our task we choose, and what wonder if so near
Looks intervene and smiles, or object new
Casual discourse draw on, which intermits
Our day's work brought to little, . . . (9.220–224)

But she grows ever more insistent, the more Adam pleads to preserve that
"talk between,\ Food of the mind, or this sweet intercourse\ Of looks and
smiles, for smiles from Reason flow" (9.237–239). She will blend Adam's
concern about a "malicious foe\ Envying our happiness, . . .\ . . . [that] seeks
to work us woe and shame" (9.253–255), with "the parting angel's" talk of
that other "enemy," passion. She takes offense, however, when Adam argues
her need of protection; she does not yet understand his own reliance on her
"peculiar graces." Nor for that matter does Adam himself. If Eve has heard
as well his clumsy enthusiasms in description of her charms (8.530–560) no
less than Raphael's subsequent rebuke of Adam's praise of them, her intran-
sigence is not hard to fathom. But chastened now Adam pleads a virtuous
influence to her looks.

I from the influence of thy looks receive
Access in every virtue, in thy sight

More wise, more watchful, stronger if need were
Of outward strength; while shame, thou looking on,
Shame to be overcome or over-reacht
Would utmost vigor raise, and raised unite.
Why shouldst not thou like sense within thee feel
When I am present, and thy trial choose
With me, best witness of thy virtue tried [?] (9.309–317).

The approach and hypothesis will be brushed aside without comment. That was not how he had spoken of her the previous afternoon. Rather, in the end Eve comes to question the very security of their condition in Paradise: "Frail is our happiness . . . ,\ And Eden were no Eden thus exposed" (9.340–341). Something has been lost. Talk with the angel has made Adam dull to Eve's "peculiar graces."

"[THEIR] HAPPY STATE" (5.234)

In spite of the happiness they have found in conversation, Adam and Eve will give up talking to each other. They will separate. On Eve's return from the fatal events at the interdicted tree, Adam in sight of her—"in her face excuse" (9.853)—and hearing of these events, falls silent: "Speechless he stood and pale, till thus at length\ First to himself he inward silence broke" (9.894–895). One might think that had he given voice to these inward thoughts, the look on her face might have rivaled the distress he observed the previous morning. One well might wonder what would have happened then. These speculations, however, are irrelevant to the tale Milton has set himself to tell. That the Raphael discourse is the appropriate means to *that* end requires explanation in a number of distinct aspects.

The discourse itself is as significant an addition to the Genesis narrative as is Milton's portrait of the pair's conversations. The motive for Raphael's commission has both a dramatic and a poetic origin. "[H]eaven's high king" looks down on the two in pity after their talk of Eve's dream and their timid request in prayer, "be bounteous still\To give us only good" (5.205–206), but Raphael's dispatch also fulfills narrative persona's yearning for a "warning voice" (4.1), without which his own task to "justify the ways of God to men" (1.26) would have been in doubt.[2] Moreover, the Father's instructions to the sociable angel are specific:

such discourse bring on
As may advise him of his happy state,
Happiness in his power left free to will

Left to his own free will, his will though free
Yet mutable; . . . (5.233–237)

These instructions suggest at the very least that in the Father's view their conversations have left them ill-informed both of their own happiness and of that discursive freedom in choice operative therein. And last and inclusive of all aspects, Milton has made executor an angel schooled in the cosmologies of the Cambridge Platonists, whose sympathies, as will be shown below, Milton by the time he came to write *Paradise Lost* no longer shared.

Adam's conversation with Eve the previous day when he woke to find her disturbed by a dream led him to derive a brilliant psychology of dreams. His reassurance *qua* commiseration with her distress revealed to him a confusion in his own past dreams of paradise and her. Yet his insight and reasoning would appear compromised by its application to this particular instance. Her dream was not the exclusive work of "mimic fancy," but required a talking toad. A dream however, is a dream whatever the source, and Adam will be cheered in cheering Eve. He dries her tears and his own, but is unsettled by an "addition strange" (5.116) that he cannot quite identify let alone explain. The conclusion of their morning prayer contains a new request to their Maker: "be bounteous still\ To *give us only good*; and if the night\ Have gathered aught of evil or concealed\ Disperse it, . . ."(5.205–208, italics added). Some uncertainty has apparently crept into their sense of the providence of the "Parent of good."

In the conception of narrative persona Raphael was then dispatched under a specific commission. He will be "that warning voice" (4.1) that is required to "justify the ways of God to men" (1.26). He appears to be unaware of the pair's recent conversations which the poem has permitted its audiences to observe. His instructions do, however, resemble the manner of other angels in Scripture.[3]

Go . . . half this day as friend with friend
Converse with Adam, in what bower or shade
Thou findst him from the heat of noon retired,
To respite his day labor with repast,
Or with repose; and such discourse bring on,
As may advise him of his happy state,
Happiness in power left free to will,
Left to his own free will, his will though free,
yet mutable, whence warn him to beware
He swerve not too secure: tell him withal
His danger, and from whom, what enemy
Late fallen himself from heaven, . . . (5.229–240)

Together with a countenanced neglect of Eve, Raphael appears to be sent to reorient Adam's sense of his own happiness. Adam's present happiness with

Eve is either invisible or beside the point. Happiness is neither a present nor a permanent condition. Adam must look to his use of his freedom of his will in the future. The threefold repetition (5.235–236) carries a note of urgency. An angel-like winged creature in Eve's dream has already attempted to raise a similar concern for her. But neither in the exercise of their freedom identify their happiness with that freedom though it surely is evident in their in their individual choices and in their talk together. Both had been promised happiness if they deferred to a voice of authority.[4] They demurred. In *that* freedom they came to discover a different source for their happiness. An inventory of these moments will be of use.

From his very first moments when he first awoke to himself in a body, Adam—and Eve no less[5]—had some sense of his own happiness. He asked those things he saw around him how he came to be. He was sure he was not the cause of his own being, but was a creature, "by some great maker": "Tell me," he asks those things, "how may I know him, how adore,\ From whom I have that thus I move and live,\ And feel that I am *happier than I know*" (8.278 & 280–282, italics added). He attempts, to state the obvious, to come to understand what he feels through talk. After he named the beasts brought to him in pairs he asks the Presence Divine, "Thou has provided all things: but with mee\ I see not who partakes. In solitude\ *What happiness, who can enjoy alone,*\ Or all enjoying, *what contentment find*?" (8.363–366, italics added). Happiness, he has a sense, is not being in a place, even if that place is a paradise. Happiness now is something that must be experienced with another. The "Presence," Adam would later tell Raphael, was not displeased by his complaint, but playfully rejoined, "What thinkst thou then of me and this *my State*" (8.403, italics added). Then owning to his imperfections before his maker, Adam came to speak of "his desire\ By conversation with his like to help,\ Or solace his defects" (8.417–419). This too pleased the "Presence," who admits, "Thus far to try thee, *Adam*, I was pleased\ And finding thee *knowing not of beasts alone,*\ Which thou hast rightly named, *but of thyself*" (8.437–439, second and third italics added). Adam knows himself enough to know what will make him happy, and so the Presence promises, "What next I bring shall please thee, be assured" (8.449). Happiness is not without some self-knowledge of what one wants and lacks.

But several days later, deceived by his own dream awareness of Eve's making and her puzzling silence since they met, he has begun to have his doubts. He apparently did not know what he thought he did. His distant gaze to the heavens in the poem's initial vision of the pair (4.287ff), queried the promise by the Presence Divine of a happiness Adam had yet to call his own. But with Eve's first words (4.440ff.), Adam is now happy that she is talking, though as ignorant of what she is talking about as of her reasons for speaking of it only now. Eve herself is delighted with her sense of "how beauty is excelled by manly grace\ And wisdom which alone is truly fair" (4.490–491). Her discovery of her own being in a body when Adam seized her hand now has made sense to her of Adam's dream-induced cry as she had turned back to the pool—"of him thou art, His flesh, his bone"—as her "other half." She is happy and she knows it. Both are free to find happiness in these discoveries about themselves and each other, but their happiness does not consist of that freedom. Though their grasp of the joyous composition of that happiness is as yet incomplete, even Satan can see in what for them it does in a sense consist: "Sight hateful, sight tormenting, thus these two\ Imparadis't in one another's arms\ The happier Eden, shall enjoy their fill\ Of bliss on bliss, . . ." (4.505–508).

That evening as they approach the wedding bower, Eve's lovely proemial epanalepsis (8.639–656)—"Sweet is the breath of morn . . . But neither breath of morn . . . without thee is sweet"—is all about her happiness only in conversation with Adam: "With thee conversing I forget all time." The question she asks him would have him talk about that decisive sense of cause for all they see and enjoy: "for whom\ This glorious sight?" She too wants to understand what she thinks she feels. As they are about to enter their bower, they stop to adore,

The God that made both sky, air, earth and heaven
Which they beheld, the moon's resplendent globe
And starry pole: Thou also mad'st the night,
Maker omnipotent, and thou the day,
Which we in our appointed work employed
Have finished *happy in our mutual help*
And mutual love, the crown of all our bliss (4.722-728, italics added)

This help and love are not habitual pleasantries but precise testimony to the aid and heart-felt affection that each has given the other. The following morning, however, Adam awakes to find Eve,

"With tresses discomposed, and glowing cheek,
As through unquiet rest: he on his side
Leaning half-raised, with looks of cordial love
Hung over her enamored, and beheld
Beauty, which whether waking or asleep,
Shot forth *peculiar graces*; (5.10–15, italics added)

This vision is made possible by those gifts bestowed by their Creator: the rational desire of the same and a nascent rational love of the other acting in concert, and a corporeal nature that bespeaks not only happiness but also its lack. Adam soon discovers by these gifts the source of his own prior discontents. "Best image of myself and dearer half,\" he names her now, \"The trouble of thy thoughts this night in sleep\ Affects me equally (5.95–97)."

He knows whereof she speaks. He recognizes from Eve's looks no less than in her account of her dream a likeness to his own dreams, first, of the garden of bliss (8.296–310) and thereafter, his dream vision of her making (8.462–478). Taken together with the false impressions he later, now awake, realized he had derived from his dreams, Adam knows now that dreams are no guide to their waking life—but their recognition as such is. Their happiness is growing still in the knowledge of themselves gained in conversation with each other.

But now each individually will be urged to seek a happiness, a happiness greater than they presently enjoy, of a different sort. In Eve's dream, mistakenly assigned by Adam to "mimic fancy," she will be invited by "One shaped and winged like one of those from Heav'n" (5.55) to think of her future happiness:

Here, happy creature, fair angelic Eve,
Partake thou also; happy though thou art,
Happier thou mayst be, worthier thou canst not be:
Taste this, and be henceforth among the Gods
Thyself a Goddess, . . . (5.74–77).

When Raphael arrives later this day to talk with Adam, as William Empson has noted, this angel will make nearly the same proposal in the same terms to him: "the voice of the mysterious dream and the spokesman of God are not merely saying the same thing (that God expects them to manage to get to Heaven, and that what they eat has something to do with it) but even using the same tricks of speech" (150).

Moreover, Milton has this "spokesman of God" describe to Adam by stages a future happiness obtained by ascent through a cosmological order that some would recognize as borrowed from Cambridge "platonism." The identification is hardly controversial.[6] This cosmology, and subsequent discourses—an account of disobedience mirrored by events in heaven, and the retelling of the days of Creation and, Adam's own enthusiastic contributions—all have been assumed to provide the philosophical and theological paraphernalia for *Paradise Lost*. In one sense they do. But that Milton himself considered this cosmology as *the* hermeneutic principle for *Paradise Lost* is doubtful. His remarks on his years of private study after Cambridge argue he did not.

AN EXCURSUS: "THE SHADY SPACES OF PHILOSOPHY"

There are two brief but oblique remarks by Milton on his studies after Cambridge in the literary record. As was noted in chapter 1, in *An Apology Against A Pamphlet* (1642) in defending himself against a slanderous portrait of his life at University and thereafter by the remonstrant author of the tract, *Against Smectymnuus,* Milton had epitomized his post-baccalaureate studies: "riper years and the ceaseless round of study and reading led me to the shady spaces of philosophy, but chiefly to the divine volumes of Plato and his equal Xenophon."[7] In somewhat similar diction and also referring to such a turning point in his private studies Milton several years earlier[8] had added to the seventh and last of his Latin elegies a "retraction" of these works which he now appeared to assign to his juvenalia:

> *Haec ego mente olim laeva, studioque supino*
> *Nequitiae posui vana trophaea meae*
> *Scilicet abreptum sic me malus impulit error,*
> *Indocilisque aetas prava magistra fuit;*
> *Donec Socraticos umbrosa Academia rivos*
> *Praebuit, admissum dedocuitque iugum*

These things at some point I came to consider[9] empty display pieces of dubious sense and a tedious pastime of my utter inconsequence. To be sure, carried away in this fashion a harmful perplexity urged me on, and an ignorant age proved to be a corrupt instructress, until the shaded school of Athens offered Socratic streams and taught me how to unlearn the yoke to which my thinking had been subjected. (numbered 1–6 in Carey, 236–237)[10]

An additional note of clarification for these remarks is provided much later by Milton's Satan of *Paradise Regain'd* as he offers the wisdom of antiquity to the Son of God. Calling Socrates the "Wisest of Men," he adds, "from whose mouth issu'd forth\ *Mellifluous streams* that watered *all the schools\ Of Academics old and new . . ."* (*P. R.* 4.276–278, italics added).

Taken together these three passages lend credence to Milton's break with Cambridge "platonism" during the period of his private studies. To what did these "shady spaces of philosophy" refer, and what therein was the focus those private studies? That there were such studies as the *Apology* mentions suggests that the *umbrosa Academia* of the retraction cannot refer to Christ College, Cambridge.[11] It would not, however, exclude the possibility that such studies were merely delayed revenue from a principal on deposit from his instruction at university. This was in essence the solution Irene Samuel offered broadly in *Plato and Milton* (1947). Samuel conceded that the platonizing of Milton's early works, "nowhere indicates that those Dialogues (i.e., on "ethical theory" and his "theory of love") have *a central and unifying doctrine"* (9, parenthesis and italics added). A Platonic 'doctrine' was her benchmark for a genuine Plato.

Milton's oblique remarks, however, suggest something different. Both contain teasing references to a study of Plato at Cambridge. The *Apology* passage mentions "the *divine* volumes of Plato and *his equal Xenophon*" (italics added). The "divinity" of the volumes of Plato is an attribution borrowed from the very beginning of first volume *The Platonic Theology* of Proclus, and thereafter, a ubiquitous attribute bestowed on Plato in Ficino's Christianized commentary of the same name[12] and in his commentaries on the *Phaedrus et alia* as well. The ironic cast of this attribute is implied by a declared equivalence of Plato and Xenophon. Milton knew that generally accepted opinion in "academic" circles would hardly have called Xenophon's volumes "divine"; in contrast with "their" Plato: there were no divinizing flights of poetry in Xenophon. Modern commentary on this passage in the *Apology* has been brief in dismissal.[13] Milton, however, ironizes hyperbole familiar to the Cambridge platonists to draw attention to that equivalence which was the focus of his private studies—the *Socraticos rivos* in both authors which Satan's figure, "streams" in *Regained* identifies with the discourses of Socrates. Milton's own poetic turns, *Socraticos rivos* and "mellifluous streams" are still more mischievous insofar as they too are sourced in Ficino.[14] But mischief aside, during this period of private study Milton was reading the dialogs of Plato and the Socratic discourses of Xenophon, not Ficino.

These remarks on his private studies now appear as an ironic judgment on an *indocilis aetas*, an "ignorant climate of opinion," he had encountered in his earlier formal studies at Cambridge. The respect in which that climate of opinion was in Milton's judgment *indocilis* is as yet unclear. The *umbrosa Academia*, however, identifies a shelter that Plato's Socratic logoi[15] provide from the heat of sun. This trope belongs to the *Phaedrus* in which, among other topics, Socrates and Phaedrus will discuss proper ways of writing. But Milton's description of his own endeavor in these private studies, *admissum dedocuitque iugum* ("taught me how to unlearn the yoke to which my thinking had been subjected"), recalls as well another Socratic discourse in the dialogs. In the retraction appended to the elegies Milton had described his own prior condition, to use Socrates's phrase, "in regard to learning and its lack" (παιδείας τε πέρι καὶ ἀπαιδευσίας [*Respublica* 514a2]), a concern which Socrates had exemplified by his remarks about prisoners in a cave. They too were bound at the neck.

"HAPPY THOUGH THOU ART\ HAPPIER THOU MAY'ST BE" (5.75–76)

Why then would Milton have employed a thinly veiled neoplatonic discourse in counterpoise to the discourses of Adam and Eve, when the latter only a "fit audience . . . though few" would recognize as *socraticos . . . rivos*? A justification can be found in Milton's desire to preserve both views of human

happiness as reasonable ends for the distinct audiences—"men" (1.26) *and*
the "fit . . . though few"(7.31)—of the poem. The two discourses of the poem,
the *socraticos . . . rivos*, and that call to obedience in the revealed word of
Scripture each makes a claim to understand and, for their own audience know
what human happiness is and how it is obtained. One finds happiness in this
life, the other in the next.

For Adam and Eve their happiness in talk is addressed to their Creator as
they walk "hand in hand" to the wedding bower: "we in our appointed work
imployed [this day]\ Have finished happy in our mutual help\And mutual
love, the crown of all our bliss" (4.726–728). Adam at this moment has yet
to recognize Eve as that "Best image of myself and dearer half" (5.95) as he
will the following morning, but their present happiness will not be devalued
by continued growth in their understanding of themselves and each other
through conversation. For Raphael, an inhabitant of heaven, however, true
happiness remains a distant prospect. As he tells Adam:

> perhaps
> Your bodies may at last turn all to spirit,
> Improved by tract of time, and winged ascend
> Ethereal, as we,[16] or may at choice
> Here, or in heavenly paradises dwell;
> If ye be found obedient, and retain
> Unalterably firm his love entire
> Whose progeny you are. Meanwhile enjoy
> Your fill of what happiness this happy state
> Can comprehend, incapable of more. (5.496–505)

This prelapsarian deferral would hardly occasion surprise among a postlapsarian audience that reads *Paradise Lost* in order to revisit a familiar story
with its sobering lessons for this life. It rhymes in a sense with what they
think they know.

Milton came to understand during his years of private study that a popular
disguise in generally accepted opinion[17]—in *Paradise Lost,* the pose of a
Christian neoplatonist discourse given voice by an inhabitant of heaven—
would be required for the call to obedience in Scripture, if it were to stand in
equipoise to his portrait of the rational inquiries of Adam and Eve. To make
its case in equipoise to rational inquiry—that "highth of this great argument"
mentioned in the proem (1.24)—it too would have to appear to have an "argument," though in fact it has none since it needs none. The voice in authority
of Scripture that calls for obedience would suffice, were it not that it lacks
an explanation why that call is necessary. That, after all, was why *Paradise
Lost* was offered as a supplement to Scripture: "to justify the way[s] of God
to men." The plural, "ways," this study would argue cannot be ignored. Thus

Raphael appears to present a detailed cosmological justification for the call of obedience. As he tells Adam,

O Adam, one Almighty is from whom
All things proceed and up to him return,
If not depraved from good, created all,
Indued with various forms, various degrees
Of substance, and things that live, of life;
But more refined, more spiritous, and pure,
As nearer to him placed or nearer tending,
Each in their several active spheres assigned
Till body up to spirit work, in bounds
Proportioned to each kind. . . . (5.469–479)

This cosmology then underpins the discourse of Adam with Raphael on food and spiritual digestion. Thus, when Adam cautiously explains his and Eve's offer of food to their guest—"only this I know,\That one celestial Father gives to all"(5.403–404)—Raphael is quick to accept and explain:

Therefore what he gives
(Whose praise be ever sung) to man in part
Spiritual, may of purest spirits be found
No ingrateful food: and food alike those pure
Intelligential substances require
As doth your rational; and both contain
Within them every lower faculty
Of sense, whereby they hear, see, smell, touch, taste
Tasting concoct, digest assimilate,
And corporeal to incorporeal turn. (5.404–413)

It is, then, an easy transition for Raphael to assimilate distinct spiritual powers to distinct powers of digestion of corporeal food, and therein obedience to God's sole command is aligned with proper self-control in eating, since, as Raphael will later observe, "knowledge is as food" (7.126). For Adam's sake he sketches the scale of ascent:

flowers and their fruit,
Man's nourishment, by gradual scale sublimed
To vital spirits aspire, to animal,
To intellectual, give both life and sense,
Fancy and understanding, whence the soul
Reason receives, and reason is her being,
Discursive or intuitive; discourse
Is oftest yours, the latter is most ours,

Differing in degree, of kind the same.
Wonder not then, what God saw for you good
If I refuse not, but convert, as you,
To proper substance; time may come when men
With angels may participate, and find
No inconvenient diet, . . . (5.481–495)

The sole condition to this spiritual ascent of Adam to the happiness Raphael enjoys with the inhabitants of heaven is, "if ye be found obedient," (5.502). This call to obedience, now couched within a then-popular discourse of Cambridge platonism, places the prelapsarian hopes of Adam for an "ascen[t] to God" (5.512) in congenial terms to the postlapsarian hopes of the poem's general audience. The stress of the conditional is familiar; it rhymes.

The discourses of Adam and Eve, those *socraticos rivos*, however, had no need of disguise because of the dominion of generally accepted opinion over the narrative of Genesis. Public opinion was in agreement about the tale. At worst, an audience of "men" would assume that the poet was simply giving somewhat new clothes to an old story that had a familiar moral—as Addison had observed—"that Obedience to the will of God makes men happy, and that Disobedience makes them miserable" (*Spectator* #369). The poem, *Paradise Lost*, on the whole then would appear to "rhyme" with what they already assumed.

A disguise for the alternative to inquiry—a neoplatonic garb for a demand of obedience to an inscrutable command would conceal to all but a "few" the stark contrast between the true alternatives for happiness: no reason can be given for the prohibition against eating the fruit of that tree save a test of their obedience; if a reason were offered, their faith in the author—whose very goodness Scripture reveals no need to explain—of the sole command would not be tested. The neoplatonic disguise appeared to offer a reason for the prohibition in the scale of ascent by a spiritual digestion: as Raphael explained, "Your bodies may at last turn all to spirit\ Improved by *tract* of time," (5.497–498, italics added). The figure was not accident, as, once again, Empson, 150, had noted. But if both Raphael and Satan offered the same figure to argue opposite acts and opposite results, eating and not eating and happiness and misery, it would be expected that a "fit few" of the audience for the poem would begin to examine the angelic alternatives more closely. Taken as a whole these differences in approach to *Paradise Lost* would "justify the *ways* of God to men" (1.26, italics added).

The call to obedience in the Genesis narrative rests on an act of faith buttressed only by a generally accepted opinion of a good of the tradition from Scripture and of the good of the author of All. As such it cannot and would not of its own appear to present a countervalent argument to and for rational inquiry because faith by definition requires no such argument. But faith is the groundless conviction that the source of happiness is revealed by the word of God. Faith would not be faith if it gave an argument for its claim to happiness. On the other hand, no rational argument can prove there is not such a source. That might explain the indefatigable confidence of faith in terms congenial to rational inquiry, but it would be irrelevant to faith. In short, the preservation of both claims, is a "great argument" (1.24) for an audience "fit . . . though few" in *Paradise Lost.*

At the conclusion of Raphael's narrative of the days of Creation, when the "filial power" returns to his great Father, a great hymn is sung to *Jehovah* and his works that concludes with:

> Thrice happy men,
> And sons of men, whom God hath thus advanced,
> Created in his image, there to dwell
> And worship him, and in reward to rule
> Over his works, on earth, in sea, or air
> And multiply a race of worshippers
> Holy and just: thrice happy if they know
> their happiness, and persevere upright. (7.625–632)

Men must be and are happy only in enjoying that delight in the three senses portrayed in the coda of the hymn: (1) the "blessing" ("Thrice happy men\ and sons of men") indicates they *are* happy—i.e., they suffer under no delusions about what they are feeling; (2) they *know* that they are by some voice of authority or they come to that awareness themselves; and (3) they *are taking measures themselves* to continue in that condition. As described this triplet surely describes the happiness that results, "If ye be found obedient" (5.502) as well as that of the recent conversations of Adam and Eve. They have been happy,[18] and they clearly both know they were so—by their own lights, that is, before the arrival of the Raphael. Their perseverance in that state is albeit brief prior to the angel's arrival, but plausible in light of their endeavors to overcome misunderstandings that are a concomitant of any conversation.

It would appear difficult for any audience of *Paradise Lost* to feel confident of any claim to happiness without still further reflection on equipoise between both "ways."

AN AFTERWORD

The exclusion in this study of one further conversation (10.867–1096) of Adam and Eve in *Paradise Lost* requires some explanation. After the Fall and their judgment by the Son and now observing the changes occurring in the world of Nature, Adam ruminates aloud (10.720–844) on ruin of his world. Totally self-absorbed, only at the very end of his soliloquy does he give a passing thought to "that bad woman" (10.837). When Eve in her own distress offers "soft words to his fierce passion" (10.865), Adam violently repels her attempt. His rebuke, "Out of my sight, thou serpent" ignorantly casts aside those "peculiar graces" which had been the engine of their accord in Paradise. But Eve will not be put off, and slowly Adam's vicious recriminations are softened by Eve's commiseration, "Now at his feet submissive in distress \ Creature *so fair* his reconcilement seeking" (10.942–943, italics added). It would appear that the corporeal element of their conversational accord in Paradise has been shaken but not irreparably damaged by the Fall.

But when narrative persona at the outset of Book 11 begins in summary of these events of Book 10, as "they in lowliest plight repentant stood/ Praying," he will offer an explanation at odds in nearly every category of description in the account of Book 10: "Prevenient grace descending has removed\ The stony from their hearts, and made new flesh\ Regenerate grow instead" (11.1–2 & 3–5). Book 10 had ended with Adam's proposal—following Eve's declared intent (10.932)—of, "to the place\Repairing where he judged us, prostrate fall\ Before him reverent" (10.1086–1088) but now, eleven lines later repeated in narrative voice: "they forthwith to the place\Repairing where he judged them prostrate fell/ Before him reverent"(10.1098–1100). To compound the puzzling evidence of an event that requires disjunctive description, the poet will even rewrite Ovid's vision of "the ancient Pair" of Deucalion and Pyrrha—*procumbit uterque\ pronus humi gelidoque pavens dedit oscula saxo* ("both fell forward\ face-down to the ground and in fear gave kisses to the chill stone" [*Metamorphoses* 1.375–376])—who now, "before the Shrine\ Of Themis *stood devout*. (11.13–14, italics added).

These particulars suggest that an account of the Socratic rationalism after the Fall will be subject to new stresses which are beyond the scope of this book. Such an account would seem to require an investigation of the Spirit which the author believes Milton undertook in two works, *Paradise Regain'd* and *Samson Agonistes*.

NOTES

1. There is no talk of Satan whatsoever in Adam's account of himself in Book 8, nor in Raphael's subsequent observations of Adam's account of his feelings for Eve.

2. See 5.246–247: "So spake the eternal Father, and fulfilled\ All justice: . . ."

3. For example, in the visit of three guests to Abraham, Gen 18, Sarah sits unseen behind the tent flap and prepares the food, until she is noticed by the Lord by her inward laugh.

4. Eve had been promised by a voice by which she was willing to be "invisibly . . . led"(4.476), "him thou shalt enjoy\ Inseparably thine" (4.472–473), but takes one look and heads back to the pool; Adam had been assured that the being that was created from his flesh and bone would be, "Thy wish, exactly to thy heart's desire" (8.451), but several days later he is not so sure, as Eve has noticed (see 4.447–448).. *CPW* 1.891.

5. See 4.461–465.

6. Merritt Hughes thought the introductory prologue, "Milton's most beautiful and crucial ontological passage," and noted that, "his ideas and imagery were drawn from a great variety of sources" (193). Fowler (311n469–90) agrees: it is "[a] highly individual, quasi-evolutionary vision of striving nature, although with distant analogues, ranging from Aristotle to Boehme, Fludd and the Cambridge Platonists. Not conceptualized elsewhere in Milton's works." Danielson (39–40) found it confirming evidence for the doctrines of *creatio ex Deo* and Milton's notorious "one substance" monism. These and other studies perhaps for understandable reasons show little interest beyond superficial echoes to investigate the pedigree and combination of sources the discourse contains. On this occasion they assign to a supposed 'Miltonic theology' matters which he merely borrowed for his angel's discourse.

From the broadest perspective there is no doubt that the basic structure of Raphael's remarks as whole is Plotinian, the metaphysical theory of emanation and return: "One Almighty is, from whom\ All things proceed, and up to him return" (5.469–470). For a concise summary of the doctrine of emanation and return with ample citations, see Wallis 61–69. But "one substance" monism is not Plotinus. "[O]ne first matter all, \ Indued with various forms, various degrees\ Of substance" (5.472–474) is a casual translation of the *materiam communissimam, id est vim formarum omnium aequaliter receptricem nominant [Platonici].* ("material most common to all, that is, the power [the Platonists] designate as receptive of all forms" [*Theo. Plat.* XVII.2.2]) of Ficino. Raphael's discourse thereafter describes in various ways a process of sublimation of physical substance: first in the abstract, "in various degrees of substance and in things that live, of life" (5.472–479); then in an analogy to the "gradual scale sublimed" in a plant (5.479–484); then, to the rise of animal spirits to the intellectual, wherein the Soul comes to receive reason in its predominantly human or angelic modes, "Discursive or Intuitive" (5.488). The terms of description of this gradual purification never completely escape the corporeal, as Raphael's summation shows:

> time may come when men
> With Angels may participate, and find No inconvenient diet, nor too light Fare:
> And from these corporeal nutriments perhaps
> Your bodies may at last turn all to spirit,
> Improved by tract of time, . . . (5.493–498)

J.H. Hanford, 159, saw the problem but historicized the fact: "Milton is expressing in this curious passage [i.e., 5.403ff], so absurd to the modern reader, [of] two profound anti-medieval convictions which constitute the basis of his thought: the metaphysical one that matter is real and that there is no sharp distinction between spirit and matter, the one passing insensibly into the other; . . ."

7. *CPW* 1.891.

8. Hughes, 61, had dated the retraction to 1630; Fowler, 236, assumes it cannot have been earlier than 1628 and notes as well that there were no significant variants in the text between the publication of the *Poems* in 1645 and the later edition of 1673. Samuel, 15, assigns the period of Milton's private studies to 1637–1642.

9. The verb form *posui*, here translated as an ingressive aorist, can equally be rendered as an historical perfect,"I once (*olim*) erected" or "raised" (so Hughes 61 & Fowler 237). The difference resides in the referent for the adverb (*olim*) : does it refer to the original composition of the elegies or to a reconsideration of their neoplatonic enthusiasms. Preference for the former rest on the assumption that *umbrosa Academia* (5) refers to his days at Cambridge.

10. Four concluding lines concern only his new and consequent disdain for amatory poetry.

11. So Agar had noted, 43, citing David Masson, (*Milton's Poetical Works*, iii. 304) "The more the general tenor of the Postscript (i.e., the retraction) is considered in connection with the circumstances of Milton's life, the more it will appear that by 'Academia' in line 5 he does not mean the University of Cambridge, as all commentators have supposed, but Platonic Philosophy" (parenthesis added).

12. See, for example, the proem dedicatory addressed to Lorenzo de' Medici, in speaking of a pious duty to see the divine light and worship God: *Neque solum ad id pietatis officium Plato noster ceteros adhortatur, verum etiam ipse maxime preastat. Quo factum est ut et ipse sine controversia divinus et doctrina eius apud omnes gentes theologia nuncuparentur,* . . . ("Not only does our Plato urge others to this duty of piety, but he himself stands out as the very best in this regard. And that is why he himself is both without disagreement called divine and his teaching among all people is called theology" (Ficino, *Platonic Theology* Vol. 1, Proem §2)

13. See Hughes 694n127; Lewis 7.

14. *Commentaries on Plato* vol.1 *Phaedrus* and Ion, "*Argumentum et commentaria Marsilio Ficini in Phaedrum*" 2.2 , speaking of the beauties of the dialog, *Inter haec artificiossima loci descripto allegorice signat Academiam, platanus, Platonem, castum arbustum amoris platonici et socratici castitttem, fons in communicanda sapientia largitiam, ornamenta cetera oratorios poeticos flores quibus Academia Platonis abundat.* "Among these the most accomplished description allegorically signifies the Academy, the *agnus castus* tree, the chastity of Platonic and Socratic love, the flowing waters the liberality in sharing wisdom, and other embellishments the oratorical and poetical blossoms with the Academia of Plato is blessed in abundance."

15. For a probing investigation of this crucial poetic figure in the *Phaedrus* (230a6–e5) especially in regard to the need of a shade described as "entirely beautiful" (πάγκαλον), from the sun provided by a tree whose name, πλάτανος, puns on the name of Plato, see Geier, 153–156.

16. Again, the emphatic pronoun, "wee," in the text of Hughes.

17. This lesson Milton would have drawn from Xenophon's account of Socrates's conversation with Euthydemus (*Memorabilia* 4.6.1–15, see Appendix) in which

Xenophon (4.6.1) endeavors to show how Socrates made his close associates more skilled in dialectic (διαλεκτικωτέρους), a skill that Xenophon himself evidently gained in listening to Socrates talk with Euthydemus. This young man, as noted above in the "Preface," was a notorious collector of generally accepted opinions gleaned from poets and sophists. In this conversation which begins with an attempt to define what piety (εὐσεβεία) is, Socrates asks Euthydemus what he believes piety to be. Socrates never objects to any statement Euthydemus makes. Evidently Xenophon learned how to listen to such conversation composed entirely of such opinions and the questions Socrates asked Euthydemus to further explain what he thought. As argued in the "Preface" one can be reasonably confident Milton was familiar with this conversation based upon his rather extraordinary remarks in the Verse.

18. See, for example, Raphael's somewhat stinting appreciation as late as 5.503–505 and the dismissive attribution of the state to God at 5.520.

Appendix A

In Paradisum Amisum Summi Poetae Johannis Miltoni

Qui legis Amissum Paradisum, grandla magni
   Carmina Miltoni, quid nisi cuncta legis?
Res cuntas, et cunctarum primordia rerum,
   Et fata, et fines continet iste liber.
Intima panduntur magni penetralia mundi,   5
   Scribitur et toto quicquid in orbe latet.
Terraeque, tractusque maris, coelumque, profundum
   Suphureumque Erebi, flammivomumque specus.
Quaeque colunt terras, pontumque et Tartara caeca,
   Quae colunt summi lucida regna poli.   10
Et quodcunque ullis conclusum est finibus usquam,
   Et sine fine chaos, et sine fine Deus:
Et sine fine magis, si quid magis est sine fine,
   In Christo erga homines conciliatus amor.
Haec qui speraret quis crederet esse futura?   15
   Et tamen haec hodie terra Britanna legit.
O quantos in bella duces! quae protulit arma!
   Quae canit, et quanta praelia dira tuba.
Coelestes acies! atque in certamine coelum!
   Et quae coelestes pugna deceret agros!   20
Quantus in aetheriis tollit se Lucifer armis!
   Atque ipso graditur vix Michele minor!
Quantis, et quam funestis concurritur iris
   Dum ferus hic stellas protegit, ille rapit!
Dum vulsos montes ceu tela reciproca torquent,   25
   Et non mortali desuper igne pluunt:

Sat dubius cui se parti concedat Olympus,
  Et metuit pugnae non superesse suae.
At simul in coelis Messiae insignia fulgent,
  Et currus animes, armaque digna Deo,   *30*
Horrendumque rotae strident, et saeva rotarum
  Erumpunt torvis fulgura luminibus,
Et flammae vibrant, et vera tonitrua rauco
  Admistis flammis insonuere polo:
Excidit attonitis mens omnis, et impetus omnis   *35*
  Et cassis dextris irrita tela cadunt.
Ad poenas fugiunt, et ceu foret Orcus asylum
  Infernis certant condere se tenebris.
Cedite Romani scriptores, cedite Graii
  Et quos fama recens vel celebravit anus   *40*
Haec quicunque leget tantum cecinisse putabit
  Maeonidem ranas, Virgilium culices.

                                      —S(amuel). B(arrow). M.D.

Concerning *Paradise Lost* of the Supreme Poet, John Milton

You who read *Paradise Lost,* lofty verses
  Of great Milton, what do you read but everything?
All things, and the first beginnings of all things,
  And things foretold as well, and ends this book contains.
The inmost secrets of the great world are revealed   5
  Described too whatever lies hid in all the universe.
And lands, and tracts of sea, and the depth of heaven,
  And that sulfered and flame-spewing cave of Erebus.
And whatever inhabits lands, and sea, and benighted Tartarus,
  What peoples the shining realms of highest heaven.   10
And whatever is ever confined by any limits,
  And chaos without limit, and God without limit:
And what more without limit—if more there is without limit—
  Than the love towards men obtained in Christ.
Who could think, who could hope, these things were to come?   15
  And yet today the land of Britain reads them
O how great the leaders in war! What arms on the march!
  What dreadful battles and numbers by trumpet called.
Serried ranks of heaven's divisions and heaven in the balance!
  And what battles to befit celestial fields!   20
How great in celestial arms Lucifer carries himself!
  And Michael so strides hardly less than him!
With what great and what deadly angers is their contest joined
  As one fierce defends the stars, the other lays them waste

While uprooted promentories as vollied missiles they hurl, 25
   And with deathless fire these rain down from above:
Olympus is in doubt to which side she will yield herself
   And fears she will not survive her own assault.
But at this moment the standards of the Messiah blaze forth—
   Wake[1] life in those chariots and worthy arms of God! 30
Wheels shriek horribly, and the wild flashings
   Of the wheels break out in grim clarity,
And flames move to and fro and real thunder mingled with flames
   Resounds to the depth of heaven:
Thunderstruck, the intent and impulse of all swoons, 35
   And vain shafts fall from emptied hands.
They flee to their punishments, and, as if Orcus were a refuge
   They strive to hide themselves in infernal shade.
Give way, Roman writers, give way, Greeks,
   And those whom recent or ancient fame has praised, 40
Whoever reads these things shall think
   Maeonides sang of frogs, Virgil, of gnats, nothing more.

S.B. M.D.

—translated by David Oliver Davies

NOTE

1. Second pers. sing. hortatory subj. as impersonal, only in early Latin and retained as poetic usage (see A&G §439a)

Appendix B

Memorabilia 4.6.1-11

[IV.6.1] But how he tried to make his close associates more discerning in conversation, this too I shall try to explain. Socrates, you see, was in the habit of thinking that those who know what each of the beings is, would be able to explain them to others. But he also said that it was not at all surprising that those who did not know made both themselves stumble and stumbled others. For these reasons, he never ceased examining in the company of his close associates what each of the beings were. Now of course it would be a huge task to go through everything in the way he defined them, but I will give an account of as many things as I think shall make evident his method of inquiry.

[6.2] In the first place tried to make an inquiry about piety somehow in the following manner. "Tell me," he said, "Euthydemus, what sort of thing do you believe piety is?" And he said, "The finest, by Zeus." "Are you then able to say what sort of person is the pious?" "To me it seems," he said, "he is one who honors the gods." "But is it then possible to honor the gods in whatever way one wishes?" "No, rather, there are laws in accord with which one ought to honor the gods."

[6.3] "Then the one who knows these laws would know how one ought to honor the gods?" "I, at least, think so," he said. "Then does the one who knows how one ought to honor the gods not think he ought do this differently than the way he knows?" "Definitely not," he said. "But does anyone honor the gods in any other way than as he thinks he ought?"

[6.4] "I don't think he does," he said. "Well then, would the one who knows the customary things honor the gods in the customary way?" "Of course."

149

"Does he who honors the gods in the customary way honor them as he ought?" "Why not?" "Is he who honors as one ought reverent?" "Of course." "Would he then who knows the customary things about the gods be correctly defined by us as pious/reverent?" "To me at least, he said, it seems so."

[6.5] But as to human beings, is it then possible to deal with them in whatever way one wishes?" "No, but in regard to them as well, he who knows what are the customary things in accord with which there is an obligation by any means to deal with one another would be law-abiding." "So then, those who deal with one another in accord with these things, conduct their dealings as one ought?" "Of course." "So those who conduct themselves as one ought are wont to do so in a fine manner?" "Certainly!" he said. "So then, those who deal with human beings in a fine manner, perform human affairs in a fine manner?" "At least, it is likely so." "So those who are obedient to the laws—these do just things?" "Certainly!" "But do you know," he said, "what sorts of things are just?" "The things which the laws command," he said. "Therefore, those who do what the laws command, do just things and what one ought?" "Of course." "Then those who do just things are just?" "At least I think so," he said. "Therefore, do you think some people are obedient to the laws although they do not know what the laws command?" "I don't!" he said. "But if they do know what one ought to do, do you think, some think that they ought not do these things?" "I don't think so," he said. "But are you aware that some people do things other than those which they think they ought?" "I'm not," he said. "Then those who know the customary things about human beings, these do the just things." "Certainly." "Then those who do just things are just?" "Well, who else are there?" he said. "Then, could we ever define correctly if we define those who know the customary things about men to be just?" "To me at least it seems so."

[6.7] "Well then, what would we say wisdom is? Tell me, do the wise seem to you to be wise about the things that they know, or are some *perhaps* (μή w/ ind. §1772) wise about that which they do not know?" "It's obvious— things that they know," he said. "How after all could someone be wise about these things at any rate which he wouldn't know?" "Well then, the wise are wise by virtue of knowledge?" "By virtue of what else could he," he said, "be wise, if not by virtue of knowledge?" "But do you think that wisdom is anything else than that by which the wise are?" "I at any rate do not." Then knowledge is wisdom?" "It seems so to me at least." Does it therefore seem to you that it is possible for a man to know all the beings?" "By Zeus, not even, as far as I'm concerned, the slightest part of them!" "Then it is not possible that a man be wise about everything?" "By Zeus, certainly not!" he said. "Therefore what each person knows, he is also wise about this?" "To me at least it seems so."

[6.8] "Well then, Euthydemus, Must one investigate the good in this manner as well?" "In what manner?" he said. "Does it seem to you the same thing is beneficial to everyone?" "Not to me at least." "What follows? Doesn't it seem to you that the thing beneficial to one person is sometimes harmful to another?" "And then some!" he said. "Could you claim that anything else is good than the beneficial?" "I can't, at any rate," he said. "Then the beneficial is good for whomever it is beneficial;" "It seems so to me" he said.

[6.9] "Would we be able to speak in any way at all differently about the noble (the fine)? Or, if possible, do you call a body or an implement or anything at all fine which you know is fine in all regards?" "By Zeus, I at least don't," he said. "Is it, therefore, the case that in that regard to which each thing is useful, in this regard it is fine to use each thing." "Absolutely," he said. "But is each thing fine in any other regard than in that regard to which it is fine to use that particular thing?" "Nor in regard to any other thing," he said. "Therefore," he said, "the useful is fine in that regard in which it is useful?" "To me at least it seems so," he said.

[6.10] "Well then, Euthydemus, do you believe that courage is one of the fine things?"

"Indeed, the finest, as far as I am concerned," he said. "Then do you believe courage is useful not in the least consequential respects?" "By Zeus," he said, "in the greatest respects, surely!" Does it therefore seem to you that with respect to the terrible and the dangerous, to be ignorant of those things is useful?" "To the very least degree," he said. "Then, if they are not afraid of those things on account of not knowing what they are, they are not courageous?" "By Zeus," he said, "in that way, lots of madmen and cowards would be courageous." "What about those who are frightened by things that aren't terrible?" "By Zeus, even less so," he said. "Then those that are good in regard to the terrible and the dangerous you suppose are courageous, but those that are bad are cowards?"

[6.11] "Certainly!" he said. "But the good in regard to such things, do you believe they are any others than those capable to deal with them in a fine manner?" "None but these!" he said. "But the bad are the sort to deal badly with these things?" "Who else?" he said. "Then do each (i.e., the bad *and* the good) manage as they think they ought?" "How else?" he said. "Well then, do those, if they are unable to manage in a fine manner, do they know how they ought to manage it?" "I at any rate don't suppose so," he said. "Then do those who know how to manage, are these capable too?" "Surely only them" he said. "What follows? If they have not been complete failures, do they deal badly with such matters?" "I don't think so," he said. "Then those who deal badly, are they complete failures?" "Probably so," he said. "Then those who know how in fine manner to make use of the terrible and the dangerous are courageous, but those who are complete failures at this are cowards?" "They seem so to me at least," he said.

[6.12]   But kingship and tyranny he supposed were both sovereignties, though he was wont to think they differed from each other. The sovereignty over men both by their own free will and in accord with the laws of their cities he supposed was kingship, but the over men both contrary to their own free will and not in accord whatsoever with laws, but in whatever fashion the sovereign wishes he supposed was tyranny. And wherever the sovereignties are established from those who bring into effect their own honored customs, he was in the habit of thinking that this regime was an aristocracy; wherever from their property assessments, a plutocracy; wherever from everyone, a democracy.

[6.13]   But if someone disagreed with him about something though he had nothing clear to say, but without proof claimed what he himself said was either more profound, or more politically astute, or more daring or some other thing of that sort, he would bring the entire argument back to the underlying supposition in the following sort of way:

[6.14]   "Do you claim that the one you praise is a better citizen than the one I do?" "I certainly do." "Well then, let us examine that first: what is the deed of a good citizen?" "Let us do this." "Wouldn't the one who made the city more resourceful in needful (or, 'money') matters be a master in the administration of those matters?" "Certainly." "In war, wouldn't he make it gain the upper hand over its adversaries?" "How could he not?" "But in an ambassadorial office surely he's one who cultivates friends rather than makes enemies?" "Probably so." "Then even in addressing the public he is one who brings quarrels to an end and produces civic harmony?" "It seems so to me." But when the arguments were brought back in this way the truth became obvious even to the very ones who disagreed.

[6.15]   Moreover, whenever he himself went through some matter in an argument, he made his way by means of those things above all commonly agreed upon since he believed that this was a sure-footed method of argument (i.e., lit., "not liable to stumbling"). Indeed, surely, of all those I with whom I am acquainted, he most of all when he spoke, produced agreement among his listeners. He said, moreover, that Homer had given Odysseus the credit of being the 'sure-footed' (lit. "not liable to stumble") orator, since he was able to conduct his speech by means of those things that seem good to men.

—translated by David Oliver Davies.

Appendix C

A Selective Chronology for John Milton

1608 (December 9)	Born in London
1620?	Enters St. Paul's School, Alexander Gill is his tutor
1625 (February 12)	Enters Christ's College, Cambridge
1629 (March 26)	Receives a BA
1632 (July 3)	Receives an MA; leaves Cambridge for his father's house in the country (Hammersmith) to pursue a life of study. "I gave myself up with the most complete leisure to reading through Greek and Latin authors." (*Defensio Seconda, WJM*, 8.120).
1635	Moves to his parent's house in Horton; 1635? (possibly as late as publication of *Poems* in 1645) adds as postscript to his love poems a retraction, *Haec ego mente olim laeva*, . . . , which speaks of the "shady academy of *Socraticos rivos* ("Socratic streams" [of discourse]).
1638 (May)	Sails to France to begin his European travels.
1639 (July)	Returns to England.
1641 (May)	First of his ecclesiastical tracts, *Of Reformation*, is published.
1642 (February)	*The Reason of Church Government* published.
1643 (August 1)	*Doctrine and Discipline of Divorce* published.
1646 (January 2)	*Poems of Mr. John Milton, Both English and Latin . . . 1645.* published.
1652	Now totally blind.

1667 (August)	*Paradise Lost* (in 10 books) published; after the fourth binding of the first edition, the publisher, S. Simmons, asks Milton to supply a prose "argument" for this work.
1667 (?)	*Essay of Dramatick Poesie* by John Dryden published.
1668	The fifth binding of the first edition now includes fourteen pages of the "argument" Simmons requested and a paragraph entitled, The Verse, that he did not ask for. With this binding, the printer adds his own ungrammatical explanation of these supplements, "The Printer to the Reader." This same as well as subsequent bindings have some copies of these additions in which Milton has corrected the infelicities of grammar and now implies that The Verse was added like the Argument at the printer's request.
1671	*Paradise Regain'd* and *Samson Agonistes* published.
1674 (July 6?)	The second edition of *Paradise Lost* is published, now divided into 12 books, with sections of the prose "argument" now apportioned to each book, and with two verse appreciations, one in Latin, *In Paradisum Amissum* by one S.B M.D., and one in English rhymed verse, "On Paradise Lost," by A.M. (Andrew Marvell), now added to the "front matters" of the poem.
1674 (November 8–10?)	John Milton dies in his house in Bunhill Fields.

Works Cited

Milton, John. *The Complete Shorter Poems*. Edited by John Carey. Pearson Education Limited. 2007.

——. *Paradise Lost*. Edited by Alastair Fowler. Pearson Education Limited. 2007.

——. *Complete Poetry and Major Prose*. Edited by Merritt Y. Hughes. Indianapolis: Hackett Publishing Co.,1957.

——.*The Works Of John Milton*. Vol. 18. Edited by Frank Allen Patterson *et al.* New York: Columbia University Press,1931–8.

——. *Complete Prose Works of John Milton*. Vol. 8. Edited by Don M. Wolfe *et al.* New Haven: Yale University Press, 1953–80.

——. The Poetical Works. Edited by David Masson, Rev. edn. Vol. 3. London: 1890.

SCRIPTURAL TEXTS

The Five Books of Moses. Translation and Commentary by Robert Alter. New York: W.W. Norton & Company, 2004

Aland, Kurt et al., eds. *The Greek New Testament*. Stuttgart: The German Bible Society, 1983.

WORKS IN GREEK AND LATIN

Anderson, W.S., ed. *P. Ovidii Nasonis Metamorphoses*, Bibliotheca Scriptorum Graecorum Et Romanorum Teubneriana. Stuttgart: B.G. Teubner, 1998.

Aquinas, S. Thomas *Opera Omnia* <http://www.corpusthomisticum.org/iopera.html> June 8, 2016 8:05 CDT. Web.

Augustini, S. Aurelli. *Opera Omnia, Patrologiae Latinae Elenchus* <http //www. augustinus.it/latino/index.html> June 8, 2016 11:45 CDT. Web.

Buxtorf, Johannes,trans. *Rabbi Mosis Maimonidis Doctor Perplexorum*, from the Hebrew of Rabbi Samuel Aben Tybbon's translation of the Arabic text, Basil, 1629.

Burnet, Ioannes, ed. *Platonis Opera.* Vol. 5. Oxford: Oxford Classical Texts, 1901 rprt. 1967.

Bywater, I., ed. *Aristotelis Ethica Nicomachea.* Oxford: Oxford Classical Texts, 1894.

Edward, William A., ed. *Seneca the Elder: Suasoria.* London: Bristol Classical Press, 1928.

Jaeger, W., ed. *Aristotelis Metaphysica.* Oxford: Oxford Classical Texts, 1957.

Kassel, Rudolfus, ed. *Aristotelis De Arte Poetica Liber.* Oxford: Oxford Classical Texts, 1965.

Lindsay, W.M., ed. *M. Valerii Martialis Epigrammata.* Oxford: Oxford Classical Texts, 1929, rprt. 1969.

Marchant, E.C., ed. *Xenophontis Commentarii* In *Opera Omnia.* Vol. 2. Oxford: Oxford Classical Texts, 1901.

Monro, David B. & Allen, Thomas W., eds. *Homeri Opera* Vol. 5. Oxford: Oxford Classical Texts, 1902.

Mynors, R.A.B., ed. *C. Valerii Catulli Carmina.*Oxford: Oxford Classical Texts, 1958.

Ross, W.D., ed. *Aristotelis Physica.* Oxford: Oxford University Press, 1966.

———, ed. *Aristotelis Topica et Sophistici Elenchi.* Oxford: Oxford Classical Texts, 1958.

Solmsen, Friedrich, ed. et al. *Hesiodi Theogonia, Opera et Dies, Scutum & Fragmenta Selecta.* Oxford: Oxford Classical Texts, 1970.

Skutella, Martinus, ed. *Augustinus Confessiones Libri XIII.* Stuttgart: B.G. Teubner, 1969.

Wilkens, A.S., ed. *Orator Ad Brutum,* In *M. Tulli Ciceronis Rhetorica.* Vol. 2. Oxford: Oxford University Press, (1903) rprt. 2012.

COMMENTARY AND CRITICISM

Agar, Herbert. "Milton's Place in the History of Platonism, In *Milton and Plato.* Princeton Studies in English no. 2, 1928. Rprt. Gloucester, Mass.: Peter Smith, 1965.

Alvis, John. "Philosophy as Noblest Idolatry in *Paradise Lost.*" *Interpretation: A Journal of Political Philosophy.* 16 no. 2 (Winter 1988-89): 263–284.

Anderson, William S., ed. *Ovid's Metamorphoses, Books 1–5.* Edited, with Introduction and Commentary. Norman: University of Oklahoma Press, 1997.

Corns, Thomas N. *Regaining Paradise Lost.* London: Longman Group Ltd., 1994.

Dowling, Paul M. *Polite Wisdom: Heathen Rhetoric in Milton's Areopagitica.* Lanham, Md.: Rowman & Littlefield, 1995.

Dryden, John. *Of Dramatic Poesie* (1668). An electronic edition edited by Jack Lynch. Toronto: <https://andromeda.rutgers.edu/~jlynch/Texts/drampoet.html> Web. 8:42 am June 2, 2015

DuRocher, Richard J. *Milton and Ovid.* Ithaca: Cornell University Press, 1985.

Empson, William. *Milton's God.* Westport, Conn.: Greenwood Press, 1961.

Fish, Stanley. *Surprised by Sin: The Reader in Paradise Lost.* Cambridge, Mass.: Harvard University Press, 1967, 2nd ed. 1997.

Ferry, Anne. *Milton's Epic Voice: The Narrator in Paradise Lost.* Chicago: University of Chicago Press, 1963.

Fiore, Peter A. Milton and Augustine: Patterns of Austinian Thought in Paradise Lost. University Park, PA: The Pennsylvania State University Press, 1981.

Froula, Christine. "When Eve Reads Milton: Undoing the Canonical Economy." In *John Milton*, edited by Annabel Patterson. London: Longman Group Ltd., 1992: 142–64.

Gross, Kenneth. "'Pardon Me, Mighty Poet": Versions of the Bard in Marvell's "On Mr. Milton's *Paradise Lost.*"' *Milton Studies.* XVI (1982): 77–96.

Hanford, J.H. *A Milton Handbook.* New York: F.S. Crofts & Co., 1926.

Hardin, Richard F. "Ovid in Seventeenth-Century England." *Comparative Literature* 24, no. 1 (1972): 44–62.

Harding, Davis P. *The Club of Hercules: Studies in the Classical Background of Paradise Lost.* Edited by Burton A. Milligan, John R. Frey and Philip Kolb. Vol. 50, In *Illinois Studies in Language and Literature.* Urbana: University of Illinois Press, 1962.

James, Heather. "Milton's Eve, the Romance Genre, and Ovid." *Comparative Literature* 45 (1993): 121–45.

Johnson, Samuel. *Lives of English Poets*, Vol. 3. Edited by George Birkbeck Hill. Oxford, Clarendon Press, 1905

Kilgour, Maggie. "'Thy Perfect Image Viewing': Poetic Creation and Ovid's Narcissus in Paradise Lost." *Studies in Philology* 102, no. 3 (2005 Summer): 307–39.

Klein, Jacob. *A Commentary on Plato's* Meno. Chapel Hill: University of North Carolina Press, 1965.

Landy, Marcia. "'a Free and Open Encounter': Milton and the Modern Reader." *Milton Studies* 9 (1976).

Le Comte, Edward. *Milton and Sex.* New York: Columbia University Press, 1978.

Lewis, C.S. *A Preface to Paradise Lost.* New York: Oxford University Press, (1942), rpt.1970.

Leonard, John. "Language and Knowledge in Paradise Lost," In The Cambridge Companion to Milton, ed. Dennis Danielson. Cambridge: Cambrige University Press, 1989.

———. *Naming in Paradise: Milton and the Language of Adam and Eve.* Oxford: Oxford University Press, 1990.

Lieb, Micheal "S.B.'s *'In Paradisum Amissam'*: Sublime Commentary." *Milton Quarterly* 19 no. 3 (October 1985): 71–78.

Martz, Louis L. Poet of Exile: A Study of Milton's Poetry. New Haven: Yale University Press, 1980.

Masson, David. *The Life of John Milton.* Vol. 6. New York: Peter Smith, (1880) rprt. 1946.

McMahon, Robert. *The Two Poets of Paradise Lost.* Baton Rouge, Louisiana State University Press, 1998.

Nelson, Max. "Narcissus: Myth and Magic." *The Classical Journal* 95, no. 4 (2000): 363-89.

Nyquist, Mary. "The Genesis of Gendered Subjectivity in the Divorce Tracts and Paradise Lost." In *Re-Membering Milton*, edited by Mary Nyquist and Margaret W. Ferguson. New York: Methuen, 1987.

Rahe, Paul A. *Against Throne and Altar: Machiavelli and Political Theory under the English Republic*. Cambridge: Cambridge University Press, 2008.

Richardson, Jonathan. *Explantory Notes and Remarks on Milton's Paradise Lost* (1734).http://books.google.com/books/about/Explanatory_Notes_and_Remarks_ on_Milton.html?id=aYOe2ZfisO4C (April 26, 2014, 11:10 am CDT).

Samuel, Irene. *Plato and Milton*. Ithaca: Cornell University Press, 1947.

Smith, Nigil, ed. "On Mr. Milton's Paradise Lost." In *The Poems of Andrew Marvell*. London: Pearson Longman, 2003: 180–184.

Solodow, Joseph B. *The World of Ovid's Metamorphoses*. Chapel Hill: University of North Carolina Press, 1988.

Strauss, Leo. *The City and Man* Chicago:University of Chicago Press, 1964.

———. *Xenophon's Socrates*. Ithaca: Cornell University Press, 1972.

Summers, Joseph H. *The Muse's Method*. Cambridge: Harvard University Press, 1962.

Toland, John, "Clidophorus" In *Tetradymus*. London: 1720.

Waldock, A.J.A. *Paradise Lost and Its Critics*. Cambridge: Cambridge University Press, 1962.

Wallis, R.T. *Neoplatonism*. New York: Charles Scribner's Sons, 1972

Wilkerson, L.P. *Ovid Recalled*. Cambridge: Cambridge University Press, 1955.

Williams, Charles. "The New Milton." In *The Image of the City and Other Essays*, edited by Anne Ridler. Oxford: Oxford University Press, 1958.

Wittreich, Joseph. "Perplexing the Explanation: Marvell's 'On Mr. Milton's *Paradise Lost.*'" In *Approaches to Marvell: The York Tecentenary Lecture,* edited by. C.A. Patrides. London: Routledge and Kegan Paul, 1978.

Wyman, A.L. "Samuel Barrow, M.D. Physician to Charles II and admirer of John Milton." In *Medical History*. 18 (1974): 335–348.

Xenophon, *Memorabilia*. Translated with annotations by Amy L. Bonnette. Ithaca: Cornell University Press, 1994.

Index

Adam's dream of Eve's creation, 112–16

Adam's dream of Paradise, 109–12

Addison, Joseph, xvi, 138

Alcibiades. *See 1st Alcibiades*

Aquinas, Thomas:
S.T. Ia qu. 75–89 & 90–102, 104;
S.T. Ia qu. 83 [*de voluntate*] art. 1, 95n1;
S.T. Ia qu. 94a.3 ad.1, 97;
S.T. Ia qu. 94a.3 ad.1 ad.2, 99–100;
S.T. Ia qu. 94a.4 co., 104n19;
Super Boetium De Trinitate pars 1 q.2 a.4 esp., co.2, 97n10

the Argument, 1–5, 136

Aristotle:
Analytica Posteriora, 103;
De Anima, 100;
De Arte Poetica, xviin17, 95;
Ethica Nicomachea, xivn10, 88;
Metaphysica, 76n8, 79, 83, 88, 100;
Physica, 41, 41n9, 81–82, 105;
Topica, xiv, xxvii, 23

audience, xv–xvii, xxi, 1–4

Augustine:
Contra Secundum Iuliani Responsum, 96;
Confessiones, xxiii;
De Doctrina Christiana, 4.9, 23;

De Genesi ad Litteram, 96, 103n18, 104–7, 104n20, 106, 106n22

Barrow, Samuel (S.B. M.D.), 12–14, 24–25

Cambridge, 133–35

Cambridge Platonism, xxvi, 130, 133–35, 138

Catullus *"Ad Fabullum"*, 36–37, 55n25

Cicero:
Orator ad Brutum, 23, 78, 99n10;
Topica, 5

"commonly agreed upon" things, 152.
See also generally accepted opinions

Delphic dictum, "know thyself," 41, 48

discursive rationality, 122

dispositio dianoetica, 101, 111, 122

Dowling, Paul, 3n3

dreaming, 108–12.
See also Adam's dream of Eve's creation; Eve's dream of the interdicted tree

Dryden, John:
Of Dramatic Poesy, AN ESSAY, 5–7

Empson, William, xviii, xxii, xxvii, 3n2, 133, 138

About the Author

David Oliver Davies teaches literature, chiefly in English, and the classical languages at the University of Dallas where he holds a joint appointment in English and Classics. A former chairman of the Department of English for nine years, at present he is the director of the PhD program in Literature in The Institute of Philosophic Studies at the University.

9 781498 532648